THE

REFERENCE

SHELF

GAMBLING

Edited by ANDREW RICONDA

THE REFERENCE SHELF

Volume 67 Number 4

THE H. W. WILSON COMPANY

New York   1995

THE REFERENCE SHELF

The books in this series contain reprints of articles, excerpts from books, and addresses on current issues and social trends in the United States and other countries. There are six separately bound numbers in each volume, all of which are generally published in the same calendar year. One number is a collection of recent speeches; each of the others is devoted to a single subject and gives background information and discussion from various points of view, concluding with a comprehensive bibliography that contains books and pamphlets and abstracts of additional articles on the subject. Books in the series may be purchased individually or on subscription.

Library of Congress Cataloging-in-Publication Data

Gambling / edited by Andrew Riconda.
     p.   cm. — (The reference shelf ; v. 67, no. 4)
    Includes bibliographical references.
    ISBN 0-8242-0871-4
    1. Gambling. I. Riconda, Andrew. II. Series.
HV6710.G315 1995
363.4'2—dc20   95-22719
                                                      CIP

Cover: A gambler watches the roulette wheel during Las Vegas' annual "Helldorado" celebration.

Photo: AP/Wide World Photos

Printed in the United States of America

CONTENTS

IV. WHEN GAMBLING BECOMES A PROBLEM

BIBLIOGRAPHY

PREFACE

The articles selected for this compilation focus on some of the economic, geographic, social and psychological factors that have given rise to a so-called "gambling nation." The United States is becoming enamored with games of chance that range from state-run lotteries to church or charity-sanctioned bingo to "Las Vegas" nights to the slot machines and gaming tables of the ever-escalating number of casinos.

Historically, our relationship with gambling has always been ambiguous. Some of our founding fathers, Jefferson, Washington, decried its place in the new America (see *Gambling Boom* and *Casino Craze*), but neither were blind to the revenues generated by lotteries. In 1931 gambling was used to combat the Depression (Nevada legalized gambling; Massachusetts decriminalized bingo), and in 1964, in New Hampshire, the first state lottery was used to generate state revenues.

Gambling seems to be following a course of manifest destiny in our country—casinos and riverboats are multiplying, lottery stakes are high and mesmerizing, and at least one airline has proposed to bring gambling *to the air*. Currently, only two states, Hawaii and Utah, still prohibit legalized gaming.

Section I explores the recent history of gambling and its move into the American mainstream. The articles also examine the effects on economies and lives. Section II looks at the gambler's world, providing profiles of low- and highrollers, as well as a glimpse into casino operations and the lives of dealers. The articles in Section III specifically examine the growth of gambling on Indian reservations, discussing the legal decisions that have led to it, while also highlighting the tragedies and triumphs of particular reservations. Section IV investigates the debate on problem gambling—which centers on whether gambling is an uncontrollable impulse disorder or a manageable, albeit often serious, proclivity on the part of the gambler. The views of either side are represented here, as is a discussion of forms of treatment and therapy.

The editor wishes to thank The H. W. Wilson General Publications staff for its assistance and the authors and publishers who have granted permission to reprint their material in this compilation.

ANDREW RICONDA

May 1995

I. AN OVERVIEW

EDITOR'S INTRODUCTION

In 1992 the total amount of money spent on gambling—called the "gaming handle" by the industry—was nearly $330 billion dollars. There is little doubt that gambling has become an "acceptable" pastime, an enjoyable way to spend time and money.

Section I looks at the proliferation of gambling in our lives. Richard L. Worsnop's "Gambling Boom," reprinted from the *CQ Researcher,* is an exploration of the legalized gambling boom. The author examines the complex relationship, past and present, between gambling and American citizenry. Worsnop catalogues the causes of gambling's rise—product demand (Americans do not want more taxes, but accept a voluntary tax in the form of legalized gambling); marketing strategy (the gaming industry's promotion of itself as wholesome, family-oriented entertainment to draw in the vacation trade); and the lack of vocal opponents (church and state, whose own gambling enterprises—lotteries, bingo halls—preclude any resonant opposition). The author further considers gambling in all its forms—lotteries, casinos, parimutuel race track betting, the Indian reservation boom, and its possible interactive future (gambling at home via television remote control)—and its possible impact on the individual and society. The article also contains a discussion of Indian Gaming regulations and policy.

"Casino Craze," by Peter Hellman, reprinted from *Travel Holiday,* explores the geographic and economic issues of gambling. Hellman looks at the expansion of gaming halls in our country and the effect on tourism and trade in local and regional economies. A key point illuminated is the cannibalistic nature of the casino boom: casinos produce a sudden influx of money to local economies as out-of-towners flock to the tables. As other casinos open gamblers are drawn away, and the local economies return to a state of economic depression.

Gerri Hirshey's "Gambling Nation," reprinted from the *New York Times Magazine,* provides brief portraits of individuals from across the country who are affected by the gambling industry—

9

the elderly gamblers who arrive at casinos by the busload; restaurateurs who have seen their businesses suffer; people concerned with the impact of riverboat gambling on their communities; dealers; the casino owner—and what is at stake for each of them.

GAMBLING BOOM[1]

Many U.S. industries slumped during the recent recession, but gambling wasn't one of them. Capping a decade of robust growth, legal wagering rose to a record $329.9 billion in 1992—compared with a relatively anemic $126 billion in 1982.

Gross gambling revenue—money lost by bettors—also surged in 1992, to $29.9 billion, or 12 percent above 1991. The rise is largely credited to the lure of new casinos and a new lottery in Texas. (The movie industry, by comparison, took in a modest $5.2 billion in box-office revenues in 1993.)

Today's U.S. gambling scene "is a world transformed," noted Eugene Martin Christiansen in his annual industry analysis for *Gaming & Wagering Business,* a leading trade journal. "A simple, lottery/parimutuel/Nevada-Atlantic City mix of traditional commercial games has evolved into an interactive device, casino/ entertainment-driven behemoth that is at once spreading across the American heartland, revitalizing Indian economies and going head to head with Orlando for mainstream family leisure spending —the market with the biggest bucks of all."

As Christiansen pointed out, gaming in facilities run by American Indian tribes has become an industry pace-setter. Despite resistance from the states, Indians have rushed to take advantage of a 1988 federal law allowing them to establish casino-style gaming (known as Class III gaming) on their reservations. In 1992, wagering at Indian casinos rose by nearly $10 billion over 1991—a 240 percent increase.

The take from riverboat gambling grew even faster. (Some of the "riverboats" are no more than huge barges moored fast to the shore.) Gross wagering in the floating casinos, licensed by six

[1]Article by Richard L. Worsnop. From *The CQ Researcher,* March 18, '94. Reprinted with permission.

states along the Mississippi and Ohio rivers, increased by $6.2 billion in 1992—a whopping 566 percent rise over 1991.

Video gambling also posted triple-digit growth in 1992, rising by $972 million, or 274 percent. Based on familiar card and number games like poker and keno, video machines attract heavy patronage because they offer virtually nonstop action and frequent jackpots. They are expected to remain a dependable state-lottery cash cow for many years to come.

Why all the growth? According to William Thompson, a professor of public administration at the University of Nevada-Las Vegas, the boom draws its energy from the gaming industry itself. "There's a public demand to gamble," Thompson says, "but there's no public demand for *legalizing* gambling." What the public wants above all, he says, is low taxes. The gaming industry senses this, "and it tells the politicians, 'Hey, here's a way to avoid taxes. Don't make the people mad, don't raise their taxes; give them gambling instead.'"

Public officials who embrace this view of gambling see it, in effect, as a voluntary tax. But they typically ignore the consequences of legalized gambling, Thompson says. "They don't look two, three, four years down the line and see that money will be drained out of other community resources—from retail sales, say—which otherwise would provide sales-tax revenue," he says.

Moreover, he notes, moral objections to gambling generally fall on deaf ears because "the public is worn out on the morality issue." And those who "are still into the morality issue are more concerned about abortion and school prayer than they are about gambling. Gambling's pretty low on the morality crusaders' list."

There's another reason for the muted moral criticism, according to a report on the gambling industry by Wertheim Schroder & Co. Inc., a New York investment-banking firm: Church and state, traditionally "two of society's moral arbiters and most outspoken critics of gaming," now hesitate to speak out "due to their dependence on revenues" from bingo and lotteries.

Meanwhile, as Christiansen suggests, the gaming industry has disarmed critics by promoting itself as a source of wholesome entertainment. This marketing strategy can best be appreciated in Las Vegas, which boasts several new spectacle properties and theme parks that appeal to the U.S. family vacation trade.

As *The New York Times* recently noted about three of the new hotels, "There are no showgirls. There are no Runyonesque souls, even if there are people with glazed eyes playing five slot machines at a time with both hands. What one notices now is the children, roaming the casinos and pumping quarters in video arcades as nimbly as their quite average-looking parents."

Las Vegas appeals to foreign tourists as well. About 15 percent of the visitors now come from abroad, compared with 4 percent as recently as 1987.

But despite the gaming industry's prosperity, and also because of it, criticism of wagering persists. Much of the opposition comes from mental health professionals who treat compulsive gamblers —many of whom became addicted to betting at an early age.

One such expert, psychiatrist Sirgay Sanger, wants the gaming industry to do more to help people who become pathological gamblers.

"No casino or gambling operation really makes that much extra money on the problem gambler," says Sanger, past president of the National Council on Problem Gambling in New York City. To the contrary, it's in the operators' self-interest to identify and help patrons who "show signs of drinking too much, spending all their money and then using up their credit cards. Those are the people who get into fights, get involved in lawsuits, sometimes even commit suicide."

Sanger also thinks states that permit gambling should do more to combat the rise of pathological gambling. "If the state is going to advocate a risky business," he says, "then the state should dedicate some percentage of its gambling profits to the rehabilitation and study" of problem gamblers.

Advocates and opponents of legalized gaming agree that the nation's long gambling boom shows no sign of losing momentum in the foreseeable future. But they disagree over its likely impact on both society as a whole and individual gamblers.

As lawmakers, industry experts and other observers consider the gambling issue, these are among the questions they are trying to answer:

Does Indian-run gambling enjoy an unfair advantage over other gaming operations?

Debates on the pros and cons of legalized wagering often center on Indian-run gaming. Since a 1987 Supreme Court decision and a 1988 act of Congress affirmed the right of American Indians to establish casino gaming on their reservations, dozens of tribes jumped at the opportunity.

However, state governments and commercial gaming interests contend the Indian Gaming Regulatory Act of 1988 (IGRA) gives Indians an unfair—and possibly unconstitutional—competitive edge. They complain that IGRA exempts tribes from state taxes while allowing them to sue states that refuse to negotiate in good faith on gaming agreements, known as "compacts."

Critics say the gaming industry playing field would be made level if it were more difficult for tribes to obtain casino permits and if there were restrictions on the types of games permitted in tribe-operated facilities. Bills thus amending IGRA are now pending in Congress.

At the same time, several states have gone to federal court to overturn IGRA on constitutional grounds. They contend IGRA violates the 10th Amendment, which essentially says Congress can't force state governments to do anything—such as negotiate gaming compacts with Indian tribes—not spelled out in state law. They also say IGRA violates the 11th Amendment, which in effect bars states from suing each other. Their reasoning is that Indian tribes, which are sovereign entities under U.S. law, have the same legal standing as states.

Tribal officials indignantly deny getting any special advantages. Indeed, they say, the fundamental issue is tribal sovereignty. As far back as 1831, they note, the Supreme Court ruled in *Cherokee Nation v. Georgia* that tribal nations had the legal right to manage their own affairs, govern themselves internally and engage in legal and political relationships with the federal government and its subdivisions. Moreover, they say, in 1987 the court removed most remaining barriers to Indian gaming in *California v. Cabazon Band of Mission Indians*, once again treating the tribes as independent nations.

In view of these rulings, American Indians say IGRA violated tribal sovereignty by requiring tribes to negotiate compacts with state governments before setting up casino operations. IGRA's legislative history clearly shows, they say, that the compact requirement was added to the law at the states' insistence.

Now, according to the National Indian Gaming Association [NIGA, founded in 1985, is a nonprofit organization of tribes and associate members representing vendors and businesses involved in tribal gaming enterprises], "The states are reneging on the deal that they proposed and Congress accepted" when it approved IGRA in 1988. "When a tribe attempts to secure judicial enforcement of the state's obligation to negotiate a compact in good faith," NIGA charged in a 1993 study, "the state asserts immunity from suit under the 11th Amendment" and the states also claim that "the 10th Amendment renders unconstitutional any resulting obligation that the compact process may impose upon the state." This strategy "has successfully obstructed and delayed many tribal efforts to use Class III gaming as a source of employment and government revenue."

Indeed, Indian leaders cite jobs and income as the main benefits of tribal gaming. Gross revenue from wagering on Indian reservations in 1992 accounted for only 5 percent of the gaming industry total. But that minuscule share represented $1.5 billion, a huge windfall for the relatively small number of tribal members involved.

Minnesota's Mille Lacs tribe, for example, financed two new schools—the reservation's first—entirely from gaming proceeds. "That means kids on the reservation no longer have to be bused to school," says Gay Kingman, public relations director for NIGA.

In South Dakota, says Kingman, Indian tribes and the state government have joined forces to promote tourism. Visitors who come to see scenic attractions like Mount Rushmore are encouraged to stop at an Indian reservation and sample American Indian culture—"and also spend some time enjoying themselves in the reservation's casino."

Such cooperative efforts benefit both tribes and the states, Indian leaders say. "Indian casinos and bingo halls have created more than 30,000 taxpaying jobs in five states alone—Minnesota, Wisconsin, Michigan, California and Washington," wrote former NIGA Chairman Leonard Prescott. "The majority of those jobs are held by non-Indians."

Meanwhile, Kingman says, many tribes are seeking to expand their gambling operations by "expanding their reservation landholdings." Some states and commercial gambling companies worry that the tactic will enable tribes to obtain more advantageous sites for casinos, draw business away from gaming establishments already in the area or discourage commercial operators from building rival casinos nearby. The IGRA provision permitting tribes to acquire more so-called "trust" lands, IGRA critics argue, is another example of the law's pro-Indian bias.

Neutral observers say fears about American Indians' expansion probably are overblown. They point out that prior approval must be obtained from the governor of the state where the trust land is located and from the U.S. secretary of the Interior. "Because of the rigor of this approval process," noted the report by Wertheim Schroder & Co., "it seems that Indians getting trust land for the purpose of gaming may happen occasionally, but will probably not become a widespread phenomenon."

Would legalized betting undermine the honesty of college and pro team sports?

Next to casino table and slot games, sports betting is considered the most popular form of gambling in the United States. But since wagering on team sports is illegal in almost all jurisdictions, nationwide data are considered imprecise.

Former *Forbes* magazine Executive Editor James Cook wrote in 1992 that illegal betting in the U.S. may run "as high as $100 billion" a year. And that estimate doesn't include the "additional tens of billions" wagered on sports events in office pools and TV parties or bar-side bets among friends, he added.

Most betting on college and pro games is against the law because politicians have accepted the argument that legalization would corrupt sports. They cite the fixed World Series of 1919 and the point-shaving scandals that surface periodically in college basketball.

Advocates of legalized sports betting retort that changes in gaming technology and higher player salaries have made it much more difficult to fix games. "This might be an instance where outrageous player salaries have made professional sports cleaner," Cook wrote. "What multimillionaire athlete would want to jeopardize his earnings by throwing a game?"

Testifying before a House Judiciary subcommittee in 1991, National Football League (NFL) Commissioner Paul Tagliabue cited four reasons for opposing legal wagering on team sports:

• "With legalized gambling, our games . . . would come to represent the fast buck, the quick fix, the desire to get something for nothing."

• "Sports gambling inevitably fosters a climate of suspicion about controversial plays and intensifies cynicism with respect to player performances, coaching decisions, officiating calls and game results."

• "Our players cannot be expected to serve as healthy role models for youth if they are made to function as participants in gambling enterprises."

• Legalized sports betting "would promote gambling among young people."

Moreover, warned Boston Celtics President Arnold "Red" Auerbach, testifying before the same panel, legalized gambling would warp fans' outlook on sports. "Legalized sports betting creates a new type of fan," Auerbach said, "the 'point-spread' fan who is more concerned with whether the point spread is covered, not whether his team wins or how the players perform." To people with that mind-set, he said, "games are not entertainment events but only activities from which they hope to profit."

Some advocates of legalized sports betting insist it would reduce illegal bookmaking. But William L. Holmes, a forensic gaming consultant and former FBI agent, believes that people who use bookmakers will not shift to a legal sports lottery because bookies offer better odds, credit, tax-free payouts and greater convenience in placing bets and collecting winnings. Moreover, they generally set few if any restrictions on the amount an individual may wager. In fact, because of these advantages, Holmes feels illegal bookmakers would eventually lure many patrons away from legal sports betting.

Advocates of legalized sports betting continue to press their case all the same. One of their favorite arguments focuses on the social benefits gambling income would provide. "State-sponsored sports-pool lotteries could raise hundreds of millions in new non-tax revenue for the important state-run programs funded by lotteries, including education, economic development . . . senior citizen programs and state general funds," James E. Hosker, former president of the North American Association of State and Provincial Lotteries, told the House Judiciary subcommittee in 1991.

Hosker also challenged the idea that legalized betting would undermine the integrity of college and professional sports and raise the risk of game-fixing. "Sports-pool lotteries are simply the 'office pool' on a slightly larger scale," he declared. Moreover, it would be no easy matter to rig a sports lottery drawing: A player would have to fix "14 or perhaps more professional sports events—practically speaking, an impossibility," he said.

But the main reason why sports lotteries are virtually tamper-proof, Hosker said, is that sophisticated computers "continually monitor the combinations that are being played, the amounts being wagered and where the wagers are being made, [and] any abnormal betting patterns would be quickly spotted."

Bookmakers, for their part, contend that no one has a greater stake than they do in the absolute integrity of college and professional sports—chiefly football and basketball. "If there was wide-spread corruption in sports, there wouldn't be any bookmakers left," said Michael "Roxy" Roxborough, president of Las Vegas Sports Consultants Inc. and the man who sets the Las Vegas "line"—the nationally consulted point spreads on games. "They'd all be broke or looking to get out of business. If there's no integrity, nobody will come and watch. If there's no integrity, nobody's going to bet."

Is compulsive gambling a mental disease?

Like NFL Commissioner Tagliabue, experts on compulsive gambling say legalized sports betting poses special hazards for teenagers. "With sports lotteries, the lottery industry is tapping a previously untapped resource, our young people" said Valerie C. Lorenz, executive director of the Compulsive Gambling Center in Baltimore, Maryland. "Compulsive gambling among our young people is already a serious problem, and we need to work together to prevent it from becoming a national tragedy."

According to Lorenz, a psychologist, sports are "uniquely attractive" to youngsters. Furthermore, "The knowledge that children would acquire through sports lotteries would quickly lead them to illegal sports gambling, once they also discover the greater odds and thrill of risk such illegal gambling offers."

Even now, says Lorenz, studies suggest that there is more compulsive gambling among teenage gamblers (7 to 11 percent are compulsive gamblers) than among adult gamblers (up to 5 percent). One reason for the disparity, she believes, is that, "We're telling our children it's OK to bet. Nowadays, a family will go to a restaurant where mom and dad can play a keno machine on the table. Or it'll take a pleasure cruise where mom and dad can gamble all the family's money away. That's what we're exposing our children to."

Compulsive (or pathological) gambling is defined by Beverly Hills, Calif., psychiatrist Richard J. Rosenthal as "a progressive disorder characterized by a continuous or periodic loss of control over gambling; a preoccupation with gambling and with obtaining money with which to gamble; irrational thinking; and a continuation of the behavior despite adverse consequences."

According to Rosenthal and other experts in the field, winning is of secondary importance to compulsive gamblers. "While money is important," he writes, "most say they are seeking 'action,' an aroused, euphoric state comparable to the 'high' derived from cocaine and other drugs."

Indeed, say compulsive-gambling counselors Arnie and Sheila Wexler of Bradley Beach, N.J., "most dual-addicted cocaine addict/compulsive gamblers will tell you gambling gives them the bigger high. Some drug addicts, who are also gambling addicts, will sell their drugs for gambling money."

No consensus exists on the cause of compulsive gambling. One theory, advanced by Arnie Wexler, views the disorder as a product of family dysfunction. "There's a breakdown of the relationship between the gambler and the father, if the gambler is male," says Wexler, a recovering compulsive gambler. "Or there's a breakdown of the relationship between a female gambler and her mother. Also, about 50 percent of compulsive gamblers have a family member with some sort of addiction, be it gambling, drugs or alcohol."

Sanger of the National Council on Problem Gambling thinks compulsive gamblers suffer from one of a cluster of related disorders. Members of one subgroup "use the excitement of gambling the way some anorexics use starvation, or some runners use running: to give themselves a high," he says. For such people, these activities "slake an inner craving or inner absence."

The problem gamblers in a second subset "have neurotic qualities," Sanger says. That is, "they're compulsive in an opportunistic way; they have to keep repeating this behavior because it offers them some meaning in life."

Sanger describes a third group as "very angry people who are determined to continue gambling—behavior that's called 'chasing.'" These individuals typically have lost large sums of money, "and now they're going to force Lady Luck" to smile on them. They aren't angry at society per se, says Sanger. "They're just angry at the way they perceive their own lack of luck."

Not everyone considers compulsive gambling a mental, or organic, disorder. A rival school of thought holds that problem gambling is "learned behavior." Two leading proponents of this view are Richard E. Vatz, a professor of rhetoric and communication at Towson (Md.) State University, and Lee S. Weinberg, an associate professor at the University of Pittsburgh's graduate school of public and international affairs.

The American Psychiatric Association's (APA) *Diagnostic and Statistical Manual* "lists no medical criteria . . . for pathological gambling," Vatz and Weinberg wrote last fall [*see*: "Refuting the

Myths of Compulsive Gambling" in Section IV], "only those referring to frequency of wagering and its social, financial and legal consequences. There is no credible evidence whatsoever of any neurochemical or neurophysiological status causally linked to heavy gambling, only changes such as increased adrenaline or palpitations caused by the excitement of the action.

Vatz rejects the view that heavy gambling is beyond an individual's control. He likens it to cigarette addiction, observing that, "millions of people have quit smoking, and studies show that the majority of people who quit did so through willpower."

If willpower is all it takes, then why do some individuals keep on gambling until they lose their homes, jobs and families? "There always is a certain percentage of people who like that kind of exciting, high-risk action," Vatz explains. "And secondly, gamblers don't anticipate losing. They're wrong, of course. Since the odds are stacked against any gambler, all gamblers will lose over time."

Vatz doesn't scorn support groups like Gamblers Anonymous (GA). He cautions, however, that "the great majority of people who go to Gamblers Anonymous do so only because they're compelled to by courts as a result of lawbreaking. Also, most people don't return after the first meeting." Consequently, GA's claims of success are based on "an unrepresentative sample of people who stayed through the entire program—people who might have been sufficiently motivated to stop gambling on their own."

Vatz sees the current interest in problem gambling as "dovetailing with the societal focus now on compulsive behavior—on whether people can resist impulses. I'm thinking of the Lorena Bobbitt situation, the Menendez brothers situation, where people's behavior is attributed to compulsions and mental illnesses outside of their control."

Ambivalent Attitudes

American attitudes toward gambling have always been deeply ambivalent—some would say hypocritical. In its first year in America, the Puritan-led Massachusetts Bay Colony outlawed not only the possession of cards, dice and gaming tables, even in private homes, but also dancing and singing. However, a century later, in 1737, Massachusetts legislators amended the anti-gambling law, stating: "All lawful games and exercises should not be otherwise used than as innocent and moderate recreations, and not as trades or callings, to gain a living or make unlawful advantage thereby."

Games of chance found little favor among the Founding Fathers. Gaming, declared George Washington, is "the child of avarice, the brother of iniquity and the father of mischief." Sounding a similar note, Thomas Jefferson warned, "Gaming corrupts our dispositions and teaches us a habit of hostility against all mankind."

Nonetheless, Washington and Jefferson appreciated the money-making potential of gaming. At a time when the nation's banking and taxation systems were rudimentary, lotteries were seen as an alternative way of funding worthy projects. All thirteen original Colonies established lotteries to raise revenue. The proceeds helped establish some of the nation's earliest and most prestigious universities—Harvard, Yale, Columbia, Dartmouth, Princeton and William and Mary.

Cardsharps on the Frontier

As the country expanded westward in the early 19th century, gambling acquired a less savory reputation. Cardsharps in the bustling river towns along the lower Mississippi, for example, were blamed for debasing local morals. Resentment exploded into violence July 6, 1835, when five accused hustlers were seized and hanged in Vicksburg, Miss.

From that time until the Civil War, gambling operations in the area shifted to riverboats operating between New Orleans and St. Louis. This was the heyday of the flashy riverboat gambler, portrayed in such Hollywood films as *Mississippi,* which starred comedian W. C. Fields as the flamboyant captain of the *River Queen.*

Today's moviegoers may assume that the nattily attired celluloid sharpers they see were figments of Hollywood's imagination. Not so. Riverboat gamblers "were acknowledged to be, as a class, the best-dressed men in the country," historian Robert K. DeArment wrote. The gambler's somber black outfit served merely as background for eye-catching accessories. These included a "snowy white shirt adorned with overlapping layers of ruffles" and a "garish flowered vest . . . studded with buttons of gold, pearl, or diamond." To complete the display, "Rings with precious stones sparkled on his fingers, and one very large stone, called the 'headlight,' gleamed in a stickpin on his chest."

Gambling in the frontier communities west of the Mississippi was more rough-hewn. Colorful characters like Rowdy Joe Lowe, Poker Alice, Diamondfield Jack Davis and Madame Mustache abounded. But the frontier gambler best-remembered today is Wild Bill Hickok.

Once, DeArment noted, "when Hickok was in danger of being cleaned out by a pair of crooked poker sharks, he called the largest raise of the evening with his last greenbacks. At the showdown, one of his opponents displayed the winning hand and Bill tossed in his cards. 'Hold it!' he said, as the sharper reached for the pot. Drawing two revolvers, he leveled them at the swindlers. 'I have a pair of sixes, and they beat anything.' The slicks watched glumly as Hickok cleared the table."

Hickok's fame was assured when he was fatally shot August 2, 1876, while playing poker at the Number Ten Saloon in Deadwood, South Dakota. According to DeArment, he was holding two pairs, aces and eights, at the time—"a hand known ever since as the 'dead man's hand.'"

Rise of Opposition

As the 19th century drew to a close, anti-gambling sentiment gathered force across the country, spurred by a series of scandals in 1890 involving the Louisiana State Lottery.

Much of the opposition to gambling at the turn of the century and later, however, came from organized religion, as in Colonial times. The Methodist Episcopal Church South declared in a 1930 policy statement: "To continue to gamble is to weaken the best qualities in the individual, no matter what the form of gambling may be, whether on the race track, in the popular sport of the day, at the card tables, or on the stock market."

Historians Reuven and Gabrielle A. Brenner theorize that foes of gambling and speculation resist "the idea that chance, rather than divine will or talent, can have a significant effect on the allocation and reallocation of property." Critics of gaming assume, they write, that "if gambling . . . was outlawed, and the laws were enforced, people would spend their time and money in more 'productive' ways."

Legalized Gambling

Such thinking colored attitudes toward gambling until the Great Depression. As financial distress spread after the October 1929 stock market crash, legalized gaming came to be seen as a way to jump-start the economy. Nevada led the way in 1931, when it lifted bans on most forms of gambling. The same year, Massachusetts decriminalized bingo. And in 1933, Michigan, New Hampshire and Ohio legalized parimutuel betting. Chain letters and movie theater "bank nights," at which prizes were awarded, also flourished during the decade.

With the return of nationwide prosperity after World War II, Nevada's fledgling gaming industry boomed. But organized crime bankrolled many of the new facilities. The first big postwar Las Vegas casino, the Flamingo, was built in 1946 by mobster Benjamin "Bugsy" Siegel. At least four other major gaming properties in "Vegas" also had underworld ties: the Desert Inn (tied to the Cleveland crime syndicate headed by Moe Dalitz); the Stardust (opened by California mobster Tony Stralla); the Thunderbird (financed by New York gangsters Meyer and Jake Lansky); and the Tropicana (linked to New York mobster Frank Costello).

Televised hearings convened in 1951 by Sen. Estes Kefauver, D-Tenn., chairman of the Senate Special Committee to Investigate Organized Crime, did much to educate the public about the extent of mob influence in Nevada and elsewhere in the country.

The mob-gambling link has long been a prime argument against legalized gaming. To sculpt a more pleasing industry profile, gambling advocates now promote vacation trips to gaming resorts as a leisure activity the entire family can enjoy. Las Vegas' growth in recent years, which has drawn broad media coverage in this country and overseas, testifies to the effectiveness of this approach.

Lottery Fever

Mounting opposition to tax increases helped usher in the modern era of state-run lotteries in 1964. New Hampshire's pathbreaking game was based initially on just two horse races a year—a concept similar to the Irish Sweepstakes. But revenues fell well short of expectations both there and in New York, which in 1967 became the second state to institute a lottery.

It remained for New Jersey to launch the first financially successful modern lottery in 1971. The Garden State offered 50-cent tickets (half the price of those in neighboring New York) and weekly drawings (New York's were monthly), thus satisfying the habitual gambler's desire for frequent action at an affordable cost. New Jersey also put a higher percentage of lottery revenues into prizes than New Hampshire or New York.

New Jersey's innovations quickly became standard lottery practice, and three new twists soon were added. The first was the "instant game," in which players scratch a thin film off the ticket to uncover the numbers or symbols hidden beneath. Then came a legal daily "numbers" game, just like the illegal version long popular in big cities, but played on a computer network.

The third and most important lottery innovation was lotto, in which players typically choose six different numbers between 1 and 40 or 1 and 54. Though the odds of making a perfect lotto match are many millions to 1, the game has proved wildly popular. That's because the jackpot is rolled over each time it isn't won. Thus, when there are no winning tickets for several consecutive drawings, multimillion-dollar prizes and "lotto fever" invariably result.

Floridians got the fever as the jackpot headed toward $100 million in September 1990. During the week leading up to the September 16 drawing, more than 100 million $1 tickets were sold. Computers showed that every possible combination of numbers had been purchased, guaranteeing there would be at least one winning ticket. In fact, there were six and they split a $106 million jackpot. But the nation's biggest jackpot ever—$118 million in California in April 1992—was split by 10 ticket holders.

Now that lotteries have spread to 37 states and the District of Columbia, including the 10 most-populous states, future revenue growth will hinge on aggressive marketing of existing products and development of new ones. In the meantime, the potential for gambling development on Indian reservations has barely been tapped.

Rulings Aid Indians

Until the late 1980s, gaming on tribal lands amounted to nothing more complex than bingo. In 1987, though, the Supreme Court's *California v. Cabazon Band of Mission Indians* decision elated Indian tribes and sent shock waves through the commercial gaming industry. In the case, the state challenged the right of two tribes to conduct bingo, poker and other card games on their lands.

The ruling held that state laws prohibiting a particular form of gambling cover tribes in the state. But if the state permits a form of gaming, tribes may operate such games, and operate them free of state control. In essence, said the National Indian

Gaming Association (NIGA), the court "formally recognized the Indians' right to conduct gaming operations on their own land as long as [it] is not criminally prohibited by the state."

Tribal self-sufficiency was at the heart of *Cabazon*. The court said federal agencies had sought to bolster tribal independence by promoting bingo and other games of chance. "Such policies and actions are of particular relevance in this case," declared the court, "since the tribal games provide the sole source of revenues for the operation of tribal governments and are the major sources of employment for tribal members."

Predictably, commercial gaming interests assailed *Cabazon*. State and federal law enforcement authorities also voiced misgivings, predicting that organized crime would infiltrate Indian gaming.

Congress tried to allay the concerns by passing the Indian Gaming Regulatory Act (IGRA) in 1988. The law defined three classes of gambling and applied differing regulatory standards to each:

Class I, consisting of traditional ceremonial gaming or social games for prizes of limited value, was placed under the tribes' exclusive control.

Class II, comprising bingo, lotto and certain card games, was made subject to oversight by a five-member National Indian Gaming Commission appointed by the president and confirmed by the Senate. Three seats on the commission were set aside for members of federally recognized Indian tribes.

Class III activities, including casino gambling, slot machines, horse and dog racing and jai alai, were prohibited unless they were legal in the state and the state and tribe entered into a "compact," as required under IGRA.

Indians denounced the compact requirement as a sop to the non-Indian gaming industry. "Regrettably, we had to make compromises and accept restrictions on our right of self-government and sovereignty in the enactment of the Indian Gaming Regulatory Act," said Leonard Prescott, then-chairman of NIGA, in 1992 congressional testimony. "Let the record be clear. IGRA did not confer any rights on Indian tribes to engage in, or regulate, gaming. We already had those rights."

Indians Cashing In

Today, six years after IGRA became law, Indian reservation gambling is on a roll. According to the U.S. Bureau of Indian

Affairs, 88 American Indian tribes in 19 states have negotiated 92 gaming compacts, and 150–175 Class II and Class III gaming facilities (mainly bingo halls and casinos) are operating. [According to the Bureau of Indian Affairs, there are 545 federally recognized Indian tribes in 35 states.]

But only Foxwoods High Stakes Bingo & Casino, in Ledyard, Connecticut, operated by the tiny Mashantucket Pequot tribe, is mentioned by industry experts in the same breath as casinos in Nevada and Atlantic City. Foxwoods, in fact, is believed to be "the single most profitable casino in the Western Hemisphere, raking in an estimated $600 million in profits in 1993."

Foxwoods opened in February 1992 after a bitter legal struggle. State officials rebuffed the Pequots' initial proposal to operate a casino, prompting the tribe to sue. The Supreme Court eventually resolved the dispute in April 1991 by refusing to hear a final appeal by the state seeking to block the project.

Foxwoods only offered roulette, blackjack, craps and other table games in its first year, yet still posted revenues up to $300 million. The Pequots subsequently negotiated a pact with Gov. Lowell P. Weicker Jr., giving them the exclusive right to operate slot machines in Connecticut. In return, the tribe agreed to give the state 25 to 30 percent of annual slot revenues, depending on the total take. [Because of their sovereign status, Indian tribes are not required to pay local, state or federal taxes on their gaming revenues.] In 1993, the state's share was $113 million.

The tribe's staggering profits have built a community center, a child-development center and new housing. "The 280 [Pequots] now have no worries about college tuitions or health insurance," Thomas B. Allen recently wrote in *National Geographic*. "Foxwoods, with 8,200 people on its payroll, now rivals Electric Boat as a major employer in southeastern Connecticut."

Deck Stacked?

For Indians, the Foxwoods story is an inspiring tale of bootstrap development. But for states and commercial gaming operators, the Pequots' success portends increasing competition—so much competition that the Indians say Congress and the courts have been asked to stack the deck against them.

That seems to be the aim of almost identical bills introduced in the House and Senate last May 26 by Rep. Robert G. Torricelli, D-N.J., and Sen. Harry Reid, D-Nev. Indian spokesmen, noting that Torricelli and Reid represent the only states with full-scale commercial casinos, promptly dubbed the bills "The Donald Trump Protection Acts"—a reference to the New York developer who owns three Atlantic City casinos.

The Torricelli and Reid bills would amend IGRA by providing that compact negotiations must be confined to games allowed under existing state law. No longer would states that offer one form of Class III gaming, such as a lottery, be compelled to negotiate with Indian tribes that want to set up full-scale casino gaming. The bills also would apply state gambling laws to Indian lands.

Torricelli and Reid said their bills were inspired partly by concern that organized crime was moving in on reservation gaming—a concern that Indian leaders called laughable. "There's no organized crime, reorganized crime or disorganized crime on Indian reservations," said NIGA Chairman Rick Hill. "What critics of Indian gaming are really afraid of is organized Indians."

The Torricelli and Reid bills are currently languishing in committee. However, Senate Indian Affairs Committee Chairman Daniel K. Inouye, D-Hawaii, is trying to fashion a compromise acceptable to both supporters and critics of reservation gaming. Inouye, IGRA's principal author, has acknowledged the law needs clarification.

With Congress moving slowly on the Indian gaming issue, federal courts have become the main battleground. In a major decision on two long-pending cases, the 11th U.S. Circuit Court of Appeals in Jacksonville, Florida, ruled January 18 that "the states retain their sovereign immunity" under the 11th Amendment, "and the federal courts do not have subject-matter jurisdiction over suits brought under IGRA."

But in what the National Association of Attorneys General called "a surprise ending" to the 11th Circuit decision, the court also held that Indian tribes blocked from negotiating a gaming compact by a state claim of sovereign immunity may appeal to the secretary of the Interior. "The secretary then may prescribe regulations governing Class III gaming on the tribe's lands." In other words, said the court, IGRA expressly provides for such redress.

The 11th Circuit decision was not the first on state claims of 11th Amendment immunity in gaming cases, and it will not be the last. In similar cases recently decided, several circuit and district courts have found for the states, while one circuit and two district courts have ruled for the tribes. The issue is also pending in the

4th, 9th and 10th circuits. And the U.S. Supreme Court may yet render a definitive judgment.

Gaming Action Spreads

Without making many waves in the national media, casino gambling has also spread in recent years to mining towns, riverboats and cruise ships. Low-stakes casino gaming returned in 1989 to Deadwood, South Dakota, the Black Hills town where Wild Bill Hickok was killed at a poker table. And in November 1990, Colorado voters approved a constitutional amendment allowing limited-stakes gambling in three old-time mining communities —Black Hawk, Central City and Cripple Creek.

Jack Hidahl, Central City's city manager, says his town's experience with casino gaming has been mixed. On the plus side, gaming revenue has spurred economic development, as was hoped. "No question about that," says Hidahl. "Our general-fund budget went from $350,000 in 1990 to $5.5 million this year."

But development and increased tourist volume have strained public services. "The police department went from two full-time guys and a part-timer in 1990 to 16 full-timers now," Hidahl reports. In all, the number of city employees has risen from 8 to 40 over the past four years.

The top challenge facing Central City, says Hidahl, is maintaining its squeaky-clean image despite the presence of 15 casinos. "We've always considered ourselves a family community," he says. "We have a lot more to offer than just gambling. We still have the summer opera, our annual jazz festival, museums and mine tours and arcades for kids.

"The gaming industry probably has not made Central City as attractive to families as it has been in the past. Initially, the casino operators were quite concerned about having kids in the casinos. And I think a number of families felt this was no longer an appropriate place to visit. So, we're making a concerted effort to change that impression, and attract even more family groups."

Riverboats Evoke Early Era

Riverboat gambling, evoking the pre-Civil War era of floating casinos, also staged a comeback. Gambling on riverboats is now legal in six states abutting the Mississippi and Ohio rivers— Illinois, Indiana, Iowa, Louisiana, Mississippi and Missouri. However, a bill that would have legalized riverboat gambling in Virginia's southeastern Tidewater region was defeated recently in the General Assembly. Advocates for the bill had said that gaming revenues would help offset defense spending cutbacks in the Norfolk-Hampton-Newport News area.

Riverboat gambling is not always what it would seem. "Some of the casinos in Mississippi are on riverboats (which are permanently moored to the dock), but others do not even resemble boats," noted industry analyst Wertheim Schroder. "The law does not require these 'riverboat' casinos to sail, but only that they be on the water."

Waterborne gaming also is prospering on passenger ships offering "cruises to nowhere." That's industry shorthand for a brief round trip to international waters, where gambling is legal. Until recently, federal law barred American-flag vessels from offering gaming. To get around the ban, gaming operators ran cruises (usually from Florida) on foreign ships.

In 1992, President George Bush signed the U.S. Flag Cruise Ship Competitiveness Act, which repealed the prohibition against gaming aboard vessels with American registry. Cruise-ship gaming revenue that year totaled $305 million, a 5 percent increase over 1991.

Sports Betting

Other legislation signed by Bush in 1992 scored big with professional sports league officials. Sports gambling generates major revenues, but nearly all the action is illegal. That's because the leagues fiercely oppose all efforts to legalize wagering on their games. The legislation signed by Bush barred additional states from sponsoring sports-based lotteries based on college and professional basketball, football and baseball. The measure did not outlaw wagering on horse and dog racing, or on the state-run numbers games that are the most common form of lottery.

However, the legislation allowed Delaware, Montana, Nevada and Oregon, which permitted sports-based lotteries or casino gambling, to continue their policies. It also ordered New Jersey to decide whether to sanction wagering on team sports, and in November 1993 the New Jersey Casino Control Commission nixed legalized sports betting.

U.S. pro sports leagues scored another knockout against gaming in February, when the government of Ontario, Canada, agreed to remove pro basketball from the province's sports lottery. The move cleared the way for Toronto to become the National Basketball Association's (NBA) 28th team, effective next season. The NBA had threatened to rescind its award of a franchise to Toronto unless league games were stricken from the Ontario lottery menu.

Keno and "Scratch" Games

State-run lotteries, which provided much of the impetus for legalized gambling's growth in the 1970s and '80s, are fast becoming a "mature" segment of the industry. The lottery market is approaching saturation, with games operating in 37 states and the District of Columbia—jurisdictions containing about 90 percent of the country's population.

Nonetheless, lottery officials remain upbeat. William Bergman, executive director of the North American Association of State and Provincial Lotteries, is betting the future on Club Keno—a video version of the familiar casino game. Club Keno represents "a whole new market because it's played primarily in age-controlled venues—taverns and bars," says Bergman. "Those places traditionally have not been lottery agents."

Club Keno is popular because it delivers payouts every five minutes—a feature that "keeps people playing for a little longer." The average increase in playing time, Bergman says, is about 30 to 35 minutes.

So-called "scratch" games based on bingo and Monopoly are also seen as bettor-friendly. These games differ from traditional ones in three ways, says Bergman: "The odds are generally higher, the payout is bigger and the cost is greater."

Moreover, says Bergman, resistance to paying more than $1 for a scratch ticket seems to have evaporated. "We've found that $5 tickets are in demand where they're available," he says. "A $2 bingo ticket that takes roughly 10 to 12 minutes to scratch everything off of also is doing extraordinarily well. Monopoly is popular because it's fun and everybody knows how to play it. And who knows what other [scratch] games are around the corner?"

An Interactive Future?

Looking ahead, industry analyst Christiansen says only one thing can hurt the gaming industry: a ban on gambling. Experience shows that the American consumer "likes to spend money on commercial games," he says. "And I think as long as these games are available, that spending pattern will continue." Christiansen is especially bullish on casinos, since "Casino games are one of the very few things . . . most consumers want that the U.S. economy does not supply in superabundance."

Harold Vogel, a gaming and lodging securities analyst for Merrill Lynch Co. in New York, expects gaming stocks to perform "above average on the whole" over the next few years, though the situation is likely to be "very volatile." Investors "have to be selective" about gaming stocks, cautions Vogel, who adds: "For now, they're doing very well."

The University of Nevada's Thompson also foresees continued casino growth, provided casinos can attract gamblers from afar. Casinos generate significant new tax revenues "only if they can export their product," he says. "The local economy doesn't benefit if only local people are gambling."

Analyzing the situation in his state, Thompson says gambling on Indian reservations in Arizona and California is bound to affect Nevada gaming. "We get convenience gamblers from California and Arizona," he explains, "and the convenience gambler goes to the closest venue. So if a casino could be positioned in Palm Springs, a couple of hours closer to L.A. than Vegas, that could definitely draw off some of our business. But it's unlikely you're going to get the synergism from reservation gaming that you get from having 100 casinos."

Besides an abundance of casinos, Las Vegas "gives the best deals on hotels and meals because of the competitive atmosphere," Thompson says. "And then we have a multiplicity of entertainment —shows and theme parks and what have you. An Indian reservation wouldn't be able to compete with all that. It could attract the convenience gamers, but people who want a little more would drive the extra two hours" to Las Vegas.

The prognosis for casino gambling in Atlantic City is more guarded. Casinos there are expected to reap continued benefits from regulations approved in 1992 by the New Jersey Legislature and the state Casino Control Commission. The rules sanctioned 24-hour gaming; new games, including pai gow, an Asian card game; an increase in the amount of floor space that may be set aside for machines; TV simulcasts of horse races; and the temporary licensing of travel representatives, designed to attract tour groups from Asia.

At the same time, though, Atlantic City casinos face rising competition. For now, the Pequots' vast Foxwoods casino in Connecticut is the main threat. Near the Rhode Island border, Foxwoods is well-positioned to attract players from Providence and Boston as well as most of Connecticut.

The approval last year of gaming compacts with New York's Oneida Indian Nation and St. Regis Mohawk Tribe amounted to more bad luck for New Jersey. Each tribe won the right to offer 27 different casino games. Though the two reservations are in lightly populated areas, their casinos are expected to lure some business away from Atlantic City. Similarly, riverboat gambling in Virginia, though recently defeated by the General Assembly, could nibble at the southern edge of Atlantic City's territory if it passes in the future.

Still farther to the south, more casino activity is taking place. Harrah's, a subsidiary of Memphis-based Promus Cos., announced in mid-February that it is planning to open the world's largest casino in New Orleans in late 1995: a 200,000-square-foot, multistory river-front operation with 6,000 slot machines and 200 table games.

The future of gaming may lie, however, not with mammoth new casinos but with interactive communications within reach—literally—of every homeowner's favorite TV chair.

"Imagine the sports bettor who will be able to gamble, using the remote control of his or her set, not only on the outcome of a game, but on every play!" wrote psychiatrist and compulsive-gambling expert Rosenthal. "The clinician," he added with understatement, "can anticipate the need to know more about this disorder."

But there is a catch. The sports lottery law enacted in 1992 bars most betting on team games. One traditional wagering sport wasn't affected by the ban, however. "By accident or design," wrote Christiansen, "the law would seem to have granted horse racing a legal monopoly on interactive sports betting. That can be a valuable franchise—perhaps a *very* valuable franchise."

CASINO CRAZE[2]

As the Mississippi River flooded Davenport, Iowa, last summer, Mike Conger worked for 10 hours straight one Sunday sandbagging a bank building against the brown water lapping at its rear

[2]Article by Peter Hellman. From *Travel Holiday*, March '94. Copyright © 1994 Travel Holiday. Reprinted with permission.

door. He rested only to feed the turtles and carp swimming at his feet. It was an ordeal that deserved some fun of a kind previously unthinkable in America's heartland.

Crossing the river to historic Rock Island, Illinois, he boarded a casino riverboat, its canopied entrance above a floating gangway that had been jury-rigged. For two hours, amid the shouts of excited crapshooters, Conger played the slot machines. With the Mississippi closed to navigation, the riverboat stayed moored throughout the "cruise." Most of the 700 gamblers aboard hardly knew the difference. They'd come for the thrill, not for the view.

That's the new American equation. Gambling fever is sweeping the country so fast that it's hard to remember when casinos (second only to lotteries as revenue sources) were confined mainly to Atlantic City and Las Vegas. By now, only two states, Hawaii and Utah, still ban all commercial gambling. Elsewhere, riverboats ply the Mississippi in six midwestern and southern states, while 179 American Indian communities operate casinos or gaming parlors on reservations in 27 states. Louisiana aims to build the world's biggest casino, slated for New Orleans in 1995. There's talk of a riverboat casino near the site of the Boston Tea Party and another a few blocks from Independence Hall, in Philadelphia. Even Washington, D.C., is considering one. Soon tour operators may be offering a combined White House visit and a night at the slots—twin fantasies in one capital package.

Americans are now betting gargantuan sums. In 1992 the national "handle" (total amount wagered) hit $329 billion, more than the GNPs of Australia and Argentina combined. Gambling revenues, including those from lotteries, reached $30 billion in 1992, one and a half times what Americans spent in liquor stores the same year.

The premise behind all this is that legal gambling is a godsend to depressed areas desperate for tax revenues and tourist dollars. The tax part is correct—at first. In Mississippi, for example, the hard-pressed coastal town of Biloxi (population: 47,000) grossed $245 million in 1993. But success breeds envy: nearby towns soon compete for gamblers, siphoning off business. Moreover, the benefits of gambling to tourism are dubious indeed.

America has long used gambling for public purposes. Lotteries were crucial in launching the Jamestown colony, founding Yale and Harvard universities, financing the Continental army, and rebuilding the South after the Civil War. Gambling is in the American grain. The whole country was a gamble: every immigrant and pioneer was a risk taker with a gold-rush faith in success, whatever the odds.

Americans, churchgoers as well as bettors, have also long felt moral confusions about gambling. Even Nevada nominally banned gambling between 1909 and 1931. But soon many churches swapped moral authority for the monetary advantages of bingo. In 1964, New Hampshire's new lottery introduced an era of state-run gambling.

The current craze started in the watershed year of 1988. In South Dakota a statewide vote allowed the remote (and presumably less corruptible) mining town of Deadwood to begin casino gambling limited to $5 bets and 30-table establishments. Equally cautious, the Iowa legislature approved casino gaming restricted to riverboats (afloat, not dockside), with bets limited to $5 and losses to $200 per player.

Ironically, these gingerly limits immediately created business opportunities for other states. The fewer their rules, they reasoned, the more their customers from queasier states. In 1990, Colorado voters copied South Dakota in approving small casinos in three mountain mining towns—but without South Dakota's limits on the number of games and machines. In the same year, Illinois launched riverboat gaming with no betting limits—and easy credit. Mississippi allowed riverboat casinos to operate dockside, not just when they were cruising. Missouri topped that—its new dockside casinos were "riverboats" in name only and never left shore.

But of all 1988 milestones the most intriguing was the Indian Gaming Regulatory Act (IGRA), passed by Congress in response to a 1987 Supreme Court decision (*Cabazon v. the State of California*). In effect, the decision required states with legal gambling to give Indian reservations an equal right to operate commercial gambling on tribal land. Because Indian lands are sovereignties—exempt from most state controls and taxes—states were left with uncertain authority over Indian gambling within their borders. Accordingly, IGRA set up a federal regulatory agency to work out agreements between states and tribes.

Unexpectedly, IGRA also ignited an explosion of Vegas-style casinos on reservations. With gaming companies clamoring for their business, dozens of reservation communities have thus far signed agreements with industry stars like Harrah's and Circus Circus to lure gamblers to tribal casinos. The national Indian "take" (gross revenue) reached some $1.5 billion in 1992 alone—an extraordinary windfall for many abjectly poor tribes. It also raises the specter of an oversaturated market and ruinous competition among those tribes.

To sample the gambling fever in America, take exit 92 from Interstate 95 in rural southeastern Connecticut, a few miles from the Rhode Island border. There's no marking to tell you that this is casino country; only a sign that says, "Mashantucket Pequot Reservation." That's the sovereign land of a tiny tribe with about 300 members. When I first took that turn, with a companion last year, I expected a sleepy Tuesday afternoon at Foxwoods, the Pequots' two-year-old casino. Instead, traffic on the winding country road turned bumper to bumper two miles from Foxwoods. It took nearly half an hour to reach the casino's enormous main parking lot. It was overflowing. Police waved us on to a second lot—also full. Much farther along (across the state line, it seemed) was a third lot, with a few open spaces.

A shuttle bus delivered us to the casino, a tasteful structure overlooking a rugged forest, home to the Mashantucket tribe for centuries. Not that anyone was admiring the view. Gambling has been so frantic at Foxwoods since the day it opened, in a driving winter rain, that the original plan to close the casino for a few predawn hours daily has proven impossible. Foxwoods has yet to shut down: attendance is 15,000–20,000 on weekdays, 20,000–30,000 on weekends. Even when we arrived on that weekday afternoon, patrons were waiting in line to get at the slot machines. To ease the crush, Foxwoods has since added a new wing of gaming areas, shops, restaurants, and theaters, making it one of the largest casino complexes in the world.

Because Foxwoods is a private tribal enterprise, it need not—and does not—disclose earnings or pay corporate-profit taxes on its reservation enterprises. But Connecticut did exact a hefty price. In return for the rights to install slot machines in its casino, the tribe agreed to "contribute" 25 percent of the slot-machine gross, or $100 million, whichever is bigger, to the state each year. The tribal ante is expected to hit $113 million in fiscal 1994.

What is Foxwoods doing for local tourism? "It saved us from becoming another Appalachia," claims Louis Camerota, executive director of Mystic Coast & Country, a regional-tourism organization. He isn't exaggerating. The Connecticut coast's economic backbone has long been the Groton-based Electric Boat division of General Dynamics, builder of almost unimaginably expensive nuclear submarines. When the cold war ended, Electric Boat began sinking fast. The area hopes that tourism will take up the slack, and Foxwoods may be the key. Last year the Pequots gave Mystic Coast & Country $1 million. "All they asked is for us to use the money to get the word out about tourism," says Camerota. "No other strings were attached."

Camerota figures that gamblers spent an additional $6 million on local attractions, ranging from Mystic Seaport to the Nautilus submarine museum in Groton, in 1992, and more than double that since then. Last fall the Pequots broke ground on the reservation for a major new museum of Native American culture—a $135 million project unique in the United States. They also plan a new theme park, built with the Chinese government as adviser and in partnership with a Malaysian investor, who financed Foxwoods when local lenders looked the other way. The park, still in the planning stages, will feature a model of the Great Wall and, possibly, a golf course and a monorail that will carry tourists past ancient statues of Chinese warriors excavated in China and lent to the Pequots by the Beijing regime.

Fascinating as all this may be, gamblers are famously oblivious to outside distractions. Twenty hours after a big snowstorm hit Foxwoods, for example, the parking lots were full of cars still covered with snow—their owners still gambling away inside.

Not everyone is pleased with the success of Foxwoods. Local folk are dismayed at the traffic overload on their once peaceful roads. Many are also unhappy at the Mashantucket tribe's efforts to add more local land to the reservation, removing it from the tax rolls. Unhappiest of all is Donald Trump, who claims that Indian casinos have an unfair advantage over non-Indian casinos, including his own three. "We are the most heavily regulated gaming industry in America, and they're the least regulated," he says. "The day will soon come," he insists, "when you are going to see an organized-crime wave like the one we had in the days of Al Capone."

Trump has sued the federal government to overturn the Indian Gaming Regulatory Act. Since the law forces most states to negotiate with Indian casinos against their will, he argues, it violates states' rights as protected by the Tenth Amendment to the Constitution. Most governors also want negotiating procedures clarified. Some states, concerned that they are missing out on potential tax revenues, are pressuring the federal government to amend the IGRA. Meanwhile, tribes with successful casinos have found a way to prosper for the first time in centuries.

Nowhere are the perils of attempting to meld tourism with gambling so starkly illustrated than in Atlantic City, a six-hour drive southwest of Foxwoods. At the turn of the century, Atlantic City was a premier family resort, drawing its core clientele from nearby Philadelphia. By 1978, when Resorts International opened the city's first boardwalk casino, all pride was gone. So were all the tourists.

Atlantic City's dozen casinos have clearly prospered, currently drawing 30 million visitors annually. They've also paid their way handsomely. Some $2.6 billion in gambling taxes have gone to such worthy causes as helping New Jersey's elderly and disabled. Yet Atlantic City, despite its double bait of sin and surf, has failed to regain its former glory. When the casino era began, unemployment was double the state average, and it remains so. Crime and poverty still vex the city. Because gamblers disappear into the enormous casinos and don't emerge until it's time to go home, the city has fewer restaurants today than it did in 1978.

Atlantic City is striving for a fallback—a $520 million corridor of boardwalk attractions, including a 1,000-room, casino-free hotel. The developer, the Rouse Company, is well known for projects like New York's South Street Seaport. Whether Atlantic City can be reborn as an exciting resort remains—in a word—a gamble.

One thing can't be denied: casinos have prevented Atlantic City's total decay. But the irony is that they've also inspired potentially devastating competition. Atlantic City gets at least a third of its visitors from nearby Philadelphia, which may well keep them home with its own new casino.

Should that happen, it would underscore the economic cannibalism that looms ahead as casinos proliferate. Casinos thrive as long as they lure out-of-towners. But once the wagering visitors get their own casinos back home, the locals tend to be left holding the bag. This boom-and-bust pattern is pandemic, reports William R. Eadington, an economist, who heads the University of Nevada's Institute for the Study of Gambling and Commercial Gaming, in Reno. In place after place, he says, a casino-based economy first soars but then slumps into a "black hole."

Gambling also prevented today decay in Joliet, Illinois, located on the Des Plaines River, 40 miles south of Chicago. When its steel and farm-equipment industries faded in the 1980s, Joliet was saddled with one of the nation's highest unemployment rates. The city's once proud downtown emptied out. Its most imposing church closed. Joliet's chief employers may have been its two state prisons.

Two years ago gambling arrived on the Des Plaines River. On Joliet's formerly grungy waterfront, Harrah's has just inaugurated a $58 million complex from which two "mega-yacht" casinos, the

Northern Star and *Southern Star,* each sail six times daily. By popular demand, there's even a night birds' 3 A.M. cruise on weekends. Six miles downriver on a wooded shore still within Joliet, the super-yacht *Empress* also packs in the gamblers with eight cruises per day, including its own night-owl sailing. Last year Joliet handled an average of 12,000 gamblers a day, nearly all of them day-trippers from the Chicago area.

Has gambling helped boost Joliet's economy? "We're not a panacea," says Phil Satre, CEO of Harrah's. "But we have added fifteen hundred and fifty jobs and a thirty-five-million-dollar payroll. It wasn't there yesterday and it is there today. Joliet is looking better than it did five years ago."

It's also true that Joliet might perk up even more if the action were in the city rather than only on the gambling boats. Crowds heading for the *Empress* never enter downtown Joliet. Those coming to Harrah's can drive directly to a new, 750-space riverfront parking deck at Harrah's Landing, often without giving a second look at Joliet. Once aboard a casino boat, a passenger finds no reason to sightsee. The Des Plaines shoreline is a hodgepodge of concrete flood walls and scrap-metal yards. The *Northern Star* sails only one and a half miles south of downtown and then turns lazy circles for an hour before heading back.

On the two-hour cruise I took, the gamblers had no interest in anything but gambling. Four slot-jackpot winners were announced over the public-address system. The biggest payoff ($2,850 on a bet of three quarters) was won by an unsmiling woman who kept right on playing the adjacent machine while coins rattled endlessly from her jackpot slot as it flashed and buzzed nonstop, like an electric alarm clock nobody could turn off. She stopped only to flash an ID and sign an IRS document confirming receipt of her winnings. A mechanic came to reset the machine. Then, still wearing a pair of soiled white cotton "lucky" gloves, she kept on playing, as state law allows, for 30 minutes after the *Northern Star* had docked. Never smiling, she seemed as grim as if she were working in a tuna cannery.

It's a three-hour drive from Joliet to the east–west meander of the Mississippi River where Davenport, Iowa, faces Rock Island, Illinois. Until two winters ago, bald eagles were the prime local tourist attraction. Now gamblers land here—all year round. They board the *President,* Davenport's handsome riverboat, or *Jumer's Casino Rock Island,* across the river in Illinois. Even such unlikely groups as the National Quilting Association, convening in the area last summer, went out for a night of riverboat gambling. "You don't have to be very old to remember when you couldn't even buy liquor by the drink in Iowa," says Mary Jo Pohl, innkeeper at the River Oaks Inn, a superb Victorian mansion overlooking the river in Davenport. Pohl, who's seen steady improvement in tourism in recent years, takes a measured view of gambling: "We don't want it to be the whole thing, but we do want it to be part of the total package."

Just as Iowa was the first riverboat-casino state, it's also been first to find out that gambling can be fickle. Unhappy with the state's $5 maximum bet and $200 maximum loss during a single two-hour cruise, owners of two Iowa boats pulled up anchor for Mississippi, where high-stakes gambling is legal. Mississippi allows dockside gambling and doesn't even require casino boats to have an engine. Gamblers merely pass over a white line on the casino carpet that corresponds to river water beneath. "From the air," says I. Nelson Rose, a gambling specialist at Whittier Law School, "they look like warehouses attached to moats."

Lately, stocks like Casino Magic and Hollywood Casinos have been hot performers, thanks largely to the gambling craze in Mississippi towns like Biloxi and Tunica, where scores of employees of a catfish-dressing plant reportedly quit to take jobs in gambling.

For now, gambling is booming in Mississippi, with 18 boats operating and more to come. But, like Iowa, the state may find that its luck won't hold for long. It's sure to lose hordes of gamblers to Louisiana, which recently began launching a fleet of 15 gambling boats and has enormous ambitions to turn New Orleans into the nation's third-biggest casino city, a plan that hardly delights Las Vegas or Atlantic City.

New Orleans clearly needs a magic bullet. The 1980s oil bust plunged 31 percent of its citizens below the poverty level. Yearning for a quick fix, New Orleans bet on the 1984 world's fair for civic salvation—and allegedly lost about $100 million. Another dubious bet was the city's Superdome, which reportedly cost nearly 525 percent more than the builders guaranteed. Now comes Louisiana's Governor Edwin Edwards's city-saver: an enormous casino of 200,000 square feet located near the French Quarter and owned by a conglomerate including Harrah's and the hotelier Christopher Hemmeter.

Many consider the proposed $700 million casino a grand illusion. The skeptics include not only the city government of New

Orleans, which won't control the casino, but also a majority of the state's voters. A statewide poll in December found that the majority would ban all gambling but the lottery if given a chance to do so.

Governor Edwards is unlikely to permit any such chance. Himself a fabled high roller, he was said (but not proved) to owe $2 million in gambling debts in 1987, when he twice beat federal racketeering charges. In 1992, according to the *New York Times,* he dutifully reported winnings of $185,000 to the IRS—a bauble he said he picked up in three days of tossing dice in Las Vegas, sometimes at $5,000 a toss.

A silver-haired charmer who had served three previous terms, Edwards was the unlikely political hero who trounced the racist David Duke in his fourth run for the governorship, in 1992. Once in office again, he rammed a casino bill through the legislature. Pointing to neighboring Mississippi's gambling bonanza, his supporters claimed that a big-time casino would attract 2 million additional tourists to New Orleans and rake in millions in state revenues. They dismissed concerns that a huge influx of gamblers would overwhelm the French Quarter. They were not worried that casino gambling might invite mob infiltration. By no coincidence, the legislature's electronic voting machine was turned off as soon as the ayes had a majority.

Governor Edwards remains unfazed, even at the recent news that his four children have allegedly sought deals in the new gambling-boat business. He apparently feels that he has simply put New Orleans on the right side of history. "In my opinion," he told the *New York Times,* "every major metropolitan area in America with a population of a million or more will soon have some form of a casino."

Chicago, a far healthier city than New Orleans, is also gunning for gambling. Mayor Richard Daley was plumping for a $2 billion casino, against the stalwart objections of Illinois's Governor Jim Edgar, who associated land-based casinos with an increased crime rate. Instead, they are now proposing an $800 million riverboat casino. Meanwhile, Indiana has authorized eleven gambling boats, including five for Lake Michigan from which gamblers will be able to step out on deck and admire the skyline of Chicago.

So far, the only major American city that has casino gambling in proximity is Minneapolis. That surprises many visitors. The whole state of Minnesota is supposedly a model of squeaky-clean rectitude. Yet, with 17 Indian casinos, the state is now third-largest in casino traffic, behind Nevada and New Jersey. Wisconsin, with 16 Indian casinos of its own, isn't far behind.

It's no more than a 30-minute drive from the Minneapolis airport to the nearest casino, at Mystic Lake, run by the Shakopee Mdewakanpon Sioux people. Also close by is the Mall of America, a vast new mecca for shoppers, in suburban Bloomington. Shopping and gambling are fostering a mighty new American synergism —though it's perhaps wiser to shop first and gamble afterward. It's not surprising that hotel-occupancy rates, countering the national trend, have been rising in the Twin Cities since the opening of Mystic Lake and the Mall of America.

Leaving suburbia swiftly behind, a gambler can now find action by heading deep into the great north woods. Three hundred miles north of Minneapolis on the Canadian border is, for example, the Lake of the Woods Casino, operated by the Red Lake Band of Chippewa Indians. This is the traditional domain of remote fishing and hunting camps—places where "a guy would go up to a cottage camp and not shave for a week," says Stephen Sherf, an executive with Marquette Partners, a Minneapolis consulting firm that works with casinos. Now, that same guy might want to shave before taking in a cabaret show or hitting one of the slot machines at, say, Northern Lights Casino, in Walker.

Casino day-trippers have never done much for tourism. Those who arrive on charter buses don't even buy gas before heading home. A heartening development in the north country, according to Sherf, is the appearance of recreational-vehicle parks at many casinos. "The roving hordes of retirees in their RVs can now stay in one place for a few days," he says. There's enough of a critical mass of casinos now that tourists can also circulate between them in only a few hours' driving time."

High in the Colorado Rockies three once booming gold-mine towns (Black Hawk, Central City, Cripple Creek) had long gone bust and dwindled down to a combined population of less than a thousand. Entire blockfronts of fine 19th-century buildings remained—many of them vacant but intact. Summer brought a trickle of visitors, notably to Central City's opera festival, held in its splendid little 1878 opera house, and to Cripple Creek's Donkey Derby Days, for a race inspired by local wild donkeys whose forebears had hauled ore wagons. Tourism, such as it was, headed for the larger ski resorts year-round and left these towns for dead.

In 1990 a few local diehards casting about for a way to revive the three towns took a cue from Deadwood, South Dakota. To the surprise of many, Coloradans approved, in a statewide referendum, limited-stakes gambling ($5 maximum bet) in Central City, Black Hawk, and Cripple Creek. The first casino to open, in October 1991, was Virginia Lewis's Jazz Alley Casino—a spot known for having the best "gambling food" in Black Hawk. The building also incorporates the town's original jail, now filled with video poker machines. Mountain-town gambling is a bonanza. With 14,638 slot machines, 70 casinos reaped about $226.5 million in 1993. As the locals had hoped, Central City, Black Hawk, and Cripple Creek are jumping year-round, even drawing visitors from nearby ski resorts. Three years ago, the joke goes, the same $20 bill was passed around town all winter long.

Yet, along with prosperity comes an undertone of disquiet. Despite the crowds, culture hasn't thrived. Central City's opera attendance has fallen. The town's jazz festival was canceled one year. The new crowd wants just to gamble. The day may come, worries Lane Ittelson, a state preservationist, when "Wayne Newton will play the opera house."

All three Colorado casino towns have ordinances protecting their historic buildings—for now, at least. Restored, they can be a pleasure to behold. But no ordinance can regulate or preserve the spirit of these essentially small-scale towns. Something unique has vanished, says Ittelson. "All these Las Vegas video noises in the night are very disquieting. It's changed these towns, completely and forever."

Not only preservationists like Ittelson question what gambling has wrought in Colorado. Late in 1992, the state's voters overwhelmingly rejected a proposed expansion of limited-stakes gambling to other towns.

When a narrow-gauge railroad from Denver to Black Hawk opened, in the 1870s, the *Rocky Mountain News* described the scenery along Clear Creek Canyon as "so variegated, so rugged and so sublime [that it] excites the greatest wonder and admiration conceivable." That's still true, as Route 6 follows the path of the now defunct railway. Clear Creek still roars, and the rugged cliffsides still soar. You can pan for gold or enjoy superb whitewater rafting less than an hour from downtown Denver. Should all this be ceded to casino-bound motorists too distracted to appreciate it?

For now, Americans display a broad tolerance for gambling. According to a study commissioned by Harrah's, 55 percent of them believe that gambling is "perfectly acceptable for anyone." Thirty-five percent believe it's "acceptable for others, but not for me." Only 10 percent consider gambling "not acceptable for anyone."

It's easy to forget that the ever greater splendors of Las Vegas, like those of lesser casino environments, are built on vast sums lost by gamblers. When losses are limited, gambling is called entertainment. Uncontrolled, it's a sickness. According to Eadington, studies show that up to 5 percent of gamblers don't know how to stop. I'm sure I saw two of them at 7:30 A.M. at a Las Vegas hotel: a man, sitting with his wife, moaning low as he banged the back of his head against a mirrored column. Her eyes were cast down, and tears rolled down her cheeks. It wasn't hard to figure out that luck had deserted them at a cruel cost. At least, their children weren't with them. But other people's children who passed by, sensing that something was wrong, eyed the couple curiously.

The most extreme gamblers, intent on keeping up a winning streak, sometimes lose their most basic decorum. Rather than move from a "lucky seat" or interrupt their streak, these gamblers, both male and female, will wet the seat beneath them. Nearly every experienced croupier can tell an unsettling tale of gambling's crossing the line from recreation to disease.

In an abrupt, multibillion-dollar turnaround, Las Vegas is now refurbishing its image as a sin city for highrolling adults only and reaching out to families, even when they're vacationing on a tight budget. The city that sparkles in the desert night long after the kids should be asleep has even begot its own, Disneyesque magical kingdom, as well as dueling pirate ships, life-size mechanical dinosaurs, a mock-up of the Emerald City of Oz, a version of pharaonic Egypt, and Arthurian characters acting out their legends.

Bugsy Siegel, the founding mobster of Las Vegas when it was raffish, would surely be appalled by such relentlessly wholesome family entertainment. So would Walt Disney have, albeit for quite a different reason. He'd not have expected competition against his Magic Kingdom to issue from the world's gambling capital. At $24.95 for dinner and a show, King Arthur's Tournament is a value you'd be hard put to match anywhere but in Las Vegas—certainly not in Orlando.

Las Vegas's turn toward Disney-style family values is shrewdly prescient in an increasingly crowded gambling market—and yet another form of brilliant denial, the emotion this desert dreamland has always worn on its glittering sleeve. But the metamorphosis has certainly astonished locals as much as it has visitors. "As kids growing up here," says Laurie Clemens, a local Mary Kay beauty consultant, "we had nothing much to do. Now we can vacation with our own kids without ever having to leave Las Vegas."

Clemens, her husband, Steve, and their three children were enjoying the Sunday buffet brunch at the Rio Suite Hotel & Casino, west of the Strip. They and many others consider it Las Vegas's best buffet. The Clemens kids barely noticed as the "Keno Lady" stopped by the table to take their parents' bet. Yet that transaction served as a reminder that, even when gambling is labeled as entertainment, it's not for children.

Laurie Clemens agrees. "We have friends who bought a slot machine for their kids and installed it in the garage. The kids could play it all they wanted. The idea was to show them that, though they could have a hot streak, over time they'd always lose." As Americans wade deeper into gambling, whether on riverboats, in old mining towns, on Indian reservations, or in great casino cities, that's a lesson to remember.

GAMBLING NATION[3]

We are the boat people. That is casino workers' slang for the millions of Americans now arriving at their portals in smelly diesel waves. We come by bus—"motorcoach," if you want to get la-di-da about it. Tonight we have been plucked from rainy parking lots all over the Houston area, and we have clambered aboard prepared: pillows, shawls, lucky trolls, full thermoses, white bread, thick stacks of Saran-Wrapped luncheon meat. We're toting worn cotton slot gloves. Intensive Care hand lotion. Insulin. Tylenol. Cash. Doritos.

"We all here? Pedal to the metal, John. Let's git!"

We are Jeanne's Bingo Buddies of Houston, driving all Friday night in a storm that has already spawned killer tornadoes. We're

[3]Article by Gerri Hirshey. From the *New York Times Magazine* July 17, '94. Copyright © 1994 by Gerri Hirshey. Reprinted with permission.

headed east, into the teeth of it; had prayers before we reached the Interstate. Voices in the dark add a gamblers' homily:

"Gonna leave our worries back in Texas, and our money in Mississippi!"

"Hallelujah."

Out east on the Mississippi Gulf Coast, strung over 30 miles from Bay St. Louis to Gulfport and Biloxi, beckons a row of floating "dockside" gaming palaces, voted in in the early 90's by Harrison and Hancock counties, some up and running within five months. These are casinos so new that construction workers must weave through gamblers, so busy that some of these $25 million to $50 million investments can pay for themselves in a matter of months.

They'll be waiting for us there in the yawning bus bays, counting heads, papering us with discount coupons. We are low rollers. Slot hogs. And we are part of the great, teeming, itchy-fingered masses that have made legal gambling—now known as "casino entertainment"—America's new national pastime.

Gambling is now bigger than baseball, more powerful than a platoon of Schwarzeneggers, Spielbergs, Madonnas and Oprahs. More Americans went to casinos than to major league ballparks in 1993. *Ninety-two million visits!* Legal gambling revenues reached $30 billion, which is more than the combined take for movies, books, recorded music and park and arcade attractions. Thirty-seven states have lotteries; 23 have sanctioned casinos. More than 60 Indian tribes have gaming compacts with 19 states. As this century turns, it's expected that virtually all Americans will live within a four-hour drive of a casino.

"Okay, Buddies, sing it *out*!
There is a bingo spirit in the air
Cause Jeanne's Bingo Buddies go everywhere
We sit together so that we can share
We're gonna WIN WIN WIN!"

Rolling toward the Louisiana state line in a big German-made bus, we are the new Gambling Nation, a yammering, munching, snoring aggregate of Italian-, Polish-, German- and African-Americans, 10th-generation Texans, Latinos—and one Comanche. Most of us work; some are retired. Between us we dabble in bingo, the ponies, the dogs, the lottery, keno, cards and the slots. We'd like to win but we sure don't count on it. And if we do hit, our expectations are modest. "Three cherries and you take the family to Red

Lobster instead of ever-lovin' Roy Rogers," a gent in a string tie explained to me recently in Las Vegas. "Hell, why *not?*"

And so we stand in lottery lines and climb aboard buses on the strength of *possibilities.* They're limitless, but with absurdist odds. America has come to count heavily on our cheerful folly. Our modest stakes have become the last best hope for budget-strapped state legislatures, for long-impoverished Indian tribes now permitted to run gaming ventures, for stockbrokers and investment bankers looking to salve the wounds inflicted by 80's excesses. To these grateful constituencies, gambling is no longer a sin, but a saving grace. It can vanquish the ugly specter of raising taxes and shake cash into shambling infrastructures, Head Start programs, fire brigades, tribal medical clinics. It can fatten portfolios with new high-performance issues.

On the strength of such boons, Mammon's had a makeover. Much has been made of the new PG Las Vegas, of the theme park hotels, the troops of Dorothys and Totos, buccaneers, knights and hunks in mini-togas who now cavort where made guys and hookers once ruled. Had any of us Buddies brought children along to Biloxi, we could have deposited them in the cheery child-care facility at the Grand Casino.

It's O.K. now, say the attitudinal seismologists. According to a national survey conducted by Harrah's, a top-tier casino company, 51 percent of American adults believe "casino entertainment" is "acceptable for anyone." Another 35 percent say it is "acceptable for others, but not for me." Even "gambling," the term that once conjured up green visors, cigar smoke and gumball-size pinky rings, has been buffed with warm fuzzies. We call it *gaming* these days. So Aspen. So Hyannisport. So very . . . *sportif.*

Why now? Exactly 100 years ago, Congress banned all state lotteries after a huge corruption scandal in Louisiana. But for the last decade, states couldn't vote them in fast enough or push them harder. The turnabout has to do with exigency, marketing and a mother lode of skepticism afflicting the national mood.

The vision of postwar prosperity that inspired Las Vegas's early gaming entrepreneurs in the late 40's has been inverted in the 90's. Possibility—the cornerstone of this upstart democracy— has rarely been so circumscribed, as the children of baby boomers find themselves competing for low-level "McJobs" and huge companies toss buyouts at once-valued senior staffers. Certainty has eroded, too, as pension plans go bankrupt and one underinsured double bypass can compromise the futures of two or three generations. With fewer and fewer "sure things," the timing is just right for a large-scale flirtation with Lady Luck.

It made all the difference that state and city governments have been her most enthusiastic procurers. Pious and public earmarks for state lottery money—education! senior citizen programs!—helped fade the taint of sin. Further sanitation was provided by the new corporate gleam of casino ownership. As I heard it explained most succinctly in the check-in line of an Atlantic City hotel: "Honey, it's not Don Corleone anymore. It's just Donald Trump."

Industry types like to remind you that gambling has long been the American way. After all, the first Continental Congress helped finance the Revolution with lotteries. Benjamin Franklin, George Washington and Thomas Jefferson each sponsored private lotteries. Our founding fathers were just numbers guys in wigs.

In "Temples of Chance," his penetrating study of gambling's transformation, David Johnston outlines boom and bust cycles in American history. One telling example: Vicksburg, Miss., now supports four riverboat casinos, with four more planned; back in 1835, local citizens, enraged by the proliferation of riverboat cardsharps and gambling dens there, smashed gambling equipment and hanged five professional cheats.

The current gambling boom is unlike any other for its size and for its mainstream status. The big winners are not outlaws, but publicly traded corporations and state and Federal coffers. Never has government been such a devoted bookmaker, taking in $25 billion a year on lotteries. The amount Americans spent on all forms of legal wagering last year—$330 billion—has set historical precedent of its own. Never has so great a fortune been staked on an itch.

Slots and the Supply Side

"I just want to see that million-dollar ladies room at the Biloxi Grand," says Maggie Smith, a Buddy. "Everybody comes back talking about that john."

"Honey, those commodes are *red* porcelain."

The Buddies tell me that folks take flash cameras into the third-floor ladies' room at the Grand Casino Biloxi, which features a hand-painted Gibson girl on each stall door and gilt carts laden with gratis cologne, lotions and jumbo cans of Final Net.

There are snowy linen towels to help with slot sludge, the shiny grime that blackens hands after 20 minutes of play. Indelicate acoustics are softened by a soundtrack of chirping birds. It's all part of what industry literature calls "feeling casino excitement."

"Some of my hard-core bingo people won't go near casinos," says our leader, Jeanne (pronounced Jeannie) Stewart. "But the ones that come to Mississippi or Las Vegas with us look at it as a mini-vacation. They gawk as much as they gamble, go walking on the beach. Look, I work in a hospital. Of a weekend, I love to see something that's not cinder block."

For more than a decade, Jeanne, a cardiologist's assistant, and her husband, Homer, a former golf pro, have regularly ferried some 500 Houston-area Buddies to the huge, high-stakes Indian bingo halls in Texas, Oklahoma, even as far away as a Cherokee operation in North Carolina, a trip that takes 17 hours each way.

The Stewarts know all about what investment bankers term "the pent-up consumer demand" to gamble. That mighty urge tops the demand side of an exhaustive report on the gambling industry by Smith Barney Shearson. The report's supply-side forces include the states' need for additional nontax revenue sources, the domino effect when states vote gambling in to prevent an income drain to adjacent gaming states and "high return on investment," at least initially, for new casinos.

The final supply factor is the proliferation of Indian gaming, which took in approximately $15.2 billion in 1992. Foxwoods, the Mashantucket Pequot casino in Ledyard, Conn., is currently the world's largest casino, hauling in more than $600 million in a year. Indian gaming is expected to grow by $500 million a year.

On the demand side, that "pent up" urge to gamble is measured partly by the estimates of illegal gaming. Gaming & Wagering Business magazine, in its most recent survey, figured the aggregate illegal take for horses and sports betting books, cards and numbers to be $43 billion. Also listed in that column: "attitude changes."

The New Saturday Night Live

Outside Port Arthur, Tex., we're still awake and chatty. Everyone is tired from the week's work—as nurses, administrative assistants, apartment house managers. But all are merry.

"*Gonna win!*" yells Malcolm Peterson, punching his bed pillow. He is the silver-haired, 52-year-old son of Sara Peterson, an elegant, witty, retired businesswoman who describes herself as "only 80." For the last half-century, Malcolm has needed his mother's 24-hour care owing to multiple Down syndrome-related disabilities. They both love the bingo trips and the casino slots. As he will prove with great glee later this morning, Malcolm always wins at the slots.

"You wait," he tells me. "I'll help you win too." Once we pass his favorite part of the drive—the refinery lights of Baytown—he curls up to nap and reaches back for a reassuring pat from his mother.

"I'm here, Malcolm. Rest now."

She lights a cigarette and leans back, looking very, very tired.

"I'm in the stress reduction business," Jeanne Stewart says. After years working in cardiac units, she can read your blood pressure in your eyes. "I see what they look like when they climb on this bus Friday night. Gray. Tense and pinched."

In workday America, the life of the soul can stagger between exhaustion and escape, with little time for reflection. For many two-career families, single parents and career-driven singles, amusements tend to be compact. Weekend trips. Movies. Fast meals out. Leisure can take on the character of the work it seeks to counterweight. And it is no accident that as jobs creating durable goods give way to the service sector, as work places become more isolationist —setting us in computer stations, telemarketing carrels, home offices—entertainment itself has become less communal, more remote.

Last year, for the first time, the solitary pursuits of video games outsold movie admissions. Even teen-age bacchanals have been tempered by technology. For most concertgoers of Madonna's "Girlie Show" tour, the Main Dish was just a series of dots on a stadium video screen. This summer's Woodstock II concert is expected to generate $20 million in pay-per-view revenues from couch potato communards.

How, then, can anyone profess surprise at the casinos' staggering numbers? They're one of the few ways left to experience Saturday night *live*, to get out amid squealing, yee-hawing humans determined to raise a wee tad o' heck.

Call it the Beyond Bugsy Effect. When he built the Flamingo Hotel and casino in 1946, Bugsy Siegel envisioned Las Vegas as an oasis for his kind of people—the restless grifters who couldn't toe that 9-to-5 line. What Bugsy underestimated was that little urge to slip the traces—if only for the duration of a bingo game, a hand of 21—laying nascent in so many of us clock punchers, homemakers and retirees.

The new casino doges understand. They pack Harvard M.B.A.'s, not heat, provide baby sitters instead of hookers. Of the scores of gamblers I talked to, few voiced resentment at their genial casino hosts. Their greatest contempt was reserved for their elected representatives. Government, they pointed out, is unsurpassed at fostering the great illusion that you can change your life with one bet. Nowhere, particularly in the hyperslick ads that show blue-collar winners cavorting on lavish estates, is it intimated that the state lotteries offer worse sucker odds than any casino or honest bookie. The house edge for slots runs from 10 to 15 percent; the lottery 50 percent.

Over the last year, news magazine stories and television specials have decried this headlong rush toward fool's gold. Thundered Walter Cronkite on a cable special, "Legal Gambling—The Dice Are Loaded": "All this while a nation once built on a work ethic embraces the belief that it's possible to get something for nothing."

Uncle Walter's stentorian moralizing makes very legitimate points about the "hidden" costs of gaming. There *are* plenty of grisly true stories about grannies gambling away pension checks. But ride the buses down here, haunt the Atlantic City bus lounges, the Texas bingo halls, and the majority of seniors will tell you they're spending more time than money. Time is cheap, time is plentiful, and in "golden" America, time can be a dubious kind of wealth. Elder testimony gathered at casinos reads like a wry, cranky litany:

"I cannot tie on those darn Reeboks my kids gave me and mall-walk one more time. I spend more that way than at the casino."

"I *talk* to people on these trips. When I stay home, it's just me and Oprah."

Boom Town in Biloxi

The sun is just rising as the Buddies pull into Biloxi. Klieg lights and welding torches flicker through the morning fog on the Mississippi Sound. This is boom town, a construction wildcatter's dream. They build around the clock here—three shifts a day. Ten casinos were operating by mid-May, with another eleven proposed or under construction.

The "architecture" affixed to these floating barges ranges

from faux paddle wheeler to mandarin palace. From the front porch of Beauvoir, the stately, white-pillared home that was the final residence of Jefferson Davis, you can see Treasure Bay, a mammoth castle-and-pirate ship. A Brobdingnagian mermaid holds up its prow, parting the gentle Gulf breezes with naked breasts as big as kettle drums.

All night, buses have been hissing to the front of Biloxi's Casino Magic, disgorging groups from Mobile, Jackson, Atlanta. And all night, perky hosts have been leaping aboard, stacks of plastic Casino Magic players' cards in hand. Before the sleepy masses can rouse themselves, they are filling out applications for the cards, which are inserted into the slot machines as you play, much like bank cards.

"Just tell us about yourselves. Birthdays, favorite colors, anniversaries. *We want to know you better!*"

Lively players, tracked by computer, can win incentives: free drinks, meals, even cash. The Buddies scribble away. Duly tagged and processed, we are released into the scarlet and fuchsia wild.

"Good luck, y'all!"

Seen at the 50's-style diner in the Biloxi Grand on a Saturday night: 60-ish parents with their young married children. When the food arrives, hands are joined, and heads bow in prayer. Spoon poised, the patriarch addresses his grown daughter:

"Now baby girl, them dollar slots is the devil. You stick to quarters, hear?"

Baby tucks into her hot fudge sundae with a right hand blackened from dropping those quarters. Nobody minds.

"I'm winning. Can't wash off that luck."

Mississippi is the nation's best petri dish for studying the effects of no-limits casino fever. And no place is there a better example of the ease with which old-time politicking has gussied up a fundamentalist's sin and elevated it to savior. This Bible Belt state has some of the nation's poorest counties, run-down agricultural areas like Tunica, dubbed "America's Ethiopia" by Jesse Jackson. By the late 80's, bankruptcies were more insidious than any boll weevil plague of yore. The tax base was on life support. The palliative? Gaming.

When it voted to legalize gambling on the waters of the Mississippi River and the Mississippi Sound several years ago, the revenue-hungry state legislature set no limits on the number of dockside casinos. And, unlike expensive and stringently regulated Atlantic City, which also has no license limits, Mississippi has a cost of doing business that is low enough to entice all comers. This has resulted in five major "gaming markets"—Tunica, Vicksburg, Natchez, Greenville and the coast. A total of 54 casinos could be operational within the year. Louisiana is mounting a challenge with boats and casinos. Next year, Harrah's expects to open the world's largest hotel casino in New Orleans—just an hour's drive from Gulfport.

The Mississippi charge was led by State Senator Tommy Gollott, a powerful, well-connected Biloxian who has long been an advocate of nearly every kind of gaming. The casino push started in the mid-80's, Gollott says, when a former state senator, Sandy Steckler ("a cousin of mine"), came to him for a little help. One of Steckler's law clients was a gambling cruise ship, the Europa Star. Its owners needed legislation to allow it to operate off the coast.

Gollott was happy to help. "We were having a terrible time," he says. "And I saw a lot of my friends going down, all types of businesses."

Gaming looked good. "I wanted to bring additional revenues into the state without adding taxes on people," recalls Gollott, whose logic is still echoed by embattled legislators across the country. He was single-minded in his pursuit. "I introduced the lottery a number of times," he says. "Horse racing. Jai alai. . . ."

Finally, Gollott looked to have a winner with dockside. But the vote seemed too close for comfort. In March 1990, on the eve of the crucial cruise ship vote, there was a strange exodus from the Statehouse.

"You oughta have seen those ol' boys run," recalls Mayor Glenn Mitchell, of Long Beach, Mississippi, describing the night when eight state senators from very conservative areas disappeared and missed the balloting.

Mitchell had driven up to Jackson, the state capital, to lobby against the casinos. (The small town of Long Beach is the lone holdout on the coast, having consistently voted against allowing casinos there.) "I caught up with one of them on his way out," Mitchell remembers. "He's from a real Bible Belt area and voting for gambling would be the end of him. Well, he just waved at me, wouldn't even roll down his car window."

Gollott, who was accused of getting the conservative senators to skip the vote by calling in heavy political favors, counters: "I don't remember asking anyone to leave."

Mitchell says: "We lost by one vote. I think it's incredible cowardice, bad politics to betray your constituency that way." Gollott insists it was just business as usual in a Statehouse where folks from unaffected counties stay out of the business of others."

There was a to-do, however, when it was revealed that Gollott's family business owned a 4.2-acre waterfront property at Biloxi's Point Cadet, bought in 1987. Gollott did not disclose his personal interest until after the Senate dockside vote. In March 1992, one month after Gollott's county voted to allow dockside gambling, his company entered into an agreement to lease the land to the Biloxi Casino Corporation for $1.9 million over the first five years, and another $47 million in options over the following 85 years.

Now Gollott chuckles and says its darn tough to argue with success—the community's and his own. "Gaming has changed this coast," he says. "We have 47,000 people working for the casino industry. Unemployment before dockside was 8.7 percent. Now it's less than 5."

He admits there are glitches. With traffic hellacious and accidents on the rise, legislators are floating more bond issues, pumping up feeder roads. And he hopes they can figure out how to help neighboring nongaming counties strained by the influx of casino workers' children overburdening their school systems.

Overall, though, Gollott says, "All the changes is positive." He predicts his low sandy Gulf Coast will rival Las Vegas in another decade. "I see a lot of high rises in east Biloxi, D'Iberville, all along the interstate." Query him about overdevelopment, and Gollott says, "I believe the weak will fall by the wayside. The strong will survive."

The Buffet Lines Cometh

Dinnertime in Gulfport, at Le Teagarden restaurant, a French-Vietnamese establishment on the main beach road that has become Casino Row. Hung Vu Nguyen, the owner and chef, has cooked only eight meals. With some time on his hands, Henry, as he prefers to be known, is listening with polite amusement to my stuttered hosannas over his astonishing catfish. In Manhattan or Los Angeles, his suave multi-cult alchemy would have foodies offering their firstborns for a reservation.

Since the casinos opened, Henry Nguyen has seen his staff dwindle from 45 to just a handful—mostly family members. "I can't compete with the wage-and-benefit packages the casinos have," he says. Business, once S.R.O., has been flatter than a Gulf flounder. Even regular customers come monthly rather than weekly. Casinos, they tell him. They all have restaurants, all-you-can-eat buffet lines. Plus games, shows, shops, nurseries, full-service A.T.M.'s. . .

"They build it so you never have to leave."

Henry Nguyen says that he is a philosophical, if weary, man. He survived wartime missions as a pilot in the South Vietnamese Air Force, has raised three children here and would just like to get them through college. "I am not bitter," he says. "I just want to hang on."

At some local residents' insistence, I also drop by to see "Miss Annie" Lutz, a restaurant owner of legend whose roots go as deep as those of the biggest live oaks here. Miss Annie has been serving up tender flounder and tough opinions since her parents opened their restaurant in 1929. "Been through recessions, been through Hurricane Camille back in '69," says Miss Annie. "Got by O.K. Not so sure about this one."

Annie's is "off the highway." Customers never had trouble finding her—until now. "Felt it right away," she says of the casino competition. "Don't let any of us locals tell you we're not hurtin'."

Atlantic City was the first gambling mecca to find that not all segments of the local economy are served by casino growth. Since the first casino hotels opened there in 1978, 100 of the city's 250 restaurants closed. Retail business dropped by one third. Tourism there has begun to dip as well. As nearby areas like Philadelphia and the New Jersey Meadowlands consider gaming, Atlantic City is making noise about "reinventing" itself as a tourist destination and convention town. After sixteen years of legalized gambling, this "city"—with no golf course, no supermarket and no movie house—is realizing the price of piling all its chips on one number.

Such is the difference between what financial analysts call the "euphoria" and "reality" phases of the gaming cycle. And it's easy to understand why they don't welcome realists in Mississippi just now. Even in casino-free Long Beach, Mayor Mitchell has been granting audiences to hotel and condo developers. "Times have changed," he says, "since I darn near stood on my head to get the K Mart into town."

Hotel operators on the coast are definitely euphoric. There are not nearly enough existing rooms to accommodate the estimated 50,000 casino visitors a day. Thus, weekends here are sheer madness. The Buddies and I had to put up at a Waffle Inn, plunked in some woods off the interstate, nearly an hour away from the action.

But downtown, little has changed. Walk down 13th Street in Gulfport and count ten empty storefronts. There is one thriving new business in a converted A.&P.: Casino Jewelry and Pawn. On the beach in Biloxi, there are four new pawnshops, each stocked with wedding and engagement rings left behind by gamblers, some on their honeymoons.

Local crime statistics are not easy to come by. Last year the Gulf Coast towns had 16 bank robberies, a fourfold increase over the year before. Law enforcement officials have reported small rises in drug arrests and prostitution in and around the boats.

The Biloxi Salvation Army is struggling to keep up with a tripled caseload of singles and families—casino Okies—who migrated here to find jobs and were shut out. Five chapters of Gamblers Anonymous have opened where there had been none. The suicide rate has inexplicably doubled in Harrison County, though no health care official was willing to tie the increase to gambling. "There is a lot of stress and a lot of change," ventures Gini Fellows, director of recovery resources at Gulf Oaks Hospital. "And people don't take to change very well."

The day I visited Mayor Mitchell, a copy of the day's Sun Herald lay folded on his neat desk. The headline blared: Big Stink Hounds Casinos. In March of this year, every casino in Biloxi was found to be violating sewage discharge laws. Illegal grease and oil dumping were clogging lines and creating noxious fumes.

But elsewhere things are still coming up aces. Employment figures have hit record highs. And there are Sun Herald headlines that read, "Biloxi Now Among Few in Black." As I left Mayor Mitchell, I ceded my chair to a smiling amusement park developer from New Orleans wearing an endangered species tie.

"Pretty country out here," he ventured. "Don'tcha think?"

Gone With the Wind?

"Well, cuss those tree-huggin', Bible-thumpin', Gamblers Anonymous, investigative, naysayin' no accounts."

My tablemate at the Pirate's Cove in tiny Pass Christian, Miss., is waving a catfish po'boy the size of a bowling pin.

"Rich N'awlins summerhouse layabouts. They don't need casino jobs."

The gentleman, who prefers to remain unnamed, says he is making $14 an hour raking dice at a Gulfport craps table, which beats the tar out of his old wages at a video rental store. I have made the mistake of describing my boat cruise with a couple of pesky women who drive around with "no casino" stickers on their station wagons.

"Agitatin' liberal *fools!*"

At town meetings and E.P.A. hearings, a coalition of local residents is lobbying to limit casino development, particularly in the wetlands near their waterfront homes on the Bay of St. Louis, west of Gulfport. Lib Duffy and Nonnie DeBardeleben admit they're "not real popular" in many circles here, where folks can do some creative cussing.

With Lib Duffy's husband John at the helm, we push off in a small motorboat to look at proposed casino sites around the bay. Despite repeated offers from a developer working with the casinos, John has refused to sell their property. When the last offer was spurned, the developer, a high-school classmate, offered some neighborly advice:

"Sell out now or you're gonna walk out Sunday morning and find Bubba passed out in his pickup, right on your front yard."

Lib Duffy was not intimidated. "I was raised here," she says. I can handle my Bubbas."

Corporate Bubbas are something else. Ally them with councilmen swooning over their new tax numbers, Duffy says, and the odds seem hopeless sometimes. Yet she vows she will not be forced out by the noise, development and traffic of 10 additional casinos proposed for this lovely, quiet bay. (Two are already operating.) She hopes her neighbors will also stand firm. Environmental issues do concern people here, according to a recent poll published in The Sun Herald. While 61 percent of local residents think the casinos' economic effects are positive, 84 percent believe more state regulation is needed to protect wetlands, the region's greatest natural asset.

The fiercest battles are being waged over development in the delicate bays, like this one, and the larger Back Bay of Biloxi, where shrimp and fish spawn in the salt marshes. Noise, dredging, heated water flushed from air conditioners, trash and sewage overload are all serious concerns in these prime nursery areas.

"We were able to rebuild when Camille destroyed our home," says DeBardeleben. "But if they muck this up, there's no going back."

At the helm, John Duffy eases the boat up to the broad, windowless back of Casino Magic. The barge settled on the bay bottom not long ago, and divers had to refloat it. Nonetheless, there are plans to add a restaurant barge and an R.V. park. "These bay locations are desirable," says DeBardeleben, "because they're more protected from hurricanes."

Hurricane safety is an issue that all these spindle-masted and pagoda-roofed "vessels" must contend with. But there have been no satisfactory answers. "Nobody wants to ruffle the casino men," says DeBardeleben.

Evacuation of 50,000 daily visitors over narrow coast roads and five bridges is a worrisome prospect. The question of moving or securing the floating casinos is still causing controversy. For more than a year, most casinos have been operating with insurance that requires evacuating the behemoths to safe harbor during storms. This month, Gov. Kirk Fordice announced that the barges would have to stay put and owners would have to build or retro-fit moorings to withstand 155-mile-per-hour winds and 15-foot tidal surges. As hurricane season approaches, casinos and insurers are vociferously opposing the plan.

Louis Skrmetta, a local excursion boat owner, has doubts that the new gaming palaces can withstand serious gales. "Some claim they can withstand any huge, ocean-going storm, he says. "During Camille, freighters built to ride storms out at sea were thrown so far up on the beach they had to be cut up for scrap."

Lib Duffy says someone made a joke at a meeting the other night. "They said maybe only God can stop corporate America," she says. "Maybe we need a hurricane."

That thought returns on a blustery evening as I head out of the Asian-themed Lady Luck Casino in Biloxi. In the valet parking area, what looks like a nubby concrete wall has been side-swiped by passing cars. Idly, I stick a finger in one large dent. Foam pellets—the kind used to fill beanbag chairs—pour out over my shoes and blow away in the wind.

That's Entertainment

"The riverboat is preposterous!" Steve Wynn is saying. "When you build a riverboat, you build a gambling hall. A gambling joint appeals to that small percentage of the public that wants to gamble. If we're looking at a cross-section of the earth, that's the equivalent of topsoil in the earth's crust."

Wynn, Las Vegas's acknowledged Wizard of Wow, is speaking from the epicenter of the Gambling Nation, his $770 million

Mirage Hotel. We are talking in the outdoor garden surrounding his elegant, glass-walled bunker on the hotel's ground floor.

"Riverboats seem to be something you can sell to the voters," Wynn mutters. All those floating delta ventures, the Iowa paddle-wheelers are just so much shifting silt to Wynn. He wouldn't touch them with a barge pole. Nor would he reconsider Atlantic City, where he sold his cash-minting Golden Nugget casino hotel in 1987—for $440 million, then a record. As a showman, he felt hamstrung by uptight Eastern regulations—no signs, no lights, no fun. He'll *never* go back. After years of casino gambling, he says, it's still a slum-by-the-sea.

Wynn flings an arm out toward the mountains. "When you talk about a destination resort like Las Vegas, you're talking about a cut that goes down deep into the igneous rock," he says. "We build places for folks who don't think of themselves as gamblers."

Steve Wynn has made a bedrock business out of helping folks maintain that deception. Much of his psychology he learned from Benny Binion, who ran the Horseshoe Casino here. "Always give a gambler a good excuse," Binion advised Wynn back in the 60's. "They'll appreciate your doing that."

At the Mirage, 20,000-plus visitors a day show their gratitude by spending more than $700,000 on nongambling pursuits. The gawk-and-gamble crowd keeps Wynn's 1,500-seat showroom sold out twice a night, six nights a week, 40 weeks a year—at $73 a ticket. They keep his 3,000-room hotel at more than 95 percent capacity, and often sold out. (The national average is 65 percent.) They bring cash for Wynn's casino, and camcorders for his white tigers, his dolphins, his $32-million man-made volcano out front.

The attitudinal sea change toward "casino entertainment" owes much to Wynn's well-executed excesses here. Nobody does it better—and with cannier timing. While Jay Sarno's Circus Circus can be credited with offering the first free "themed" entertainment in the mid-70's, with trapeze artists and clowns cavorting over the casino area, it was Wynn's far grander vision that jump-started the Vegas transformation. Listen to Wynn explain the simple lines of what he calls his "better mousetrap":

"The name of the game here is who gets the walk-in," Wynn is saying. "Your brain says you're in the harsh, inhospitable desert of southern Nevada." How to bend that? Casting about for a theme, he seized on a beloved American musical. Wynn says he was thinking about the director Joshua Logan's first shot of Bali Ha'i during the film version of "South Pacific." "Juanita Hall as

Bloody Mary is singing, they've got the filters on. Orange. Amber. . . .

"I said to my buddies: look, you'll see 150,000 gallons a minute of the most beautiful, lush, tropical thing we can do. Shrouded in trees, with a boulevard going up to it. And you'll say *this is funky*! Could the inside be as fanciful as the outside?"

He claps his hands.

"That's the roll of the front. That's the hook."

Wynn is all but yelling his corporate mantra: "*We've got to keep the promise!*"

They walk into an atrium that smells like Bali Ha'i. Flown in from Hawaii: live orchids, elephant ears, banana trees and coconut palms, intermingled with top-of-the-line silk facsimiles.

"We're gonna chevron the casino around the atrium. . . . When they come out, they'll already be in the middle of the casino."

Gotcha.

In its first month of operation, December 1989, the Mirage beat Caesar's 1988 Atlantic City gaming revenue record of $38 million, taking in $40 million. The Mirage's unprecedented success led to other multi-million-dollar hallucinations, like the MGM-Grand with its yellow-brick road, the Egyptian-themed Luxor with a tour-boat-laden Nile River in its lobby and Wynn's own pirate-themed Treasure Island. It also led to that Miss Kitty ladies' room at the Biloxi Grand. And you can't tell me that Vegas va-va-vavoom didn't infuse the lagoons and atriums of Minnesota's stupefying Mall of America. Vegas has even spun off a PG, homogenized version of itself in the dewey bosom of Branson, Mo.

Steve Wynn and the Branson bunch, from Loretta Lynn to Tony Orlando, know why management will never take down that Elvis memorial in the lobby at the Las Vegas Hilton: we are all members of the Lost Tribe of Elvis, wandering here to his neon desert in record droves. Over the last decade, we have made Entertainment—the *Big* E—our No. 2 export, behind jet airplanes. We watch E! network, display an alarming capacity for receiving our news with a rimshot. From "A Current Affair" to the grits 'n' Jesus "gospel brunch," *we will be entertained.* Product has taken a back seat to Production Values. So build it big, build it outrageous *and we will come.* Some of us may be summoned to worship, others to hoot. But everybody pays the cover charge.

"This place was a no-brainer," Wynn says. "It was like spitting and hitting the sidewalk." This, he says, is because of the big E factor so many people discount when sizing up his town, where gambling and entertainment achieved that crucial meld.

"In my view, Las Vegas has been an entertainment attraction since the 50's," Wynn says. "Gambling was what you did while you were here. But the *shows*, the *characters*! The attraction has always been the mystique of the town, the Sinatras. You come to see the lights. You can stay up all night."

Lord knows they come dressed to play. Earlier I stood at the bottom of an escalator next door at Wynn's Treasure Island hotel and counted 14 adults in a row descending in bright nylon jogging suits and fanny packs. From Biloxi to Bettendorf, Iowa, the fanny pack is the official badge of the Gambling Nation, riding high above cholesterol-belted radials, or weighted low by three rolls of quarters.

You see more silk shirts and the occasional Rolex in the more upscale Mirage. High-roller table games—blackjack, roulette, craps and baccarat—rake in 30 percent of the Mirage gambling revenues. By way of example, Wynn plops yesterday's profit-and-loss statement beneath my nose; the gaming take is more than $3.6 million, skewed upward, he says, by just one high roller.

"An Asian gentleman," is all he will say. "Playing baccarat. He won $1.5 million then gave it all back—$7 million—last night."

For years, all the big casinos have staffed sales reps specializing in the huge Asian market here and abroad. When I visited Las Vegas on Chinese New Year, every room was sold out within 10 miles of town. To better service his biggest fish, or "whales," as high rollers are known, Wynn already has offices in Kuala Lumpur, Tokyo, Singapore, Seoul, Kyoto, Hong Kong and Jakarta.

As American-style gambling goes global, Wynn won't have any difficulty financing overseas expeditions. His current line of credit, somewhere over half a billion dollars, is provided by 17 domestic and foreign banks, including Bank of America, Bankers Trust, Société Générale of France, Long Term Credit Bank of Japan. Even a decade ago, such an all-star lineup would have been unthinkable for a casino stock.

The road to respectability and boundless credit lines started when a couple of young turks in denim—Wynn and Michael Milken—took a casual meeting in August 1976. Wynn was 36, and struggling to finance a second Golden Nugget casino, this time in Atlantic City. Milken was 30, an ambitious bond trader for Drexel Burnham Lambert. Wynn blue-skied the Victorian candy box he wanted to build, top rung, going straight for the custom-

ers who still order their steaks bloody and their Lincoln Town
Cars once a year. Milken was intrigued. Though Drexel had refused financial requests from other gaming companies, Milken
had a new vision of the bond market that was built around risk.

Junk bonds, all but unsecured, high-yield issues, would become the financial community's hottest 80's gamble. Milken and
his traders would grow impossibly rich on Americans' willingness
to finance a long shot at high interest rates with huge built-in
bonuses (the Trifecta!), should these companies actually pay off
their debt on time. For Milken's raiders, it was indeed morning in
America. And the casino industry was happy to stay open 24
hours to service those millions in new debt.

With Milken's intercession, Wynn got a $20 million debt issue
for the Golden Nugget Inc., then worth only $35 million. It would
set the stage for quarter-billion-dollar forays into the junk market
by other emerging gaming outfits like Elsinore (Hyatt's gaming
branch), Trump, Hilton, Circus Circus and Merv Griffin's Resorts
International.

"In '87, when we started the Mirage," Wynn recalls, "I phoned
in 525." Meaning he raised $525 million easily, quickly and at
"attractive" rates. "The gaming industry had an instant love affair
with the bond market, primarily because Michael Milken made
the commitment," he says. "He vouched, they listened, then the
gaming industry kept the promise."

In the mid-80's, he says, he could scarcely believe his own
good fortune: "You could sell gaming to these major companies
and sell their debt for any amount of money. You never saw half a
billion show up as fast as it did for this place, and it wasn't guaranteed by the parent company. All I did was guarantee to finish the
building."

'We're in the Political Business Now'.

If there was any resistance left to gaming as an acceptable
divertissement, it wasn't in the state capitals. The industry could
now count government among its most forceful allies. Wynn
thinks attitudes were tenderized by all the pounding from those
television lotto ads—served up by Madison Avenue's best—on
government contracts. *You gotta be in it to win it. Hey, you never know.*

"The states pummel citizens with the benefits of the easy dollar in gaming, which is not the right thing to say, because it's *not*
that way," Wynn says. "But the states did it."

For years, he had to answer to hectoring gaming commissions.

Now when Steve Wynn talks, government listens. After word leaked that the Clinton White House was considering a 4 percent gambling tax to finance welfare reform, Wynn called Representative Dan Rostenkowski at home, at 11 P.M., to register his deep displeasure. Recently, during a drive through Philadelphia with that city's mayor, Ed Rendell, Wynn told hizzoner that the riverboat gambling being proposed for the Delaware River there was a "cockeyed, ridiculous idea." He told him that nothing would fill his new half-billion-dollar convention center like *committed* hotels downtown.

"If the Mayor could announce that anyone who builds 1,500 rooms can have a gaming facility inside, and if he had an agenda where that neighborhood near Market Street was to be developed, my prediction is that in Philadelphia, it might take 60 days to get three of us there. We might cut loose a billion. A billion two. . . ."

Soon, pending approval, Wynn will be constructing another one of his lavish, tender traps in Vancouver. He's also preparing a joint venture on South Beach in Miami, anticipating a casino referendum in Florida. And he's headed for the Lone Star State, with the hearty encouragement of Houston's Mayor, Bob Lanier. In April, Lanier, in the company of Gov. Ann Richards, opened the new Sam Houston Race Park, declaring "There's a lot of tax revenue out here."

The race track was built by Maxxam Inc., which will be Wynn's partner in a new venture there. When I visited Houston, a Maxxam executive drove me through the proposed casino site, a weedy, not-so-sprawling urban park that currently holds the dilapidated Sam Houston Coliseum and an exhibition hall. The whole sorry package is wrapped in freeway ramps, and set at the edge of a very moribund downtown. Wynn is unfazed by the mess, and by the fact that casino gambling must still go up for a vote next year. With Mississippi and Louisiana casinos sucking Texas wagers over the border, it's expected that the vaunted domino effect will carry the day.

Meanwhile, the Maxxam-Mirage consortium will construct an "interim park," with "grass berms, graceful walks" and a performance stage as a "gift" to the citizens of Houston. And they will assume the $5 million cost of demolishing the old buildings and removing asbestos. Should gaming be passed, Maxxam-Mirage will guarantee rents and taxes of $15 million a year for the city coffers.

"Bob Lanier's got this really nice project of ours," Wynn says. "We'll get licensed all right."

Wynn says gambling's estimable new position in America is making him reassess his own. "This spread of gaming, the complexity of new jurisdictions and the issues raised are going to put a new requirement upon fellas and ladies like myself. A requirement to be very circumspect. To learn how to think dialectically, on a number of levels besides just operational."

It's come a long way from cost-per-servings and high-roller comps.

"We're in the political business now."

Everyone Into the Pit

Leon Gilliam, designated Party Animal, is working his cheering constituency in front of the Big Six wheel in Harrah's "Party Pit." It's his afternoon shift. Peer in from the blinding sun out on the Vegas Strip this 87-degree day, and rockin' Leon is one exotic vision, a tall, model-handsome black man with many moving parts and a very long ponytail currently whipping time to that polyester chestnut, "Y.M.C.A." For some reason, the Village People are tops in the Pit.

Gilliam deejays, sings, dances, deals and takes bets on the wheel—all with boundless energy and wit. Stationed right inside Harrah's front door, directly across from the entrance to the Mirage, he and his T-shirted fellow Pit vamps constitutes Harrah's latest weapon in what's called "capture"—enticing bettors in off the street. Harrah's, considered by many market analysts to be the best-run, most solid casino company in the game, is putting friendly faces up against Wynn's volcano. They don't go for kaboom —just consistency. The hook used by the Party Animals is straightforward enough: *Let's boogie.*

Bunches of helium balloons mark the Pit—six blackjack tables where party dudes and dudettes deal, joke, whack careless bettors with rubber hammers, ring bells and joust with collapsible plastic swords. Poker faces have no place here. And on Saturday nights, the wait is five deep for a seat.

"Call me a dealer-slash-entertainer," Gilliam says, mopping his brow during a break. "Cause that's the job description these days."

Though Gilliam has a couple of "jammin'" octogenarians among his devoted fans, most of the Pit patrons seem to be in their 20's and 30's, women in cutoffs and halter tops, men whooping and high-fiving over the payoff on a sweet pair of queens. Revenues for this area of the casino are up more than 50 percent since employees dreamed up the Pit last year. The "capture" has increased from 35 to 52 percent of passers-by. And now the fun is being franchised at other Harrah's casinos. *That's* entertainment. And it's good business. In 1992, the stock of Harrah's parent, Promus, Inc., soared 150 percent.

Brand-name entertainment is Harrah's stock in trade, thanks in large part to its 4.5-million-player data base (users of Harrah's gold cards) that lets management fine-tune its customer "relationships." Beginning in the mid-80's, Harrah's was the first to use the plastic cards, which have the same sort of magnetic strip used to identify customers on credit cards. In the casino war room, a "hot screen" flashes the names and locations of customers playing here on their birthdays, along with their favorite drinks.

Out on Harrah's casino floor, "celebration stations" produce the beverage, balloons, a cake. When someone hits big on a slot machine, "win committees" converge like cheery commandos, toting a boom box that plays Kool and the Gang's "Celebration." Glittery "lucky dust" is sprinkled over the area—a salt lick to draw slot hogs foraging for a hot machine.

'Call Me Odell'

Here in the no-smoking, quarter-slot section at Harrah's, the gentleman to my right has just been personally greeted ("Hello, Odell!") by a small message screen on the "Fourth of July" slot machine. His gold card is attached by key ring to a gaudy clutch of others from Caesars, the Mirage, Bally's, Grand, the Hilton, Casino Magic. . . . "Just call me Odell," he says, confiding that he's playing hooky from his mechanic's job in Milwaukee.

"All these places," Odell says, "they know my grandbabies' names. They know I drink Wild Turkey straight up, Sprite when I'm serious. They know when I took my lovin' bride—in May of '58. Gave us Champagne on our anniversary. They know how much I've lost on what machines and to the penny."

"I like these people," Odell says of Harrah's, as a waitress delivers another free bourbon. "They treat me right. And I can't say that of my phone company, my bank. Hell, I don't expect them to let me win. But they bust butt to make sure you have a good time."

Harrah's aims for the heartland, not the whales. It has cut way down on highroller events and incentives and has even installed a McDonald's in some of their casinos. As the truly corporate casino, Harrah's is state of the art.

The facade of Promus's Memphis headquarters is an upscale version of the Southern decorators' chintzed roost in "Designing Women." The mansion, exquisitely appointed with mahogany sideboards, Persian rugs and priceless Chinoiserie sits on five acres, heady with enough azalea and magnolia to fell Rhett Butler. Inside a tasteful modern cube behind the mansion, the Big Brain hums. Harrah's data base, a property as valued as its formidable real estate, is tended by scores of market researchers, product developers, direct-mail geniuses and cost managers.

The president and chief executive, Phil Satre, has his office in the Big House, a clubby, paneled room with many photographs, including one of Bill Harrah, who started the chain as a Reno bingo parlor in 1937. Leaving the high rollers to others, says Satre, "has been a philosophy from Day 1—Bill Harrah was the first to emphasize slot machines versus table games." His slot logic now prevails throughout the industry. Satre recalls a certain snootiness when the slot-heavy Harrah's Marina first opened in Atlantic City. The East Coast was supposedly high on table games. Within three years, Harrah's was the most profitable casino in town, with slots representing 70 percent of the revenues.

"Most casinos are getting on the slot bandwagon," Satre says. "They recognize that it's the most stable customer base. They're not trying to win real big. It's people who are there for fun. They'll be back if they have fun."

He likens the lure of slots to that of fishing or golf. "I'm convinced that golfers only need one good putt in eighteen holes," he says. "People are willing to have intermittent reinforcement of what they *want* to have happen. And if there's enough, it'll keep them excited about it."

This is one reason that Harrah's decided to help slot winners celebrate their triumph over the house. Hollering and boom boxes make images of the Big Payoff flash in a hundred nearby brainpans. So does the sound of money. One selling point of a Bally Pro Slot machine, claims an ad, is "a noisy stainless steel tray, so that payoffs are truly exciting."

Harrah's is more upfront than most gaming companies on the issue of gambling addiction. The Harrah's casinos I visited had large posters advising "Know When to Stop," with a hot-line number, 1-800-GAMBLER, that is partly financed by the company. (Other casinos post the number, some in small stickers on slot machines. At Trump Castle in Atlantic City, I found it in tiny type in the same folder with the room service menu.)

At Harrah's, a special employee-training program helps spot

customers losing control. Estimates on the percentage of the American population at risk for the problem vary between 1 and 3 percent. With 28 million households visiting casinos annually, management has labeled it a significant corporate concern.

'It's Getting Kinda Ugly'

Tugging at the bill of his Tomball Cougars cap, Buddy Bates is addressing the nagging question of the S.P.—saturation point—"the thing politicians don't want to talk about." When will the big machine read "tilt?"

Bates, publisher of The Bingo Banner News, has cast his lot with what the industry trades call a "mature" form of gaming. Houston bingo looked fat and happy a couple of years back, but now he's wondering if it's going to get his son through college.

"Lucky the boy's a fine baseball player," he says. "Probably get a scholarship."

In the vast roiling sea that is now legalized gambling, Bates says he's no killer whale, like Steve Wynn. He's just a modest bottom fisher, putting out his free newspaper, with ads and schedules for Houston's dozens of bingo halls. He's making a decent living off people's need to know when and where they can gamble.

Texas is a big bingo state, and until recently, there was plenty of action for everyone. Voters approved it as the first form of legal gambling in 1981. A decade later, they were spending $1.5 billion a year on bingo—but then it leveled off. High-stakes Indian halls started yanking them over to El Paso and across the state line to Oklahoma. Last year, the state government dealt local operators the greatest blow. "As soon as the lottery started, we felt it—bad," says Bates. "Now Louisiana has casino bingo. Hall operators all up and down the pike tell me attendance is way down. And now you've got the race track open. Steve Wynn wants to put that casino downtown. Good night."

Bates made the tough decision to accept ads from the track and from the tour operators running buses to the Choctaw, Chickasaw and Otoe Indian halls, to the Gulf Coast boats and casinos. Some outraged local bingo operators pulled their ads.

"Everyone's snapping at one another," he says. "Lowering card costs to where it hardly pays, just to get them in there. Moose, Eagles, V.F.W.'s, the little charity guys, they're hurting bad. It's getting kinda ugly."

I saw this for myself the night I dropped into the Golden

Nugget bingo hall in southwest Houston to play an evening session. The crowd was sparse for a Thursday night, according to the bookkeeper, Jackie Madeley, and they were dying at the snack bar. Nobody was spending.

"I can't even sell a full box of pull tabs anymore," grumped Madeley. She was talking about the instant bingo games sold in the hall—pull up the cardboard tabs and see if you've won instant cash. Pull tabs are gamblers' popcorn, so addictive, Madeley says, she used to sell two boxes of 2,300 tabs a night.

"The pull tab money," she says, "goes to the lottery now. They've got us in some kind of vicious cycle."

From Bingo Ladies to Bookies-in-a-Box

What's happening in Buddy Bates and Jackie Madeley's little pond is an apt microcosm for the tensions afflicting some other gaming markets across the country. Struggling horse tracks are agitating to install slot and video poker machines to hold the railbirds firm. Already riverboats are weighing anchor and trolling new waters. Even conservative states like Iowa are considering easing gambling limits imposed on their cash barges. Donald Trump is bawling "no fair" over his Indian competition. Investment banking houses issue monthly reports projecting increasing competition. And more and more state legislatures are jumping into an already crowded field, introducing gambling bills to help dying mill towns, crumbling cities, stricken farm areas.

Given the nature of this huge, runaway industry—that it's built on an ancient but mercurial urge—no one is willing to predict whether and when the gambling boom will level off or crap out spectacularly. Many smaller outfits are operating on dangerously slim margins, throwing what Phil Satre of Promus calls "stupid money" at dense-packed casino areas like the Mississippi Coast. Satre likens this investment influx to the boom that created the hotel glut in the 70's. "It's like any industry that gets hot, like the athletic apparel industry," he says. "Financial institutions get swept up in it and make some bad judgments."

Nonetheless, the big wheel keeps on turning. The cable industry, perhaps in an effort to finance its interactive ventures, is aggressively investigating pay-television gambling on "gaming channels." The goal: a "bookie-in-a-box" atop every television. Slide some popcorn into the microwave and your Visa card into the slot atop your cable box. Punch in your wager for the Knicks-

Bulls game and sit back. No more meeting Big Louie at the Blarney Stone steam table—the check or the corporate debit will be in the mail.

There is evidence that this gambling pandemic is going global. England is about to have its first lottery since 1826, something that has the racing and football touts up in arms. It's also experiencing a tremendous bingo boom; Sloane Street debs and street kids in nose rings and Mohawks are invading the bingo halls there. Moscow is now honeycombed with busy casinos. And Lebanese gamblers are literally risking their lives to patronize West Beirut gaming houses that draw equal fire from militiamen and religious fundamentalists. Big winners are escorted home by casino guards armed with machine guns.

Air space—domestic and international—is the final frontier. Harrah's, working in tandem with a company called Sky Ventures, is angling to put video gambling equipment on commercial flights. After all, bored passengers are already swiping credit cards through their seat backs to make phone calls and catalogue purchases. Virgin Atlantic Airways is weighing plans for in-flight casino-type games, so the race is on. John Boushy, Harrah's marketing vice president, says, "It wouldn't surprise me if somebody has something in the air by early '95."

Buddy Bates says he's trying a high-tech tack, too. He has installed a gaming news fax service—just dial up the Moose Hall bingo schedule—but the fax phone rarely rings. He has a sideline—bingo fortune cookies—though he allows "that's a spotty sort of a thing." So he's moving his operation out of two tiny rooms in this northwest Houston office building back home to suburban Tomball.

"Hedging my bets," he says, smiling. "And counting on those hard-core folks who're gonna bingo no matter what. They're bedrock. Those bingo ladies started it all."

You See It All Out Here

I'm reading about the demise of Spanish Raymond as I ride my very last bus, the morning Casino Express from Memphis south to Tunica. The New York papers have chronicled the investigation and arrest of Raymond Marquez, the most successful and legendary numbers king the city has ever known. Spanish Raymond ruled for more than 30 years, taking in an estimated $30 million a year from the barrio poor. No one could touch him. So how did Raymond get caught? After years of building an empire on tiny scraps of paper, he tried to go high-tech. The police intercepted fax transmissions from his office manager to Raymond and his wife at their motel in Fort Lauderdale, Fla. Like the new casino moguls, Raymond liked his profit-and-loss statement with his morning café con leche.

Raymond isn't the only oldtime oddsmaker feeling the pinch these days. "Too much heat now" was the reason several veteran bookies wouldn't talk to me for this article, even with promised anonymity. I can remember when newspaper sports departments had to eject these guys regularly, shooing them out like so many flapping, cackling crows. Now they are hard to flush out. Though illegal gambling still pulls in billions, the guys in those flashy sport coats have opted to blend in with the working stiffs.

It's not as if they're out of business. Sports betting, one of the most common, casual and evergreen forms of gambling, is still the most prohibited. Consider the official opprobrium that rained on Pete Rose, or the huffy editorials decrying Michael Jordan's golf wagers. No effort has been spared by league offices to preserve at least the illusion of sanctity on the gridiron and diamond. A 1992 Federal law banned sports betting in any state where it wasn't already legal, and since New Jersey was unable to pass a pro-betting bill before a December 1993 deadline, that left only Nevada for a legal bet on the N.F.L. playoffs—and a lot of busy bookies everywhere.

I'm still thinking about Raymond, arrested in his light blue bathrobe, when our bus turns off Highway 61 to Commerce Landing, the cluster of casinos closest to Memphis. Rising up out of cotton fields that have been flooded to create placid dockside lagoons off the less stable Mississippi, the Tunica casinos look much the same as their coastal sisters: Pirate ships, Wild West towns and Harrah's ersatz Tara.

At 9 A.M. on a weekday morning, Harrah's Tunica operation is quiet: a few holdouts from last night, lots of seniors and a noticeable contingent of wheelchair patrons. In fact, throughout my casino days and nights, I've never seen such a public concentration of the American disabled. At Caesars Palace in Las Vegas, I saw a wheelchair patron with his forehead strapped to a board support, and an IV bag swinging overhead. I saw a quadriplegic woman playing the slots by hitting the "spin reels" button with a device held in her teeth.

You do see it all out here in the Gambling Nation, people of different races, incomes, playing skills and ages having a swell time rump to rump. By and large, people are friendlier than they are at airports, bars, even some churches I've been to. It is startling how many life stories tumble out in between spinning reels. If you make your living questioning people, the forthrightness is astounding.

This may sound a lot like the up-with-people, rainbow vision of the Gambling Nation that Phil Satre described in a speech to the National Press Club in December. It's what you see in a lot of the gaming companies' glossy annual reports—clutches of well-dressed, ebony-and-ivory casino patrons photographed in mutual ecstasy over a brimming bucket of coins. It's what I heard from Steve Wynn, delivering an Emma Lazarus-like description of his customers: "The inhibited, the introverted, the noisy, the quiet, the aggressive, the meek! They all find something here."

That vision is also, in many places I visited, quite true. People who wouldn't make eye contact in a mall or gas station do commiserate over a balky Lucky Seven reel. Bouncing along Highway 61, listening to the easy conversation between strangers—a black mother and son and a couple of elderly white "Driving Miss Daisy" types across the aisle—thinking about Jeanne Stewart and her mixed bag of Buddies, I have to concede that gambling's clientele has changed as much as its image. For the most part, and at least while they're playing, the new gamblers are a pleasant, noncombative counterweight to the "ordinary people" who fume and scream at one another from those pit-bull audiences on the afternoon talk shows.

Is it genuine tolerance, or a marketing conceit? Is it a spurious neighborliness, or are partisan-weary Americans simply longing for a gaudy, giddy cease-fire zone?

Standing amid the relentless din, the pinging and the halooing, counting the deflated fanny packs, the full Snugli's, the acres of rapt newlyweds, homemakers, pipe fitters, dentists, paraplegics and granddads, I have to wonder: how'd we *get* here? As American fair play dissolves, as the gap between rich and poor widens and the middle class gets squeezed from both sides, are we just pushing our chips toward that primal equalizer—chance?

I think part of the answer may lie in a conversation I overheard in Tunica between two women sporting identical bouffants. One was tsk-tsking cattily at the spandex exuberance of a well-endowed patron. The other reproved her, firmly but smilingly:

"Sister, we all stand naked before the Odds."

EDITOR'S INTRODUCTION

Section II explores the reality of the gambler's world. James Popkin's "Tricks of the Trade," reprinted from *U.S. News & World Report,* clues us in on the persuasion techniques used in some casinos to keep the gambler gambling. These techniques range from the merely innocuous, pumping of pleasant odors into the casino air and pushing dealers to shuffle as quickly as possible, to adopting behavior techniques to reinforcing slot players' continual feeding of the machines, to high tech computer systems that track gamblers and their gambling activity.

In article 2, Jon Nordheimer reports on the pressure felt by dealers in "Casino Burnout, Behind the Bright Lights," reprinted from the *New York Times.* Popkin's article touches upon what the casinos and pit bosses expect from their dealers; this article outlines those expectations more fully, and delineates the emotional hazards of their stressful albeit lucrative positions.

Most Americans can attest to the dreams and expectations excited by nothing more than a dollar lottery ticket purchase, but may find unimaginable the idea of losing sums, vast or small, on a toss of the dice or a hand of poker. The next three articles, profiles of gamblers who describe the lure of the game. Edward Allen, in "Penny Ante," reprinted from *Gentlemen's Quarterly,* comments on the magic of chance and fascination with the odds even on a small scale in the casinos of Las Vegas. Although he is a man who "prides himself on his common sense" the writer is paradoxically drawn to the blackjack table because of its inherent irrationality, the belief that "Lady Luck" might shine on him. A. Alvarez, in "No Limit," reprinted from the *New Yorker,* explores the thrill of higher stakes during the Las Vegas World Series of Poker. The intensity of the tournament events essayed and the machinations of the professional players versus the amateurs seeking fortune and fame will prove interesting to player and lay person alike. Finally, in "Watching Dad Gamble," reprinted from *Yankee,* Pat Jordan takes his father on a gambling jaunt to Foxwoods Casino in Connecticut and reminisces on growing up with a father who was always gambling.

TRICKS OF THE TRADE[1]

"Our goal is not to get more out of a customer in three hours but to get him to stay for four hours."

—Bob Renneisen
President and CEO
Claridge's Casino, Atlantic City

At precisely midnight on Oct. 11, 1991, an obscure Chicago neurologist slipped behind a row of quarter slot machines at the Las Vegas Hilton and switched on a homemade contraption of cardboard, black metal and old fan parts. For the next 48 hours, the hidden device pumped a pleasant-smelling vapor into the stale casino air.

The neurologist was not an intruder but a scent expert invited to the Hilton by casino manager Lee Skelley to test whether certain smells can subtly influence slot machine players to wager more. Over the next two days, Hilton gamblers poured thousands of quarters into the 18 nearby slot machines—45 percent more than usual for an October weekend.

If you give a guy a $100 bill he looks at it like a round of golf, a golf cart, two beers and a hot dog. But if you give him chips, it's just betting units and it loses its value."

—Bill Zender, Operations Chief
Aladdin Casino, Las Vegas

The days of shaved dice, missing face cards and rigged roulette wheels are long gone. But the pursuit of profitability in the corporate era of gambling has turned the average casino into a financially hazardous place for bettors. In Nevada and Atlantic City, for example, confidential documents reveal that five casinos now pump Chicago neurologist Alan Hirsch's secret scent—Odorant 1—into the slot machine pits 24 hours a day. (The Las Vegas Hilton never took the idea beyond the testing stage.) Some casi-

[1]Article by James Popkin. From *U.S. News & World Report,* March 14, '94. Copyright © 1994 by *U.S. News & World Report.* Reprinted with permission.

nos have even studied how the controversial psychologist B. F. Skinner altered the behavior of rats and pigeons. But of all the tricks in the casino manager's Psych 101 handbook, the subtle manipulation of time is by far the most common.

In 1980, a math whiz named Jess Marcum spelled out exactly how time affects a gambler's odds. Marcum, who helped to develop radar and the neutron bomb before becoming a casino consultant, figured that a craps player who wagered just $1 every bet for two months straight would have only one chance in 2 trillion to win $1,000 before he lost $1,000. On the other hand, by decreasing his exposure at the craps table to just 25 minutes and wagering $200 every bet, that same gambler would increase his odds to 1.15 to 1. Even the lowest-ranking casino official knows the concept: Since all casino games give the house a mathematical edge, the longer a player gambles, the greater the house's chance of winning.

That helps explain why gamblers frequently get lost in a maze of slot machines and why down-home gambling halls offer free "Ladies Breakfasts" at 6 a.m., a slow point in the casino day. Over a year, a special promotion or interior-design element that somehow keeps gamblers at play for just five more minutes a night can add millions to a casino's gross, or "hold." The Harrah's Casino spends tens of thousands of dollars a year studying whether fresher air, wider aisles and even back supports on slot-pit stools will make customers comfortable. And slog it out longer, too. "We're now developing technology that's just lighting the felt" on blackjack tables, says Harrah's president, Phil Satre. "We're trying to keep [light] off the forehead of the customers, which is draining on them from an energy standpoint."

Hidden purpose

Such sensitivity to customer comfort abounds. For example, nearly all new slot machines sold in the United States have built-in bill acceptors. Gamblers like the devices because they no longer have to wait in line for change, and casino managers love them because they keep slot hounds glued to their stools.

Like car plants, casinos also stress productivity. The hidden cameras above the casino floor scan for fast-fingered dealers and card cheats. But the ubiquitous "eye in the sky" also enables casino officials to conduct regular "game-pace audits." At the Aladdin Casino in Las Vegas, blackjack dealers are instructed to deal at least 75 to 80 hands per hour. They are also supposed to shuffle six decks of cards in less than 80 seconds. The reason: Shuffles can eat up eight rounds of playing time an hour. In a year, the Aladdin could earn an extra $1.2 million if its blackjack dealers never had to shuffle.

Penny-pinching casinos set faster production schedules, especially when the nightly cash hold tumbles. "We don't instruct people to deal faster," says Bob Stupak, owner of the Vegas World Casino in Las Vegas. "They better deal as fast as they [expletive] can or they're gonna work someplace else."

Casinos have become pop-psych laboratories. When a player at a low-limit blackjack table flashes a $100 bill and asks for chips, for example, dealers at many casinos are under orders to dole out chips of the lowest-possible denomination. Partly a convenience for gamblers, the practice also is meant to discourage low bettors from pocketing higher value chips when they leave the table. Such players are likely to blow all 20 of their $5 chips one at a time, the thinking goes, but might hold onto a $25 chip and never gamble it away. "Psychologically, casinos don't want gamblers to realize how much they're losing," explains one Atlantic City dealer.

But slot pits are the true training grounds for casino mind games. Deep, dark colors like black, red, purple and blue trigger a strong response in slot players, research shows. So, slot machine manufacturers like IGT, based in Reno, Nev., prominently feature those hues. IGT North American President Bob Bittman says research also shows that gamblers no longer associate winning with the cherry and plum symbols on many slot machine reels. Poof, they're gone. "Fruit is a dinosaur. Ninety-nine percent of the machines we sell now will not have fruit," Bittman says.

Some casinos go to even greater lengths to exploit gamblers' subconscious preferences. Casino consultant David Britton says that after surveying dozens of Nevada-based slot players he confirmed a hunch that they are drawn to bright-red machines. But after several minutes, the players subconsciously tire of red and seek softer hues. Since casinos want to avoid "transitional periods," when players leave one machine in search of another, Britton devised a new system where players are now lured to the brightly colored machines at the end of a long row of slots. But the machines closer to the middle of the row feature softer colors, like blues and greens.

Sometimes casino operators look to actual psychology for in-

spiration. In 1966, University of Nevada undergrad Larry Andreotti was studying Skinner, one of the first scientists to demonstrate how positive reinforcement can influence animal behavior.
Andreotti told his father, the late Rome Andreotti, who at the
time was one of the rising stars on the operations side of the
growing Harrah's chain. "A lot of the behavior I saw in the lab
seemed comparable to the control one has over behavior in casinos," explains Larry Andreotti, who today is a college psychology
professor and Skinner specialist in Canada.

Smart rat

In 1937, Skinner taught a white lab rat named Pliny to operate a rudimentary slot machine. After Pliny pulled a chain with its
teeth, a marble would fall. The rat would then drop the marble in
a slot and receive its reward, 1/20th of a gram of a dog biscuit. By
tracking Pliny's reactions over time, Skinner learned that the rat
became more motivated when he got a biscuit only occasionally,
and randomly. Pliny would drop even more marbles into the slot,
in other words, when he was not sure when the biscuit would fall
next.

Rome Andreotti applied Skinner's findings to the casino. If
most slots were set at about the same payout rate, recalls a former
Harrah's president, Richard Goeglein, Andreotti would slip in a
few machines with a much more generous jackpot percentage.
The casino wouldn't indicate which machines offered better odds,
but gamblers soon learned that there were a few ringers in the
crowd. And the search for those machines sent gamblers into a
Plinylike, quarter-dropping frenzy. "Rome knew how to reward
people for continual, consistent play," says Goeglein.

Coincidentally, slot machine makers have also put Skinner's
theories into practice. Modern slots reward players with frequent,
small payoffs—often as inconsequential as one quarter—that entice gamblers to keep chasing their dream. Thirty years ago, by
contrast, small, frequent payoffs were unheard of, says slot machine historian Marshall Fey. The new payout system works. "It's
like eating popcorn. It's very hard to stop playing," says Jeffrey
Lowenhar, senior management consultant with the Resorts casino
in Atlantic City.

One firm took gambler manipulation too far. In 1986, Universal Distributing began selling slots that produced "near miss"
combinations. Instead of running randomly, the slot reels often

stopped so that players could see the symbols of a payout just above or below the pay line, giving the false impression that gamblers had missed a massive jackpot. Although the machines quickly became a hit with customers and slot managers, Nevada gaming authorities outlawed the near-miss illusion in 1989.

It was a Sunday afternoon, and Pennsylvania jewelry salesman Sam Roberts was bellied up to a roulette table at his favorite Las Vegas casino. Dressed in what he described as his "Mr. T starter set"—three gold necklaces, four gold bracelets, a gold watch and four gold rings—Roberts seemed to epitomize the successful Vegas man about town. When asked whether he was ahead after three days of roulette, Roberts said he wasn't "paying any attention."

But the casino certainly was. On a computer screen just off the casino floor, the file on Sam Roberts (not his real name) was extensive. Not only did it reveal his exact losses on his current trip ($2,092) but it had already figured his average bet ($20.88), time spent gambling (11 hours and 39 minutes) and "average worth," or how much Roberts should lose ($528) based on time and the house's 5.26 percent edge at roulette. It also contained personal data like Sam's height (5'10"), weight (300), hair color (brown)—even whether he needed corrective eyewear (yes).

Casinos amass personal information to enhance customer service and reward steady players with "comps"—complimentary meals, show tickets and hotel stays. (They never reveal internal data, although Roberts agreed to for this article.) But there's a hidden agenda. Casino marketers need detailed histories to keep old customers loyal and, more important, to "capture" new ones.

If marketers learn, for instance, that divorced slot players from Cleveland who love boxing lose big and often, the casino will buy mailing lists and try to find sucker clones. Gamblers who can be lured to the hotel are especially prized. "If we can get you to stay in our hotel we can bump up your average trip worth," one marketer says. Everyone gets in on the hustle. When a casino hotel is nearly full, reservationists will scan the computer and open remaining rooms only to known gamblers with a high trip worth.

A decade ago, most casinos bothered to gather data only on high rollers. Now they use slot-club cards to snare the meat-and-potatoes guy, too. After filling out a survey and receiving an ATM-like card, slot junkies insert them into a "reader" built into almost all slot machines. In a distant computer room, casinos track the action 24 hours a day, down to the last quarter.

Giveaways

Players who use the cards the longest get the most comps, somewhat like a frequent-flier giveback. At the Trump Castle in Atlantic City, an internal document shows that 64 percent of all slot players now use the Castle slot card. The cardholders lost $109 million to the slots last fiscal year, or about $101 per player per trip. Slot players who never bothered with the card, by contrast, lost $31 per trip on average.

For an industry governed by odds, casinos leave little to chance. To line their pockets just a wee bit more, they've added games with stunning house odds. Many casinos now offer "double-exposure blackjack," for example, in which the dealers reveal all their cards; players keep trying to top the dealer's hand without going over 21. Novices fall for the ruse, overlooking the rule allowing the house to win all ties. "That one rule change is worth about 8 or 9 percent in favor of the house," explains Arnold Snyder, editor of the *Blackjack Forum* newsletter.

Many riverboat casinos also offer "multiple-action blackjack," with complex rules that encourage gamblers to place three bets on every hand. "It causes players to play dumb and put more money on the table," Snyder says. If gambling critics can be believed, that neatly sums up the danger of America's latest entertainment craze. As any old Vegas hand will tell you, "If you wanna make money in a casino, own one."

BEHIND THE LIGHTS, CASINO BURNOUT[2]

ATLANTIC CITY, July 28—The night the high roller dropped dead and casino workers rolled his body beneath the craps table so the game could proceed was Vinnie Springer's confirmation of the relentlessness of the game.

"Even when the paramedics came to remove the body 15 minutes later, the dice kept rolling," said Mr. Springer, a tall, amiable 40-year-old man who has worked as a craps stick man and blackjack dealer at Atlantic City casinos for the last 10 years.

[2]Article by Jon Nordheimer. From the *New York Times*, Aug. 5, '94. Copyright © 1994 by The New York Times Company. Reprinted with permission.

Mr. Springer is part of the elite of Atlantic City's work force, the men and women who work the casino tables, winning or losing millions of dollars for the house on each eight-hour shift.

It is high-pressure work, as stressful on a daily basis as being a big-city cop or an emergency room nurse, and signs of wear and tear on casino workers is becoming more pronounced as Atlantic City enters its 16th year as a gambling paradise.

"Behind the bright lights and the glamour are a lot of unhappy workers who earn white-collar pay for what are essentially blue-collar jobs," said Sandy Festa, an alcohol and drug counselor who also treats casino workers for a number of job-related complaints like depression and anxiety.

"They make too much money to leave, but they can't stand the thought of doing the same thing day after day for the rest of their lives," Ms. Festa said. "It's what is known in the trade as casino burnout."

Her husband, Elliott, who has been a blackjack and craps worker for 14 years, added, "You reach a point where you either take the job one day at a time or else quit and do something earning less money, but without all the stress."

Among the chief complaints are casino work shifts, which are shuffled as often as decks of cards in the round-the-clock operations. Working on weekends and holidays. Boredom in roles that require a degree of cleverness in counting but not much more. Little chance for promotion.

Add to that the constant audio and visual overload of a casino floor—glittering lights, the clatter of coins and ringing bells from slot machine payoffs, the stutter of roulette wheels and the whoop of joy or anguish from players—and the casino can be a very demanding workplace.

Casino officials say the complaints are similar to grievances that arise in any workplace about unsympathetic supervisors or slow advancement. What adds new wrinkles are the dynamics of gambling, said Michelle Perna, vice president of human resources for Merv Griffin's Resorts Casino Hotel.

"Our workers are paid well to make sure people have a good time," Ms. Perna said. "And that can be stressful if people are losing money."

Many casino workers, Mr. Springer included, count themselves lucky to hold jobs that can pay $40,000 a year, mostly in pooled tips—though the average may be closer to $30,000—and that place them in the center of the action.

"Each day working in a casino is like New Year's Eve anywhere else," he said with a broad smile.

He rattled off the names of celebrities and sports stars he has met on the job.

His co-worker, Billy Sullivan, nodded in agreement. "Real good people who treat you right," said Mr. Sullivan, who was joining Mr. Springer for an after-work round of drinks, shortly before 5 A.M., in the Chelsea Pub, a half-block from the boardwalk and the bright lights of Atlantic City's 12 casino towers, which employ 50,000 workers.

But they also described venemous encounters with players who blamed them for their losses, as well as big shots who treated them like dirt.

They and other casino workers all recall high rollers who years ago were given the red carpet treatment everywhere they went and today are broke, scavenging through the payoff basins of slot machines for overlooked coins.

"They're all searching for that lucky streak that'll win back what they lost," said a woman who quit working as a croupier after three years to return to college. Like many other past and present casino workers, she spoke only on the condition of anonymity. "I may want my job back some day," she explains.

She said she left the casinos because job pressures were getting to her.

"My mother was a pit boss and it was her whole life," she said. "I couldn't take the constantly changing hours and constantly being caught between management and the customers. Everyone's watching your every move, including the surveillance cameras in the ceiling, and one mistake really puts the heat on you.

"If your table is losing unusual amounts of money, the pit bosses start sweating and watch you even more closely to see if you're trying to 'help out' a customer."

Moreover, she said, there were the "guard dogs" or "blue coats"—dealer parlance for the Casino Control Commission agents stationed on every casino floor to enforce state regulations—who, she said, could "nit-pick on every rule in the book."

She was also bothered, she said, by the antipathy of some gamblers for women dealers, especially at the craps tables, where superstition rules just about every decision of some players. "They think women are unlucky and they don't want you to touch the dice," she said.

Her worst moment: A high roller on a hot streak refused to

leave the craps table to go to a rest room after hours of play, and he relieved himself under the table, sending her and other croupiers scattering. "He went on playing as though nothing had happened," she said. "On my break the pit boss complimented me on not making too big a fuss."

Kelly Hass, who left her job as a casino coin-change supervisor to tend bar at the Chelsea Pub, said casino bosses could be friendly with the workers as individuals but ultimately had little regard for their welfare.

"They treat you like a number and ignore you, or treat you like a dog and fire you," Ms. Hass said. "There's absolutely no job protection."

Casino workers, unlike hotel and restaurant workers, have not organized a union and work at the pleasure of management.

"Some dealers have been fired on their break for their attitude —not for something serious like stealing," Mr. Festa said. "Management knows they have people lined up for each job opening."

Despite all that, the hardest part of the job can be boredom. Most casino workers say that blackjack dealers face the most acute problem of keeping focused on repetitive action and the changing faces of players, even with a 20-minute break for every hour worked.

The most serious occupational hazard dealers face is gambling itself. "If you're constantly in the company of high rollers who throw tens of thousands of dollars around, you start thinking your salary is not that great after all," said Harvey R. Fogel, a counselor for compulsive gamblers who has treated scores of casino workers.

"A majority of the dealers won't spend one minute more inside a casino than they have to, but quite a few spend their off-hours at other casinos losing what they had just earned," he said.

"The problem is I can't tell them to quit a $40,000-a-year job to get out of that environment and take a job for less elsewhere," Mr. Fogel added. "And if a dealer goes to his boss and says he's a compulsive gambler, it's worse than admitting you are an alcoholic or a drug addict in their eyes."

Ms. Perna of Resorts Casino Hotel said that the casinos contract with companies to provide employee assistance programs to help workers with personal problems. Such programs are confidential, she said.

For those who feel trapped in a golden web and do not want to leave the casino industry, there are some alternatives, including taking better jobs as pit bosses or shift supervisors in new casinos that have been opening from Mississippi to Illinois.

Mr. Fogel says he believes the change of scenery may be illusory.

"The ones who are really troubled feel every decision they make is mechanical and every move supervised by someone waiting to pounce on them for screwing up," he said.

And the basic rules of the game, he observed, are the same no matter where one chooses to roll the dice.

PENNY ANTE[3]

I can't understand it. I've done everything right all day: left my ill-starred blue shirt home, brought along the sunglasses that have been so good to me, avoided abbreviating any of the items on my grocery list. And, of course, I have labored carefully over the exact placement of that certain hidden object, which I have pinned with much seriousness beneath my clothes.

What's more, I have been a careful driver, covering the fifty miles between my house and town without causing a single Toyota to honk at me angrily. I have taken care to be equally well-mannered with my shopping cart, there in the corridors of the bag-it-yourself discount warehouse, where love songs, nothing but love songs, filter down all afternoon, soft as asbestos, from the barnlike ceiling. Those tender lyrics, mostly about individuals learning to live with or without someone else's precious love, still echo through my head as I wheel my week's groceries through the parking lot, wandering in search of my car through the vague, frostless chill of a winter night in Las Vegas.

Now, with shopping over, half my supper eaten and the other half doggie-bagged, an inconclusive fortune-cookie chit folded in my shirt pocket and a clump of third-rate Mongolian beef sitting heavy on my stomach, I am an unhappy man. I am unhappy in that crushed and chastised way of a student who has been yelled at unfairly in front of the class. I can feel my face flush with the shame of it—the shame of someone who has no reason to deserve

[3]Article by Edward Allen. From *Gentlemen's Quarterly*, May '92. Copyright 1994 © by Edward Allen. Reprinted with permission.

the kind of humiliation I see laid out on the table in front of me, hand after hand, here in a room where all the other blackjack players and crapshooters and roulette-wheel watchers seem, from their buzz and clamor, to be getting as rich as sweepstakes millionaire David Brumbalow.

I want to tell you that these are the thoughts of a man who prides himself on his common sense, who likes the efficiency of combining this weekly Las Vegas shopping trip with a quick and strictly budgeted run at the casino tables, a man who answers no chain letters nor dreams of buying real estate for no money down, someone to whom Nostradamus is nothing, someone who will never call in to Time-Life Books to order its *Illustrated Encyclopedia of Spooky Noises*. In short, I am a reasonable American, registered to vote, sitting at a blackjack table, losing, with a $2 bill safety-pinned to the front of my underpants.

What I like most about gambling is that it does not make sense. I find it comforting that in pursuit of its admittedly fraudulent promises, I don't have to pretend to make sense myself. The hobby of gambling, even at my wimpish betting level, allows me to believe things that I know are not true. It lets me be a devotional weirdo, without requiring me to dress funny. It gives me a chance to apply the most-Byzantine rules and structures to my most ordinary actions, all in search of that compelling fiction known as luck.

In short, gambling invites me to take an hour's recess from adulthood, to play in a well-demarked sandbox of irrationality and to look at the world as a magical place, which, of course, it is when the light hits it at the right angle. Those people who stubbornly remain adults and who look upon gambling's happy meaninglessness from within the logic of the real world will see something quite different. They will see a phalanx of games controlled by the indomitable law of averages, games that from an adult's wintry perspective you cannot hope to master. Those adults will see me, and the people sitting next to me, giving our money away week after week to people who do not love us.

One reason it's so hard to keep from getting angry tonight is that this casino has been very good to me on occasion. I do not believe in telling you the name of this establishment or how well I have done before, but I will say that in the past, on a summer night, I have stepped out onto the Las Vegas Strip with a smile on my face that you couldn't have wiped off with a shovel. I have walked past where the Caesars Palace loudspeakers blend flutes and drums to produce what I guess is supposed to sound like Cecil B. De Mille slave-sacrifice music, have walked with the kind of stride that can only indicate the presence of multiple hundreds in the wallet. If I were a mugger, I would pay close attention to the way people walk.

But tonight, everything is terrible: The air is thick with carpet shampoo and cigarettes; the happy voices around me seem as empty and shrill as untrained parrots. Nothing falls together right. I choose this dealer for her kind face, yet there seems a ferocious hopelessness to the cards she tosses me. As she deals me a jack to bust another hand, I can hear, at the far end of the casino from beyond a bank of slot machines, the strains of "I've Got to Be Me" in the amplified voice of a lounge singer who I'm sure would rather be almost anybody else. Everything around this little $5 blackjack table seems wounded, like a country that has just devalued its currency.

One of the reasons I find gambling so much fun is that the adventure is not limited to the times when you are doing it. In fact, the moments when you are actually doing it will frequently stink, as they do tonight. For me, the subsidiary thrill is just as important, as well as much less expensive.

The surrounding excitement can stretch out in either direction. For hours before, on a Las Vegas shopping day, as the time draws near for me to leave my house in the desert and drive into town, I find an almost-religious excitement in the preparation for a session, complete with my own private rules, rituals, prohibitions. And coming home, blessed or wounded, I am allowed to wrestle again with the mystery of what I did wrong and what I did right; I must also try once more to find some way to recognize the difference in advance.

One of the things I know, though it doesn't matter on these local trips, is that I must never again permit myself to drive through another state and out again without stepping on the ground of that state. This is a superstition that I developed on my own, and I am rather proud of it. Somehow it seems right, a mandate for some kind of geographical integrity. I would be even prouder of it if it worked.

Particularly important in the moments of preparation is to avoid putting on any article of clothing in which I have had a bad night in the past. Unfortunately, a too-strict observance of this rule always leads to a problem with shoes because I have only a limited number, and I've had terrible nights in every pair I own.

The best I can do, as a sort of nervous compromise, is always keep a second pair in the car so that if I get hurt in one casino, at least I can change shoes before trying the next.

Do I really believe any of this stuff? I do, in the sense that within the skewed world of gambling it is no crazier to believe it than not to. And at the purest level, the irrationality is its own payoff. I don't know if anybody in the world shares this feeling, but for me, to walk around in a place as public as a casino with a $2 bill fastened to the front of my shorts is an unqualified pleasure, whether it works or not. (It doesn't work. I will be honest now and admit that this account is narrated retrospectively and that I have since retired the $2 bill, which is the only reason I'm willing to mention it. That bill let me down one too many times—meaning somehow that it must have lost the power I knew it never possessed. I am trying to be scientific about these things. As I said, I pride myself on my rationality.)

So here I am, delivering more of my money to the absentee investors in a casino I won't name, on a night I could be reading a good book or maybe writing one. Why do I bother? This question always comes up when I talk to non-gamblers, and I never have a decent answer. Why is an activity with so little to offer so appealing to so many people, enough to make it one of the few growth industries in a retreating economy? Why would so many people fly so many thousands of miles to stay in rooms where the drapes never quite come together in the middle, and drop so many thousands of dollars at games that really aren't very interesting, all in pursuit of a chance that anybody with more brains than a state-lottery player knows is mathematically remote?

In my experience, what makes it worthwhile is the idea that something as tyrannical as the law of averages can be turned upside down, if only for an hour or a weekend, and that what does not make sense can be forced to make sense. That logical turnabout is in itself a pleasure worthy of any number of spongy hotel mattresses. Deep down we all know, unless we are of the intellectual caste who smoke cigarettes but find airplanes too dangerous, that we are suckers. But that's okay; we're in good company, and we're here to have fun. All day and night, the law of averages grinds away at our frail chances, immutable in its pronouncement that if you keep playing long enough at a game that has a negative expectation built into it, you will have to lose.

In other words, you can't even break even. But we also know that people have been known to have astonishingly good nights, even when they are playing like idiots. And the best players can, and will, get slapped in the face. It's not fair. That's another thing I like about gambling. It's value-free. You'll have a great night sometime, and the greatest thing about that night will be that you did nothing to deserve it.

I suppose that when I described some of my own private superstitions, I might have sounded like someone who has forgotten to take his medication. But I think I can demonstrate that such craziness makes at least some kind of sense.

Superstitious gambling behavior makes sense because even the smallest and most meaningless actions can be shown to affect, in some way, the random interconnectedness of all physical processes. By this logic, everything you do can be said to transform the world. If I cough once at the card table, or lean back in my chair, or audibly riffle my chips, I may distract the dealer during that magically important process of shuffling the cards. The outcome of the game will thus be changed completely—every hand, every possibility, turned upside down.

The example I use in my forthcoming novel has to do with what will happen if you bend down to pick up a penny as you are walking into a crowded casino.

The first thing that will happen is that you will get to the crap table a few seconds later than you would have without having bothered with the penny. A man who walked in the door before you, who would have been behind you if you had left that penny alone, will now get where he's going a few seconds earlier. The shooter about to roll the dice at your table will see you out of the corner of his eye and will shake the dice in his fist one less time, and the throw will come out showing a different number.

Because of that last throw, or because of all the throws following it, which have been changed as well, somebody will eventually leave your table. And it is a physical law that whenever someone leaves one place, he or she has to move to another place. When that happens, the progress of the game at whatever table that person ends up at will be changed utterly. Because of that change, a few who would otherwise have left their tables will stay, and others who might have stayed will leave. Where will they go? It doesn't matter. Wherever they go to will never be the same.

In time, every game in the whole casino will be changed utterly, because of that penny. The change will be so pervasive that eventually a man who would otherwise have been lavishly in the money will get discouraged and grab a taxi downtown (and, of course, the interference of that cab in traffic will delay by a few seconds another cabload of gamblers bound for Caesars, whose night, now, will never be the same, and they will never know it).

Thus, when our discouraged man gets downtown, Binion's Horseshoe Casino will be transformed by his effect on the games he buys into there, which effect again will multiply from table to table in a chain reaction, a process something like that film they played for us in elementary school to illustrate atomic fission, showing a floor covered with thousands of mousetraps armed with Ping-Pong balls, onto which one triggering ball (the neutron?) is dropped. Those people chased out of Binion's by the change this man has caused will wander around Fremont Street, extending the process you have begun, carrying it from street to street, mousetrap to mousetrap, from Pioneer to Golden Nugget to Four Queens.

When you look around town a few hours after picking up that earthshaking penny, everything will seem normal. But I believe that if you were able to go back, like George Bailey in *It's a Wonderful Life,* and see both worlds, with penny and without penny, the Strip would be a different place. People would still walk in and out of the same doors, but they would not all be the same people; cars gliding up and down the Strip would catch the traffic lights in a different sequence. Those two possibilities of the Strip would look much alike, but they would in reality be as different from each other as Jimmy Stewart's old Bedford Falls was from the soulless alternate reality of Pottersville. (Actually, I have to admit that I've always liked Pottersville better; every time I see that movie I wish I could drop into the Indian Club for a Christmas Eve martini.)

And more: I suspect that in one of these casinos there is a man who because of that penny will have the luck of his life. This guy will end up with so much money that he will choose to spend some of it on a young woman who is not his wife. If the girl does not turn out to be a police decoy, this man's casino session will culminate in her arms, with the result that later, on the too-soft Beautyrest, he will disappoint his wife by turning over and going to sleep—which means that the baby who would otherwise have been conceived that night will never be born to fulfill his appointed destiny, whether that be to develop sugar-free cotton candy or to blow up the world. That child's existence is now canceled, as thoroughly as all the other Pottersvillean ghosts have been canceled by all the other people who have bent down to pick up pennies in front of all the other casinos.

Like many other trains of thought, this one takes us to only a limited number of terminals. As crazy and metaphysical as the idea of interconnected events is, there's not much you can do with it, mostly because we can't ever see the alternative possibilities that our actions have preempted. All we can do is pay attention, go on with our strategies, not worry too much about what could have been and try to play as intelligently as we can. We will find, among other things, that intelligence does not help us.

Although the mathematics are pretty clear, any psychological observations I can make about gambling will be almost as shaky as the hands of a poker novice holding the first full house of his life. The reason I know so little about anybody else's gambling experiences is that, even though it doesn't look that way, gambling is a profoundly solitary activity. In the crush around the casino tables, surrounded by the high spirits and apparent camaraderie of players, one is really walking among thousands of strictly private experiences. When I mention the irrational (or maybe I can be fancy and say *pararational*) behavior that I have taken such pleasure in, I have no idea if it applies to anybody else. It's not the sort of thing we talk about.

I feel the same ignorance whenever I get into a discussion about the phenomenon of the compulsive gambler. From within my minimum-risk style, the cruelty of that disease seems incomprehensible. And although I don't think I'm likely to end up like that, the picture frightens me. Among those of us who consider ourselves noncompulsive, the specter of the toxic gambler, the driven and tortured person we have seen on television, with his face hidden from the interview camera, and who down deep we all fear we could turn into, waits at the edge of every table, his flamboyant sickness looming over our careful play the way the shadow of alcoholism hovers over the early social drinking of every young man with a family history.

Whenever the subject of compulsive gambling comes up, it is usual for someone to cite the many sources who believe that what the compulsive gambler really wants to do is to lose, that he is trying to reconnect with a distant parent, who will comfort him in his hour of loss and take him in. I don't know. I wonder if in some cases, the problem has more to do with rationality.

My admittedly unstudied theory is this: If "healthy" gambling is in part a vacation from rationality, then perhaps sick gambling is for some a failure to escape that rationality. Perhaps the sick gambler suffers from bringing too much rational baggage along, into a part of the world where it does not work. I am thinking in particular of the principle of fair play, the idea that there exists some sort of moral balance sheet between getting and deserving.

A normal gambler knows the dice and the cards and the wheels and the video chips will play anything but fair; cards will fall (as they have been falling for me on this rotten night) in a sequence that only a malevolent deity (or the always-suspected, but highly unlikely, crooked casino) could have engineered.

The healthy gambler winces, gets disgusted and finally writes it off, knowing the universe is unfair. I think some compulsive gamblers fail to understand this. The compulsive, frantic on a losing night, seems to believe both in fair play and in the inherently balanced nature of the universe—and so goes on losing disastrously, laboring under the conviction that the universe will relent, will show just a touch of human decency and will force the cards to pay the wronged player back for all those previous acts of cruelty.

I suspect also that some compulsives are simply drawn into their illness by the pure sensuality of the betting moment. When we see the misery that the compulsive gambler brings down upon himself, it is natural to imagine him the worst of masochists. But just because he almost always ends up ruined doesn't mean that the ruin itself is what he sought. To use an example from another illness: If we were examining the case of an alcoholic who every night gets so drunk that he throws up, we probably would not be taken seriously if we concluded that this person's real problem is that he's addicted to vomiting.

Instead of being a masochist, perhaps the compulsive gambler loses control because he is enjoying himself so much. Even if he seems miserable most of the time, there is something very powerful about the instant the dice are thrown, the second the deciding card is turned over, the moment the little ball takes its last spastic bounce into the numbered slot.

In my own timid experience, I've felt something of that thrill a few times. On those rare occasions, when a series of successful blackjack hands has allowed me to increase my bet to the grand total of, say, $30, the moment when the card comes down, while everything hangs in the balance—that's where the thrill is. It is a neurological jolt made up of greed, lust and excitement mixed together with a strong dose of fear. Whenever my game gets raised to such a level, then I can feel myself coming alive in a way that seems to redeem all those previous hemorrhogenic hours I have spent on those stools, busting sixteens.

There is another thing that attracts me to casinos, and it may help explain why it felt so appropriate for me to pin that $2 bill to my shorts. For many people, and on many levels, gambling is strongly associated with sex.

On one level, it's easy to understand why that should be so: Money gained through the accident of luck comes with few restrictions on how it is to be spent. And even though Las Vegas is trying to put on a clean face for the benefit of its most profitable tourists (meaning the retirees and the young parents, devoted slot-players all), there remain plenty of young women ready to provide more-traditional forms of entertainment—after they have checked your ID and asked you all sorts of questions to make sure that you are not a cop.

But even for those players who would never call the Room-Service Showgirls escort agency nor board the free limousine that ferries patrons to the out-of-town, legal brothels, something of the old sexiness still hangs in the air above the real games, the ones still played on green felt instead of video terminals. I'm sure it is no accident that the prettiest employees in a casino are always the women who bring gamblers their free cocktails, encouraging them, without saying a word, to drink more, bet more, lose more.

Although the narrow-tied swagger of the Rat Pack is long forgotten down the endless corridors of Circus Circus RV Park, although the city seems determined to insulate the "slots-and-tots" crowd from any disturbing memories of how sexy this place used to be, although the public-relations industry seems bent on changing the symbol of Las Vegas from the painted showgirl to the painted clown—still, something filters through here and there, in the agitated light of the Strip when it catches your eye from an unexpected direction, in the climactic squeal of a Chicago secretary blessed with beginner's luck as she rolls another winning number.

And then there is the ubiquitous $100 bill, the controlling scrip against which all clattering chips and wrinkled twenties are measured. It is the only piece of American currency that cannot be called ugly. The reverse side is especially attractive, with its leafy green and that sort of Frederick's of Hollywood laciness in the scrollwork around the edges.

Even the most uxorious conventioneer knows that if an escort-agency transaction ever should occur, it would involve bills of this denomination. To handle one bill is perhaps to be remotely involved in all the adventures that that bill has helped to capitalize. That moment at the casino cage, as the cashier counts your chips and crisply deals out the stacked hundreds, remains, I think, an erotically charged moment—no matter that you have already earmarked that money to resurface your driveway.

NO LIMIT[4]

When poker players get together, they don't talk about the hands they have won. They talk instead about "bad beats"—the hands they should have won but didn't, because the cards were freakish or, more often, because some other player made a stupid call. Bad-beat stories are long-winded and bad-tempered, and their punch line is always roughly the same: "I mean, what was the schmuck doing in the hand anyway with a pair of lousy deuces?" Bad beats haunt you like bad dreams. You brood about them, you complain about them, you play them over in your head again and again. And this is how it should be, because while it is happening a truly bad beat feels like a waking nightmare.

This is a poker story, so it starts with a bad beat. The setting is Binion's Horseshoe Casino, in Las Vegas, during the World Series of Poker; the event is the World Championship; the game is Texas hold 'em, ten-thousand-dollar buy-in, no limit. In Texas hold 'em, each player is dealt two cards face down, in the hole. The two players to the left of the dealer are forced to bet blind—before they see their cards. The other players either call the blind bet or raise it or fold. Then three communal cards, called the flop, are dealt face up in the center of the table, and there is another round of betting, although this time the players may check. Then two more communal cards—known as Fourth Street, or the turn, and Fifth Street, or the river—are dealt face up, one at a time, with a round of betting after each. The five cards in the center are common to all the players, who use them in combination with their hole cards to make the strongest possible hands.

Like most nightmares, this one begins sweetly. I am playing

[4]Article by A. Alvarez. From *The New Yorker,* Aug 8, 94. Copyright © 1994 by A. Alvarez. Reprinted with permission.

with great discipline, my stack of chips is building nicely, I am in control. Then the scene darkens and the horrors start. I am in the dealer's position—"on the button," the classic position in which to make a bet in the hope of stealing whatever money is already in the pot. I cup my hands around my hole cards and peer at them: two aces, the strongest starting hand in the game. I raise, but modestly, as though I were "on the steal." To my delight, an early caller who has a lot of chips in front of him reraises. This is what I was hoping for. "Raise," I say. I put my hands behind my stacks of chips and move them all into the pot. (In no-limit poker, you can bet as much as you want whenever you want as long as the money's on the table.) My opponent thinks for a long time; he looks at me; he looks at the mass of chips in the middle of the table; he studies his cards. I have more chips than he does; if he calls the bet and loses, he will be out of the tournament. Finally, he shrugs and pushes all his chips forward. The pot is huge, and whoever wins it will be the tournament's chip leader. Since there can be no more betting, the tournament coördinator asks us to turn over our cards for the benefit of the TV cameras. When the other player sees my aces, he shakes his head despondently, turns over an unsuited king and queen, and rises from his seat, ready to make a humiliated exit. I settle back smugly, unable to believe my luck. The dealer pauses dramatically, thumps the table with his fist, and deals the flop: king, king, deuce of different suits, giving my opponent three kings. Another pause, another thump, another card: seven. Only a third ace will save me now. But the last card is a jack, and from being one of the tournament leaders I am now down there at the bottom, scrabbling to stay alive. A few hands later, I am out.

The nightmare really happened, but not at Binion's, and not even at a poker table. It happened at home in London, while I was warming up on a computer game of the World Series, two days before I left for Vegas. I took it as a good omen: bad beats like that tend not to come in pairs.

This year, the World Series of Poker, which takes place annually at Binion's Horseshoe, and runs from mid-April to mid-May, celebrated its silver anniversary. It is the Wimbledon of poker tournaments—the most popular, the most illustrious, and the longest-running. It began in 1970, when Benny Binion invited a handful of his high-rolling poker-playing cronies to get together at the Horseshoe in order to compete in various forms of poker at stakes that only they could contemplate. When all the games were over, they voted democratically for who should be named the champion of champions. The man they elected was Johnny Moss, who celebrated his eighty-seventh birthday during this year's tournament, and is still competing.

Since that first tournament, the event has grown exponentially. By 1990, the entry to the main event—the ten-thousand-dollar no-limit Texas Hold 'Em World Championship—was approaching the magic number of two hundred people. Two hundred buy-ins meant two million dollars in prize money to be distributed—about forty per cent to the winner, the rest according to finishing place. The Binions, who understand what makes gamblers tick, stopped fussing with percentages, and guaranteed the world champion a million dollars as well as the 14k.-gold bracelet with his or her name on it that is also given to the winner of each of the subsidiary events. For the silver anniversary, Jack Binion, who has been president of the Horseshoe since 1964, added a further attraction: the champion would win his weight in silver as well as his million dollars, and whoever got into the money in the minor events would receive a commemorative silver bar.

Like the World Series, the Horseshoe Casino itself has grown enormously in recent years. When I first went there, in 1981, it was a shabby little place, dark and narrow, and in terms of décor it had nothing to offer at all. It was also overpoweringly noisy, for the simple reason that it was always packed. If you wanted action—real action, with no upper limits on the bets you made—you bypassed the ritzy palaces on the Strip; the Horseshoe was the place to go.

Somehow, the Binions had worked out the right formula for serious players. It helped that Benny Binion was the boss of gambling in Dallas until 1946, when, as he dourly put it, "my sheriff got beat in the election" and he had to leave town in a hurry. The Dallas connection guaranteed him the loyalty of the high-rolling Texans after he moved to Las Vegas. Supporting Benny was the patriotic thing to do, and anyway the Binions were their sort of folk. The Binions responded by providing outsized gambling action, along with the best steaks and the hottest chili in town. Yet even the most loyal Texans drew the line at staying in the handful of poky rooms above the casino. They gambled at the Horseshoe, but they stayed across the street at the Golden Nugget.

The Binions eventually solved their accommodation problem by buying the casino next door, a great, echoing barn of a place called the Mint, which was nearly always deserted, and had just two things to recommend it, both of them on its roof: a small swimming pool (the only one downtown in the early eighties) and a huge illuminated clock (also the only one downtown, then and now, in a city where time has been officially banished in case it interferes with business). The Mint had a lot of rooms, none of them particularly luxurious, but considerably more comfortable than the flophouse above the Horseshoe. The Binions did almost nothing to tart the place up or improve the amenities. They simply knocked down the wall between the two casinos, remove the giant illuminated "M" from the clock, put a horseshoe in its place, and called the whole block Binion's Horseshoe. And that was all it took. Overnight, the wastelands of the Mint were jam-packed with gamblers, whooping it up and having a great time.

During the World Series, amateur poker players fly in from all over the world to compete in the tournaments, which cover most current forms of poker and vary in expense from the thousand-dollar-buy-in Women's Seven Card Stud to the ten-thousand-dollar-buy-in World Championship. The Las Vegas professionals play in the tournaments, too, but often simply as a courtesy to Jack Binion and because their status as champions requires it. Their real business is in the side games that go on day and night while the World Series is in progress.

These cash games are listed in a kind of shorthand on a roster at the back of the tournament area. The smallest is "PLH 1-2-5"—pot-limit hold 'em, in which the compulsory blind bets are one dollar, two dollars, and five dollars, and the buy-in is five hundred dollars; from there, the size of the games climbs steadily toward the stratosphere. The biggest game of all is off in a corner at Table 61, where ex-champions like Doyle Brunson, Johnny Chan, and Stu Ungar hold court. According to the board, the game at Table 61 is "2/7 NL, 100 ante, 200–400"—that is, deuce-to-the-seven razz, a particularly brutal form of lowball, in which each player antes a hundred dollars before every hand, the two players to the left of the dealer are forced to bet two hundred and four hundred dollars blind, and there is no limit to the size of the subsequent bets. The buy-in for that game is twenty-five thousand dollars, but usually no one sits down with that little. One night during my stay, someone at the table won a single pot of nearly a hundred thousand dollars. In other words, the World Series is not just the foremost poker tournament; it is also a hustlers' convention.

Over the years, the World Series acquired a great deal of

glamour in the poker world and inspired a large number of imitations. But one major problem remained: how to attract all those good players who were out there yearning to get in but were never going to build up enough money for a stake. In 1984, someone had the smart idea of organizing "satellites"—competitions for the competitions—in which ten players would ante up a thousand dollars each and play a freeze-out, winner take all. But even a thousand dollars is a substantial sum to invest in a nine-to-one shot, and it was still beyond the range of many hopefuls. The next step was super-satellites—multi-table events in which each player paid two hundred and twenty dollars for two hundred chips and, during the first hour, could rebuy additional stacks of two hundred for two hundred dollars a throw. If enough people entered —and they entered by the hundreds—there would be sufficient money to guarantee everyone at the final table an entry to the main event. There are now satellites for all the events. At the Horseshoe, they start a few days before the beginning of the World Series, but for months before that they run in casinos across America and around the world. The World Series is no longer the exclusive preserve of the top professionals and the millionaires; it has been democratized.

Like all poker players, I have dreamed of playing in the World Championship. This year, I got my chance. I had been training for it for fifteen months, playing in tournaments once or twice a week in London. Although I often reached the final table and occasionally won an event, I knew that in Vegas they marched to a different tune. I would be like a good club tennis player with a wildcard entry to Wimbledon: the game played by the top players has no relation to the game played by the likes of me; it just looks the same. But at least I could try not to make a fool of myself. I would pace myself, get used to the pressures, work out some strategies for survival.

Poker is a game of many skills: you need card sense, psychological insight, a good memory, controlled aggression, enough mathematical know-how to work out the odds as each hand develops, and what poker players call a leather ass—i.e., patience. Above all, you need the arcane skill called money management: the ability to control your bankroll and understand the long-term implications of each bet (how to avoid the casual five-dollar call that ends in a five-hundred-dollar disaster), so that you don't go broke during a session. All good players have these skills, but the pros have them to a far greater degree than the amateurs. Another difference between the two groups, however, is not often mentioned: somewhere along the road, the pros have lost their sense of urgency. Their lives are one long poker game, which began when they turned professional and will end—if it ever ends—when they retire. Mostly, they expect to win, but sometimes they lose, and when they do they shrug and leave the table and come back the next day or the next week, knowing that the game will always be there. Amateurs are less philosophical: because they usually play no more than once or twice a week, they want to cram as much action as they can into the limited time at their disposal, so they stay too long at the table and play until they can't think straight.

In order to survive in Vegas, you must divest yourself of the sense of urgency. Day or night, the game you want is always in progress, and you must treat it as the professionals do: when nothing is going right, when you sit for hours folding unplayable hands, or, worse, when every time you are dealt two kings someone else has a pair of aces, you must learn to get up from the table, swallow your losses, and come back another time. Quitting when you are ahead is easy; to cut your losses and run takes far greater discipline.

It is particularly hard during the World Series, when a flood tide of money is washing around the Horseshoe. Even the language spoken at the tables is calculatedly unreal. Whatever the size of the game, the general rule is: Never call a buck a buck. Over at Table 61, when someone bets "a dime" he means a thousand dollars, and even in the small games they divide by a hundred. Treating money like small change somehow adds to the pleasure. When the dealer says, "Your nickel," the player on the big blind obediently pushes forward a five-dollar chip. The first player to act says, "A quarter to go," and throws in a green twenty-five. An elderly man wearing a white Stetson flicks a hundred-dollar bill into the pot and says, "Make it a dollar straight." The dealer thumps the table and deals three spades into the center. Without hesitating, the man who had originally bet the quarter now bets two hundred and fifty dollars. The man in the white Stetson looks at him, looks at the exposed cards, shrugs, and throws his cards face up into the center: an ace and king of hearts. "Right string, wrong yo-yo," he barks. But the very next deal he comes out raising again before the flop. "Don't mess with him," another player says as he folds his hand. "He's hotter than a polar bear in the Mojave Desert." Three players call, however, then fold docilely when White Stetson bets five hundred dollars after the flop. "It's like picking fresh grapes," someone says admiringly. "The bigger they are, the easier it is." White Stetson beams.

The atmosphere is curiously festive, and disdain for money is part of the festivity. Large sums are changing hands, yet the poker tables buzz with the pleasure and excitement and good humor that come when people get together to do something they love doing and do well. When someone wins a hand because another player checked when he should have bet, the winner scoops in the chips and says, "Only in America can a guy get a free card and make money. Only in America."

The revels end abruptly when you sit down to play a tournament. There are twenty-one open events in the World Series, and each of them is like the last-chance saloon: the atmosphere is gloomy, the faces are tense and unsmiling. The reason is simple: if you make a mistake or suffer a bad beat in a cash game, you can always reach into your pocket and pull out more money, but if you make a mistake in a tournament, you are out. (In two of the events, Deuce to Seven Draw and the biggest of the Omaha tournaments—Omaha being a four-card variant of hold 'em— rebuys are permitted during the first three hours of play if, at any time, you have fewer chips than you started with.)

For players like me, there is another cause for anxiety, and it has to do with pride. The tournament events are our chance to sit down with the champions on equal terms—or, rather, on equal financial terms at the start. "We're ambitious amateurs, and we don't want to be humiliated," my friend Julien Studley, a New Yorker who plays regularly and successfully in the big tournaments, said. "The great players don't have that problem. They'll go for the brilliant, do-or-die move, and if it doesn't come off and they get eliminated, so what? It doesn't bother them. We are different. We want to stick around because our egos are very much affected by being able to say we were still there on the second day of play or past the dinner break, or whenever it was. Even if we have no chance of winning the championship, we want to hang in. It's a mistake to give up hope. Every time someone is eliminated, it's a benefit to you. The point is to survive."

Johnny Chan said much the same, but from a different point of view. Chan is small and trim and compact, with a heart-shaped face and unnervingly sharp eyes. He has won the World Championship twice, in 1987 and 1988, and this year he became the first player to bring his total earnings in the World Series to more than two million dollars. Chan tends to talk in imperatives, a style that goes with his commanding presence, and he reacts to amateurs the way a great white shark reacts to blood. "No-limit is a game to trap people," he told me one afternoon when he was taking a break from the monster game at Table 61. "When you find a weak player, try to get everyone else out. Now it's between you and the weak player. You need to trap him, make him lose something. You don't have a hand—who cares? Bluff him out. He's weak. Make a play. When you sit down, you look around the table and see how many weak players there are. Who is the weakest? That's the one you go for. You try to avoid the good players until you get to the final table. That's what you've got to do to win."

When Studley talked about not giving up hope, he made me understand how hopeless my position was at this level of poker. Chan's staccato commands deepened my despair. So did Artie Cobb, but after I talked to him one evening over dinner in the Sombrero Room, at least I began to understand the measure of the difference between the small fry and the great whites. Cobb has ginger hair, a big belly, and a mournful face. He is a talented poker player, who has won three tournaments in the World Series, but he is not up there with the champions, and has thought deeply about why this is so. "There are a lot of fine players out there, but the great player always has that little edge on them," he said. "The player who is not great has tendencies he always falls into when he has a good hand, a mediocre hand, or a weak hand. The great players can spot them easily. They read the table like a walking computer. They understand when they have to gamble more and when they have to gamble less. The average player doesn't always understand that. When the game starts, everyone has the same number of chips. The favorites are favorites because they know what they have to do to win the tournament. They can't stay idle and hope they're going to double up their stack along the way. They try to increase it a little bit at every limit, sometimes even with marginal hands most people don't want to play, like an ace with a doubtful kicker." (A kicker is the "side," or subsidiary, card to a more powerful card.) "I remember an extraordinary hand played by Stu Ungar and Doyle Brunson. Both of them had ace-queen in the hole, and Gabe Kaplan, the actor, was there with king-jack. The flop was ace, ace, king. Stuey made a small bet on the flop and the others called. The next card was a three. Stuey came out betting, Gabe folded, and Doyle just moved all-in. It was a huge bet, and if Stuey called and won, Doyle would be out of the tournament. Each of them knew the other had an ace, so it was down to the kicker. An amateur might have thought that an ace was good enough or that Doyle would only move all-in with a full house—with ace-king or ace-three in the hole. But somehow Stuey sensed that Doyle was making a play. He thought a long time, and if he had had less than ace-queen he might have folded. It was possible that Doyle had ace-jack, but that was un-likely, knowing how well he plays. So Stuey figured they must have the same hand, ace-queen. He called, and they split the pot. And that's a mind-set only great players get into. That's the deep part of the game, which the average player has no concept of."

I played in three events in the World Series—the fifteen-hundred-dollar-buy-in Texas hold 'em (pot limit), the twenty-five-hundred-dollar-buy-in Texas hold 'em (no limit), and the ten-thousand-dollar-buy-in World Championship itself—and each was grimmer than the last. That made good sense to me, since the prize money shared out among the finalists grew steadily more serious in each event: three hundred and seventy thousand five hundred dollars in the fifteen-hundred-dollar tournament; five hundred and fifty thousand dollars in the twenty-five-hundred-dollar game; and two million six hundred and eighty thousand dollars in the World Championship. It also made sense that I played less freely as the grandeur of the occasion increased. But while the World Series was in progress I was also playing in cash games, and what didn't make sense was how my play in them was like a mirror image of the way I played in the tournaments. Hold 'em is, among other things, a game of calculated aggression: if your cards are good enough for you to call a bet, they are good enough to raise with. According to Don Williams, a small, bearded, fast-talking, and successful professional, "When you're betting, you've got two chances of winning: you can take the pot there and then, or you can have the best hand. When you're calling a bet, you've only got one chance: you've got to have the best hand. But you don't win tournaments just by showing the best hand." I followed his advice in the cash games and did very well. Whenever I had bet before the flop, I bet again after it, if the other players checked, even when the exposed cards had not helped my hand. More often than not, the original callers meekly folded, and I took the money. But I played only in the modest pot-limit cash games, with other amateurs and small-time professionals. The heavy hitters were busy elsewhere.

The weekend before the World Championship, Binion's Horseshoe was like a pressure cooker with the heat turned up beneath it. The casino was packed with gawping spectators, and the poker pits swarmed with TV crews, with self-important people flashing press cards and asking dumb questions, with players short of funds working the crowd, trying to hustle deals. In the cash games, tempers frayed, and there was a final feeding frenzy in the thousand-dollar satellites. People were buying in, losing, buying in again, as though a thousand dollars truly were no more than a dime. Behind them, a group of professionals lounged against the rail like hawks in a tree, waiting to pick off an easy satellite to save themselves the ten-grand entry fee on Monday. The air-conditioning seemed unable to cope, the voices on the intercom never let up, the sheer predatoriness was battering. I ground out some money in a cash game and went to bed early.

The morning of the big day was chilly and overcast. A brisk wind was blowing, and I had the pool to myself. Around twelve-thirty, I wandered down to the casino. Although crowds were gathering in the tournament area and journalists bustled about, the frenzy of the last few days was over. The players stood around in little groups, talking in subdued voices, eying the opposition. Off to one side, Jack McClelland, the tournament coördinator, sat at a table drawing the seat numbers and droning them out on the intercom. The big board behind him had space for two hundred and forty names, but that was not enough. Because of the satellites and the fact that this was the silver anniversary of the World Series, two hundred and sixty-eight players, a record, had signed up for the World Championship. The sight of my own name, at No. 182, up there with all those champions whom I had watched for years, from a safe distance, should have been exhilarating. Instead, it filled me with gloom.

We all dispersed to our appointed seats. Mine was Seat 1 at Table 56; at ten thousand dollars, it was the most expensive seat I had ever sat on. Next to me was Billy Baxter, a famous high roller and one of the great deuce-to-the-seven players. Jack Keller, the 1984 World Champion, who had that day been inducted into the Poker Hall of Fame, was in Seat 6. Ken Flaton, another expert, was in Seat 8.

Finally, the chatter subsided, and Jack McClelland gave the starting orders: "Dealers, shuffle up and deal."

Mick Cowley, an Englishman I know, once made it to the final table. "In the early stages, I came in with nothing lower than a pair of jacks," he said later. Two jacks are strong enough to call with and easy to throw away. A pair of queens is a trickier hand to play; I was dealt them four times—twice in the first fifteen minutes—and in the end they were my undoing. But my first mistake occurred an hour or so into the game. I was dealt an eight and seven of diamonds when I was in the big blind. There were two or three callers but no raise. The dealer thumped the table, burned the top card, and dealt six, nine, ten. The seven and eight in my hand gave me a straight. It was an almost perfect flop, except that the exposed nine and ten were both hearts. I checked, in the hope of trapping someone, and a young woman named Barbara Samuelson came out betting. She was tall and rangy, with a mannish figure, a small face, and large hands, and her style of play was fearless and aggressive. I should have moved all-in immediately, in order to shut her out, but greed overcame me. So I raised a paltry thousand, and she called. The next card was bad for me: the queen of hearts, making a possible flush and a higher straight. When I checked, she checked. The last card was a king, and this time she bet strongly. I should have folded—any good player would have folded—but I was in love with my puny straight, so I made a crying call. She had a pair of jacks in the hole and had made a higher straight than mine. (Samuelson eventually placed tenth—the highest-ever finish by a woman in this event.)

At least I wasn't the only one making mistakes. Within two hours, three former world champions had gone. Jack Keller slow-played a pair of aces, moved all-in when a king and a ten flopped, and was called instantly by Billy Baxter, who had king-ten in the hole. Minutes later, Stu Ungar, who won the title in 1980 and 1981, stalked past, looking furious. Phil Hellmuth, Jr., winner in 1989, followed. "I had two aces, but I ran into a pair of tens," he said. Billy Baxter watched them go. "I'll tell you one thing," he said contentedly. "They sure knocked some whales out already."

At three-forty-five, there was a ten-minute break. As we settled around the table again, Baxter and a pal were chatting together about hold 'em. "Not my pond," Baxter was saying. "Hell, man, you just busted a guy in the Hall of Fame."

"That just shows you I'm not long for this world."

For the next hour and a half, my chips bled away in antes while I folded unplayable hands. Then, for the fourth time, I was dealt two queens. I bet a thousand, and Baxter instantly reraised another thousand. Maybe I should have moved all-in to shut him out. But he had position over me and a lot of firepower. So I just called. The flop was king, seven, deuce. When I checked and he bet two thousand, I knew what his hole cards were: an ace and a king; with anything stronger, he would have checked to trap me; with less, he would have checked for fear of being trapped. My only hope was to catch one of the two queens remaining in the deck or to bluff him. I suppose I should have folded then and there and kept my last three grand for a better spot. But the antes were eating me up, and that pair of queens in my hand seemed like a mountain after the cards I'd been seeing. I thought and thought, then called, hoping my long pause might have puzzled him. The next card was another deuce. That was my chance. I pushed in what was left of my stack and said, "Come on, Billy, let's gamble." He looked at me slit-eyed and hesitated. "You got a deuce?" he said. And for a moment I thought I'd bluffed him out. But the pot was large and the bet was small, so he called. The last card was a jack. Without waiting, he turned over the ace-king I knew he had.

When Adlai Stevenson lost to Eisenhower in 1952, he said that he was too old to cry, but that it hurt too much to laugh. I understood how he felt. I had been preparing for this day for fifteen months, and when it came I blew it. I made the classic mistake of a newcomer to the big league: I played what the pros call "tight-weak"—afraid to bet without the stone-cold nuts, and easily scared out. But at this level players can smell your fear, and they run all over you. I couldn't even complain about bad beats. On the contrary, I knew justice had been done. I am a good pot-limit player, but in pot-limit you can make a big enough bet to bluff an opponent out without putting your whole stack in jeopardy. No-limit is different. You get few chances, and the smallest mistake can destroy you. I failed to take the chances I was offered, and ended by making a big mistake.

The first person I saw when I left the table was Nic Szeremeta, an Englishman who knows all the odds. "At least you were beaten with the best hand," he said consolingly. "Two queens are a fifty-five to forty-five favorite over ace-king offsuit."

A few minutes later, as though to prove his point, I watched a replay of the identical hand at an adjacent table: someone bet with ace-king offsuit, then called a huge all-in reraise by a guy holding a pair of queens. But this time the first card to be flopped was a queen, giving the raiser three queens and making him chip leader of the tournament at that point.

At breakfast the next morning, I saw Herb Bronstein, who was considered a strong contender for the title. He, too, looked stricken. "Yeah, I'm an also-ran," he said. "You wait a whole year for your chance and then it's gone."

"I've been waiting all my life," I answered.

When I called my wife in London with the news, she burst into tears.

The World Championship is a four-day event, and, like the other also-rans, I could not bring myself to watch it with any interest until the last day, when the field had been reduced to six and show biz took over. The final table was set up, as though for a prizefight, in a fenced-off square, its entrances blocked by security guards. Around the table was a cordon sanitaire for the television crews and the press photographers. Behind it, and flanked by two big TV screens, was a dais where the players were interviewed as they were eliminated from the game. There were two blocks of reserved seats—one for the players, the other for the press—but no matter how close you sat all you could see was a slumped back, a profile, a foot tapping secretly below the table. The things that really mattered—the cards, the facial expressions, the size of the bets and the manner in which they were made, the dealers' deft, eloquent fingers as they handled the cards—could be seen only on the TV monitors.

In best prizefight style, there was a weigh-in before the start, so that the winner's weight in silver would be ready at the end. By ten-twenty-five, the ceremonies were over. For the last time, Jack McClelland called, "Shuffle up and deal," and the cards were spun out. Within two and a half hours, three finalists had been eliminated, two of them when they moved all-in against players holding ace-queen, and a queen came on the flop. Each time, I thought, Where were you when I needed you?

Then the action froze. The chip leader was Hugh Vincent, a scrawny, chain-smoking, bespectacled amateur, with a goatee, a cheap white shirt, and a blue cap. He had begun the day with almost a million and a half dollars in chips—more than half the money in play—and he used his muscle to harry the other players, pushing his luck, living on the edge, playing brilliantly by the seat of his pants. Close behind him was Russ Hamilton, a Las Vegas professional. He weighed three hundred and thirty pounds, and when he climbed onto the scales before the start, they ran out of silver ingots. He had pale hair, a ghost of a beard, and sharp, calculating blue eyes. At the table, he was a thoughtful and forbidding presence, biding his time, making no mistakes. He sat for what seemed hours without stirring; only his eyes

moved, missing nothing. A long way behind came John Spadavecchia, a Miami businessman who looked as if he had just walked
out of a Scorsese movie: a creased face with a lot of mileage on it,
dark hair, dark patterned shirt, gold watch, gold bracelet, gold
ring.

The 1994 World Series had already broken all sorts of records, including the total number of entrants into all the events
(thirty-eight hundred and thirty-two) and the total prize money
distributed (nine million nine hundred and sixty-nine thousand
five hundred dollars). In the World Championship event, more
records went: it had the largest entry (two hundred and sixty-
eight), the highest-placed woman player (Barbara Samuelson), the
largest single pot (a million nine hundred and eighty thousand
dollars), and, in the closing stages, the biggest-ever blind bets
(twenty-five thousand and fifty thousand dollars). Another record broken was the three-handed marathon that ended the
game: more than five hours passed without a player being eliminated, as Spadavecchia tried to claw his way back to level terms
and Vincent leaked his money away, little by little, to Hamilton.

Spadavecchia went, finally, at six-twenty-five. Five minutes later, Hamilton was dealt a pair of queens, saw a third queen appear
on the flop, and trapped Vincent into the largest pot in the history of the event. Ten minutes later, it was over. Russ Hamilton had
the title, a million dollars, twenty-eight thousand five hundred
and twelve dollars in silver ingots, the winner's gold bracelet, and
the honor of having his picture up on the wall of the poker room
along with all the other greats.

That evening, I had dinner with the English writer Anthony
Holden, an old friend and a fierce poker player. Afterward, we
wandered back to the tournament area to find a game. But there
was no tournament area. The tables had gone, the players had
gone. All that was left was a cleaning man wearily vacuuming a
stretch of leaf-patterned carpet.

We stood there for a while in silence. Then I said, "Why do
they always get the queen when they need it and we don't?"

"That's the mystery of life and poker," Tony said. "I guess the
answer is they invented the game, so they deserve it."

WATCHING DAD GAMBLE[5]

When I told Dad that *Yankee* would pay for us to go gambling at the Foxwoods Casino on the Mashsantucket Pequot Indian reservation near Ledyard, Connecticut, he didn't act thrilled. I should have expected that. He knew I had never been much enamored of his gambling.

When I was growing up, my mother nagged my father daily to quit gambling. But he never did. I remember all those times our house was put up for sale after Dad's losses and how terrified I was I'd have to leave my friends. And then, just as suddenly, our house would be off the market and Dad would be buying me a $100 Herb Score model baseball glove. I remember our Sunday afternoon rides in the country, to look at the fall foliage, that always ended abruptly with my mother and me sitting in the car by the side of the road while Dad shouted into a pay telephone, "I want 50 times on Frisco!"

I remember the time I got into his drawer of dice and mixed them all up. That night my parents had a terrible argument because I had caused Dad to lose a lot of money shooting craps. I remember the time I played with a book of matches, lighting the whole book. I was punished doubly—for playing with matches *and* for incinerating the betting line Dad had written on the inside cover of that matchbook.

Most vividly I remember the time I broke Dad's finger. I was 12, the best Little League pitcher in town. Mom and Dad went to all my games. They sat in the stands and watched proudly as I pitched yet another no-hitter. People congratulated them on my success. In a way, my pitching made my family respectable in town in spite of my father's gambling. Always before the last out, I'd look to the stands and give my parents a little wink, as if to say, "It's in the bag." Then I'd pump, kick, and catch, out of the corner of my eye, my father leaping down from the stands and running toward the pay telephone in the parking lot to place a bet.

He used to catch me on the sidewalk in front of our house while my mother sat on the porch and applauded my efforts.

[5]Article by Pat Jordan. From *Yankee*, Jul '93. Copyright © 1993 by Pat Jordan. Reprinted with permission.

Then one day, Dad was distracted. Maybe he was thinking about dealing cards that night? Whatever. I cut loose with a fastball. He caught it on his bare hand. Dad ran bellowing into the house. When I finally got the courage to go inside, I found him sitting at the kitchen table, trying to deal a poker hand to my mother. The cards slipped in his bleeding hand, fell to the floor. With a look, my mother sent me to my room where I said a host of Hail Marys that Dad would be able to deal cards tonight to make the money we needed so desperately.

Years later, a grown man, I sit at the kitchen table in their apartment, and we laugh at such memories. My father's gambling is now a personal idiosyncrasy rather than a debilitating vice. It is our family history, funny now that we've all survived.

We left Bridgeport for Ledyard, a two-hour drive, in a driving snowstorm at five o'clock on a Saturday morning—Dad and I going to gamble together for the first time in our lives. He was 84, an old man by some standards, but as young, vigorous, and quick-witted as always. I hated to admit it, but it was his gambling that kept him young.

"We've got $300 to gamble with," I said.

"Well, then we'll go right down the line like Maggie Kline."

I looked across at him. "Now what the hell does that mean?"

"It's a Prohibition expression." He smiled. "It means we'll shoot it all."

Jeez, I thought. The old man will never change. Just a few weeks ago he'd shot pool with his 16-year-old grandson, and it inspired him to go to a pool hall in Bridgeport to hustle up a game. He found a black guy named James. Well dressed, Dad said, whatever that meant.

"He was a pretty good shooter," Dad said. "So I made him spot me the eight and nine in nine-ball. He said, 'You may be an old man, but you might make me stand up and take notice. How do I know you ain't hustlin' me?'" Dad just lowered his head, fingering the fedora in his pudgy hands, trying to look as pitiful and harmless as he could. James bought it. "I guess I'll take a chance," he said.

Dad let him win five dollars. "The setup," Dad said. "Next time we'll play for more money." I couldn't help but laugh. The old man was still hustling. That's what he loved about gambling—the hustle.

My father first began hustling pool when he was 15, just discharged from the orphanage. He had never known his parents.

He quit school and turned to pool for his livelihood. His gambling cronies became the family he never had. They were like him—outside the mainstream of conventional society. A place he'd always be.

He played nine ball for $100 a game, a lot of money in the twenties, especially for a 15-year-old kid. But Dad was good at it, with his maddeningly methodical southpaw stroke, the balls dropping with a thudding monotony game after game. His reputation spread, and pretty soon he couldn't scare up a game anywhere in Connecticut. So he quit pool and turned to other games. He liked shooting craps the best, he said, because it was a fast game. Fast and loose, the way he liked it.

"I gambled because of the excitement," he said, as we drove past New Haven. The snow was thick on the highway now, and I could feel the car drifting on me. I slowed to 40 miles per hour. It was starting to worry me, but Dad didn't seem to notice. He was too intent on talking to me, for the first time, about his career.

"Gambling was a shortcut for me," he said. "Illegal gambling was the most exciting. Even if the only game in town was fixed, I had to play. That was the kick. Not winning, but the possibility of loss. Hell, for a gambler, is a game he can't lose. The money I won, well," he made a backhand toss of his hand, "I lived good. But mostly I gave it away."

When he was younger, he gave it to his cronies, never letting them pay for a meal or a drink. When he was older, he gave it to me. Now he gives it to his grandchildren. It's a lesson I learned about money from the old man. My father is a smart man. More than that: He's one of those brilliant self-educated men who spend their lives trying to make up for a lack of education. He still reads Plato and Socrates and Kafka and especially Dostoyevsky. *The Gambler* is his favorite book, he says, because it perfectly captures a gambler's masochism. "Gamblers love to lose," he says. "The more they lose, the more of a man they think they are."

My father's lack of education has always frustrated him. "It's the one thing I miss the most," he said. "Sometimes people would use a word I didn't know, and I'd run to the dictionary to look it up. I tried to fake it. As a kid, I dressed collegiate, but I wasn't thinking collegiate. I was thinking wise guy."

I remembered a few old pictures I'd seen of my father in his twenties. He wore a double-breasted Chesterfield topcoat, a regimental striped tie, and brown-and-white shoes. He looked like a dandy out of an F. Scott Fitzgerald novel. Not the Jordan Baker crowd with their easy inherited wealth and comfortable, preppy way of dressing. More like Gatsby, the parvenu, trying so desperately and pathetically to look as if he'd gone to Princeton and then on to a seat on the New York Stock Exchange, but overdoing it.

Since my father had no legitimate outlet for his intelligence, he turned that intelligence to gambling. It was the secret of his success. He always found an edge. "The percentage is in your favor when you know something the other guy doesn't," he said. Sometimes what Dad knew was the percentages of a winning poker hand, and sometimes what he knew was that the dice were loaded or that he was dealing cards from the bottom of the deck.

"It's not how well you gamble," Dad went on, "but how many mistakes your opponent makes. That's why I don't like to gamble at casinos. You can't beat the 'iron,' the house winning percentage. The casinos win because they don't make mistakes. You can't outwit a casino like you can a guy in a private game."

But mostly he knew his opponents. He read them—their angers, their frustrations, the insecurities that made them bet stupidly, something he never did. In a way, reading people is something I inherited from Dad. It's how I make my living now as a writer. Yet I have never gambled—because of my father. When I told him this, he laughed. "A free-lance writer all your life," he said, "and you say you never gamble."

Twenty miles from Ledyard, the snow was falling so heavily that dozens of cars had drifted off the Thruway. State police directed traffic and tow trucks pulled cars out of snowdrifts. I was hunched over the steering wheel like an old man myself, driving barely 30 miles per hour. But Dad was still talking, oblivious to the snow.

He said he'd already been to Foxwoods a few times because, "It's my style. It's not like Vegas or Atlantic City where people expect a show, girls, liquor, a steak. It's for hard-core gamblers who can't help themselves. There are few recreational bettors at Foxwoods."

His only complaint was that the games weren't fast enough for him. The dealers were so slow in counting cards, or dealing out money, that the casino managed only thirty decisions an hour instead of sixty. "Volume counts," he said.

He never saw any evidence of pickpockets or prostitutes or Mob control, he said, the common fears of most people when casinos open in their area. "The Mob only comes in before the casino starts up," he said, "never after." As for the other vices, women and liquor, he said, well, nobody much cared about them at Foxwoods. The gamblers at Foxwoods were his kind of gamblers, he said, because they had room in their lives for only one vice. "There are drinkers, womanizers, and gamblers," he said, "and if you're gonna do it right, you have room for only one vice."

Ledyard is a typical New England village of 15,600 with a big white Congregational church on its green and a reputation, before Foxwoods, of having the largest oak tree in New England, which died a decade ago. It's off the Thruway, along a narrow two-lane blacktop road that rolls past snow-covered woods and old clapboard-sided Colonial homes.

"Turn here," Dad said. I'd almost missed the casino because it was set back off the road in a little valley surrounded by hills thick with fir trees. No one could complain it was an eyesore in this pastoral setting. We reached the parking lot at 7:00 A.M. It was already filled with cars, most of them piled high with snow, as if they'd been here all night.

Inside, at first glance, the casino looked like a shopping mall. It was painted pale purple, green, and beige. There was a towering rock-waterfall in the lobby, a gift shop that sold Native American crafts that looked as if they had been made in Taiwan, and a deserted bar. There was a dining room to the right of the waterfall with only a few people eating there and behind it a cafeteria. It was only when I looked to the left and right of the waterfall that I realized I was in a casino. To the right were hundreds of slot machines and beyond them a huge bingo hall. To the left were the gaming tables, already packed with gamblers.

Dad checked our coats and gave me a tour. He took me first to the slots. Most of the players were women, mechanically pulling the iron levers and, even as their winnings hit the metal tray with a clatter, feeding more money into the machines.

"Here's where the profit is," Dad said. "The casino can regulate the percentage of payoffs. Most of the games, roulette and craps, earn the casinos between five and six percent, but the slots are higher. If a casino eliminated the slots, it would have a tough go."

I approached an unoccupied slot machine to look at it. A woman with teased, frosted hair, wearing a bowling-league jacket, stretched her arm across the machine like a school crossing guard. "That's for my husband," she said. "He's been playing it all morning. He just went to the john."

"Oh, I'm sorry," I said. Dad just shook his head and led me past the waterfall to the gaming tables that stretched as far as the

eye could see. Blackjack. Chuck-a-Luck. Craps. Baccarat. Roulette. "The poker games are downstairs," Dad said. Waitresses
dressed in skimpy outfits were circulating among the gamblers,
offering them free drinks as long as they gambled. They wore
short skirts and shiny, orthopedic-looking hose, and most of their
high-heeled pumps were too big for them so they had stuffed
wads of paper in their backs. Nobody paid them any attention.
"They don't look like much compared to Vegas and Atlantic
City," Dad said.

He led me over to the crap tables, his game. There was a lot of
shouting after each roll of the dice. A good-looking blond guy
with a beard was making a great production of shaking the dice in
his hand, exhorting them, "Come on, baby," before flinging them
across the green felt. His pretty girlfriend was massaging his neck
in between throws, but he didn't seem to notice. Some of the men
looked as if they had been playing all night. They leaned against
the table as if for support. The air was thick with cigarette smoke.
Dad said, "You know, you could put six police dogs in a room
filled with smoke, and they'd be dead in 12 hours. But crap shoot-
ers," he shook his head, "could stay alive for days."

One of the pit bosses stopped play to check the dice. He was a
burly man in his late twenties, dressed in a double-breasted suit
too big for him. He held the dice up to the light. Dad said, "He
doesn't know what the hell he's doing." He called to the pit boss,
"What are you checkin' for?"

The pit boss smiled. "Too many people been winning with
these."

Dad said to me, "The pit bosses here don't know how to deal
with a complaint. They always have to go to a higher authority. It
slows down the game. In a good professional game, the boss is
respected so he can deal with complaints quickly, and you get
more play." Then he added, "Still, no matter how inefficiently it's
run, you can't beat the 'Tiger,' the house percentage."

Just then, one of the stick men was replaced at the table by
another. He raised his hands to the ceilings as if presenting an
offering before he left. "He's showing the guy upstairs," Dad said,
pointing to a window in the ceiling, "that he's not taking any chips."

"You're a good reporter, Pop," I said. He smiled.

The baccarat tables were in a small room behind the crap
tables. Baccarat is a card game favored mostly by Europeans in
places like Monte Carlo. The gamblers here, however, were
mostly Orientals. In fact, I noticed that almost a quarter of the
gamblers at Foxwoods were Orientals.

"They're the best," Dad said. "They're control gamblers. They'll come with $500, and if they lose it, they'll quit. If they win, they'll break the bank. They'll knock the casino right through the ceiling."

One of the Orientals playing baccarat was a fresh-faced girl who looked no older than 19. She had short lustrous black hair, big round eyeglasses, and a brightly colored ski parka. She looked like a Wellesley student, except for the cigarette dangling from her lips and the fact that she was betting $100 chips on every hand. Throughout the day, I would come back to the baccarat table, and she would still be there.

Alongside the baccarat table were the high-stakes blackjack tables. A lean, grizzled man wearing a black trucker's cap was betting $1,500 a hand and losing every one as we watched. A well-dressed Oriental woman beside him was also losing heavily. She kept glaring at me and Dad standing behind her. Finally Dad said, "We'd better go. We're bothering her."

"We're not doing anything," I said.

"It doesn't matter. She's a player, and she's entitled. Any whim she has, the casino will accommodate." He paused. "Until she busts out, and then she won't exist."

We went downstairs to the high-stakes poker room. Most of the players were men, unshaven, looking as if they had been playing for days on end. Dad went over to one of the casino managers and asked a question. He came back disgusted. "No one here knows anything," he said. "If you asked them how to get out of this place, they couldn't tell you."

We stood behind a game and watched. The men were silent, intent, calculating. Dad whispered to me, "They play against each other. The house gets a fee every half hour."

One of the players, a man named Scott, had a little fan in front of him to blow away the other players' cigarette smoke. Scott was losing, so he changed chairs for luck. He looked like a young college professor with his reddish beard and wire-rimmed spectacles. A voice over the loudspeaker announced a call for Mr. Scott. He jumped up, hurried to a nearby phone, and answered it. He listened for a moment, glancing anxiously back toward the game, then shouted into the receiver, "I'll be home when I'm home!" He hung up and hurried back to his seat. Dad looked at him and said, "Degenerates! It's the only outlet they have."

I sat down at one of the empty poker tables. The chair was plush. Dad stood over me, smiling. "That chair comfortable?" he asked. I nodded. He said, "They're the most expensive you can buy. They fit your back so you can sit for hours. They'll contain you in a den of vice. The casino doesn't care if you drop dead while you're playing."

We went back upstairs. I asked Dad if he wanted to shoot craps now. He put his head down as if embarrassed. "I don't have to," he said.

"Go ahead. I want to watch you."

"If you insist. If it'll help your story." I gave him $180 to start out with. He went over to a table, bought $100 in chips, and began to play. I moved back, away from his line of vision, to watch. He was just another old man, bald, with a little friar's tuft of hair around his ears. Nobody noticed him. He began to win. A chip here, a chip there. His eyes were quick and alert as he calculated the odds after each throw. He stretched his neck the way an athlete does in the heat of competition. He didn't look so old now.

The shooter shook the dice in his hands, whispered to them, and fired them across the table. Dad lost. I felt a sinking in my stomach. The dice were handed to Dad. He picked them up, turned his head away, and flung them, backhanded, as if with disdain. He won. Someone shouted, "You're on a roll, old man!" Dad flung the dice again and won. "All right! All right!" the players shouted. They noticed him now. Not an old man, but a winner, ageless. My old man, competing in his sport the way I used to compete in mine. It was funny, I thought. I can't pitch anymore, and sometimes that thought makes me feel old. But Dad can still gamble—which, in a way, makes him younger than me.

He tossed again and lost. My heart sank. He tossed again and won. The chips began to pile up in front of him. I got excited, rooting for him the way he rooted for me all those years that he sat in the stands watching me pitch. For the first time I knew how he must have felt, how unbearable it must have been to see me lose, how joyous it was to see me win.

But I didn't have his stomach. I couldn't take the pressure. I drifted away toward the blackjack tables. The exhilaration of watching Dad gamble made me want to gamble, too. So I sat down, bought some chips, and began to play. I lost a hand. Then another. I looked across the room for Dad. I could see his tufts of hair, hear the shouts from the table as he flung the dice.

The dealer dealt another hand, and I won. He counted out the chips for each winner so slowly that the woman beside me whispered, "So slow. It's not like Atlantic City. I hope they get better."

I won again. And again. Hours passed. I was so lost in the

game that I was barely conscious, every so often, of a voice beside me. "Can I get you a drink, sir?" I glanced up to see a smiling waitress. "Something to eat?" she said. I shook my head no, annoyed at her interruption, and went back to my game. By the time I was ahead $375, I had completely forgotten about my old man. He was right. It was addictive. Then I began to lose. My pile of chips shrank. I began to sweat.

I heard a voice behind me. "I hope you bust out." I turned around. It was Dad.

"Just in time," I lied. "I was ready to quit anyway."

"How'd you do?" he asked.

I counted my chips. I had won $100.

"Too bad," he said.

"What, are you afraid I'm gonna get hooked on gambling like you?" I asked. He just shook his head. "Pops, it's not my idea of fun to drive four hours in a snowstorm and sweat all day, just to go home with $100. What do you think, I'm crazy like you?"

He smiled. "You know, sometimes I had such bad luck I hoped I wouldn't wake up in the morning. I had no more doors to knock on to get money. I had tapped out everyone." He made an angry, sweeping gesture with his arm to encompass the whole casino. "They're gonna ruin the whole damned state with this!"

"Except for the Indians," I said.

"What Indians? Did you see a goddamned Indian in here all day?"

I hadn't. "By the way," I said. "How'd you do?"

"I was up big for awhile. I finished $100 ahead."

We cashed in our chips and headed for the door. It was late afternoon. I threw my arm over the old man's shoulder. He looked up at me and said, "Was I helpful, son?"

"The best, Dad. You make a great reporter."

He smiled shyly, thrilled that he could use his intelligence in a way that he respected. "I had a wonderful day," he said.

Then I remembered something. "You know, Dad, watching you shoot craps, I realized how it must have been for you watching me pitch."

He looked up at me, startled, as if I'd said something outrageously stupid. "What, are you crazy?" he said. "You watched *nothing!* I watched a *thunderbolt!* I watched a *talent!*"

EDITOR'S INTRODUCTION

The sudden growth of gambling is quite evident on Indian reservations. Tribes have embraced gambling as a way to raise funds for education, health, and housing and raise the expectations for Native American self-sufficiency and pride.

In 1987 the U.S. Supreme Court, in a decision to foster tribal sovereignty, ruled in *California v. Cabazon* that tribes could operate gambling facilities if gambling were legal elsewhere in the state. The decision led to the start-up of many gambling facilities and acted as a clarion call to the industry at large, fearful of possible lost revenues. In 1988 Congress passed the Indian Gaming Regulatory Act (IGRA), which set up licensing regulations and required states to negotiate in good faith compacts with the tribes. Purportedly passed to protect Indian gaming from outside influences, like organized crime, and to ensure that the operations were run by and for the tribes, IGRA was in fact regarded by many tribal leaders as a caving in—by virtue of its regulatory nature—to the pressures of the non-Indian gaming industry and its cries for an even playing field.

This section highlights the successes and failures of reservation gaming. David Segal, in "Dances With Sharks," reprinted from the *Washington Monthly,* looks at tribal gaming around the country and finds that even when successful, "[it] is no panacea for deep social ills that could be billions of dollars and decades away from a cure." Segal discusses organized crime involvement on the reservations, employment, and the federal bureaucracy of the National Indian Gaming Commission (NIGC), which he feels impedes change for the better. In "Incident at Akwesasne," reprinted from *Gentlemen's Quarterly,* Daniel D'Ambrosio discusses the war over gambling that broke out among the Mohawks—In this instance, gambling proved morally and economically divisive within the tribe's ranks—and led to two deaths in upstate New York.

Kim L. Eisler's article, "Revenge of the Indians," reprinted from the *Washingtonian,* looks at the phenomenal success of the

Pequots Foxwoods Casino in Connecticut and how it has benefitted the tribe and the state. Lastly, Jon Magnuson visits two flourishing gaming establishments, one in the Northwest, and one in the Midwest, in "Casino Wars: Ethics and Economics in Indian Country," reprinted from *Christian Century,* and discusses some of the complex moral issues that tend to get lost in the wake of success stories. More than a polemic on good versus evil, the debate involves serious issues of economics, history, ethics, racism, and self-determinism.

DANCES WITH SHARKS[1]

Plastic garbage bags stand in as roofs; faucets along a dirt road serve as showers. A 12-year-old might call this a scout camp, but the Kickapoo tribe of Eagle Bend, Texas, calls it a nation—and it's clearly a nation in trouble. A quarter of the population is unemployed, more than half is illiterate, and much to the embarrassment of tribal leaders, the signal crop in the community vegetable garden is marijuana.

By the looks of it, the Kickapoo reservation needs several basic things, including electricity, plumbing, and a school. But it *wants* only one thing: bingo, and step on it. "We're desperate for the money," says Julio Frausto, a tribal leader. And the Kickapoos are not the only ones. In the four years since Congress passed the Indian Gaming Act, which guaranteed tribes the right to run gambling enterprises on their reservations, more than a hundred tribes from North Dakota to Florida have gotten into the act, eager to translate blackjack and bingo into better education and opportunity.

But while the Kickapoo look to Las Vegas for inspiration, they might be wiser to first glance a few hundred miles north, to Miami, Oklahoma.

When the leaders of the Seneca-Cayugas there hired Wayne Newton Enterprises to run their high-stakes bingo parlor in October 1990, they thought their troubles were behind them. The

[1]Article by David Segal. From *The Washington Monthly,* Mar '92. Copyright © 1994 by The Washington Monthly Company, 1611 Connecticut Ave., N.W., Washington, D.C. 20039 (202) 462-0128. Reprinted with permission.

parlor had been shut down for several months after the tribe terminated its contract with a British management company that failed to turn a profit after running the hall for a year. But now they had a real Las Vegas concern working for them, and Wayne himself—half American Indian—came to the grand opening to give away the evening's big prizes. Sure, the tribe was asked to throw in $224,000 to help restart the operation—over and above the $300,000 it had already spent to build the hall—but Wayne was going to ante up $125,000, he was sending his best people, and anyway, business during November was good. No worries.

By December, worries. On most nights the huge hall, with its mirrored ceilings and pastel interior, was packed with 1,400 players. But profits were nowhere to be found. Neither, for that matter, was Wayne's $125,000. In December 1991, Newton Enterprises' own ledger sheets reported a gross of $12.5 million for the year, improbably offset by enough expenses to leave a debt of $360,000, which the company asked the tribe to cover. For the whole year the Seneca-Cayugas received $13,000—barely a seventh of the salary of Newton Enterprises' on-site manager. The final outrage came in December, when two jackpot winners were unable to get their checks cashed at the bank. The tribe retaliated by surrounding the bingo hall with pick-up trucks while Newton's security forces barricaded themselves inside. After a tense five-day standoff, a federal judge ruled that the hall was to be returned to the tribe. The question of who will pay the hall's debt is now headed for arbitration.

Although tribes have always kept criminal and financial data to themselves, and while the government seems equally disinclined to discuss the subject of troubles in Indian gaming, there's a growing body of evidence that what happened to the Senecas is not unusual. Since high-stakes, Indian-owned bingo parlors made their first appearance in the late seventies, tribes with gaming operations have been beset by difficulties ranging from graft to fratricide. What Congress envisioned as a fast track out of poverty and unemployment for American Indians has evolved into a billion-dollar-a-year industry that has added precious little to social services on reservations throughout the country.

"If we get the money from bingo, we're going to set up a vocational training program," says Kickapoo administrator Frausto. "Even if the kids don't go to college, they'll have a trade." Perhaps. But they may also get more than they bargained for. In one extreme instance, the Mohawks of upstate New York split into pro- and anti-gambling factions and commenced a brief civil war because profits from their seven on-reservation halls were going exclusively to hall owners and their non-Indian management team. Two tribe members were left dead.

While it's easy—and partially correct—to blame American Indians for the unfolding gambling fiasco, the real culprit may be bureaucrats in Washington, D.C. After all, Indian gaming is an experiment that might convince even Milton Friedman that government regulation is in order: inexperienced, financially desperate Indians entering a slick and crime-infested business. But the Indians don't want help, and the commission the government created to regulate Indian gambling, the National Indian Gaming Commission (NIGC), is equally disinclined to provide it, preaching laissez-faire as tribe after tribe gets taken. The shame is that a few tribal success stories suggest that, if properly run and carefully regulated, Indian gambling can pay off as promised—in housing and modern plumbing, scholarships and jobs. Instead, as the Kickapoos break in the tables without expertise or government assistance, the deck has quietly been stacked against them.

To anyone familiar with the effects gambling has had on other communities that have legalized it, the Indians' venture into gaming may sound less like a shortcut to prosperity than a quick way to finish off tribal life once and for all. Wherever it's been tried, gambling has been accompanied by a dramatic increase in violent and property crimes, alcoholism, and drug abuse. Yet there is surprisingly little breast-beating on the reservations about how gambling could destroy what is left of Indian culture. (Could names like "Stands With 17" be far behind?) One reason is that Indians are a little more modern than we think. Another is that, after a decade of penetrating budget cuts, they have few other options.

Indian gaming took hold in the eighties, as most everything else on the reservation was withering away. While funds for education decreased only slightly in the Reagan-Bush era, other aid programs plunged. In 1980, the National Health Service Corps sent 155 physicians to reservations; a decade later it was sending seven. Housing and Urban Development, which had authorized 6,000 new units of Indian housing during Carter's last year as president, was building only 1,500 new units by 1988. The Economic Development Administration, which had funded bricks-and-mortar projects, was slashed to near extinction, while the

Community Services Administration, which granted money for development projects, was wiped out altogether.

"The Reagan cuts devastated tribes," says Frank Ducheneaux, who served as counsel on Indian Affairs for the House Committee on Interior and Insular Affairs during this period. "Since most have high rates of unemployment and poverty and rely heavily on the government for social services, Indians had to find alternative sources of funding." And as the need for alternative funding became evident, the legal grounds for gaming were being won.

The first test came in Florida back in 1979, after the Miami Seminoles defied a state law prohibiting bingo prizes of more than $100 and began offering $10,000 jackpots in a 1,200-seat hall. The state sued, but in 1982 a federal appeals court ruled that since the Seminoles were a sovereign nation, state civil regulations did not apply to them. Tribes nationwide took note, and within five years, 113 bingo operations around the country were grossing $225 million annually. Legal challenges from states abounded, but in 1987 the Supreme Court decided that Indians could operate any form of gambling already permitted by the state—and could do so with their own regulations. In the 14 states that allowed groups to run highly restricted "Las Vegas nights" for charity, the door was opened for Indians to start up full-blown casinos.

A year later, Congress bestowed its approval with the Indian Gaming Act, which advocated gambling as "a means of promoting tribal economic development, self-sufficiency, and strong tribal governments." Yet Congress wasn't altogether sanguine about gaming—nor should it have been, considering the then-vivid example of Atlantic City, where the felony crime rate skyrocketed in the first few years of legalized gambling. (Las Vegas was steadier, ranking either first, second, third, or fourth in per capita felonies in the country's metropolitan areas between 1960 and 1984.) Nevertheless, Congress agreed that the Indians had both the legal right to establish gaming parlors and little prospect of raising badly needed money from other sources. So to shield Indians "from organized crime and other corrupting influences" and ensure that "the Indian tribe is the primary beneficiary of the gaming operation," it devised a complicated system of regulation. Yet to date, no government or private agency has examined the successes or failures of Indian gaming—Congress didn't apparently have much of a plan for overseeing how its well-intentioned rules would work. According to the FBI, troubles began almost as soon as the gaming did—and those troubles have included organized crime.

Grift horses

When Stewart Siegel, a dealer and manager at casinos from Las Vegas to the Caribbean, was hired to run the Barona reservation's bingo hall in San Diego, he brought a pro's touch to the reservation's games: Grand prizes like cars and $60,000 in cash were regularly won by planted shills, who then gave the money back to Siegel. After pleading guilty in 1986 to four counts of grand theft, including bilking the tribe of $600,000 a year, he joined the witness protection program and started talking. Testifying before the Senate Select Committee on Indian Affairs with a hood over his head, he claimed that he knew of at least 12 halls that were controlled by the Cosa Nostra but guessed that nearly half of all Indian casinos were tainted by it, either directly through management and investors or indirectly through suppliers.

The allegation is hardly far-fetched, given the economics of starting up a gaming hall. Indians are especially vulnerable to mafia infiltration because few banks make loans to tribes; their land, which is sovereign, cannot be foreclosed. So when tribes look elsewhere for start-up money, well- and not-so-well concealed mafiosi are often their most willing backers. According to the FBI, the trendsetting Seminoles unwittingly hired the mob when they opened their hall in 1979. (The FBI routed them out.) Two years later, the Cabazons, a tiny tribe in Riverside County, California, retained Rocco Zangari, a member of a Southern California organized crime family, to run their card room. When tribal vice-chairman Alvin Alvarez accused the management of skimming profits, he was forced out of office. Months later, he and two other critics were found shot to death. The case has yet to be solved.

Disorganized crime may be just as threatening. Under the most common contracts that tribes negotiate with management companies, the Indians are promised 60 percent of "profits after expenses," a clause that often means the tribe gets nothing. Examples of management companies cooking the books are legion. On the Mohawk reservation where the intratribal gambling war broke out, non-Indian investor Emmet Munley was found by his Indian business partner to have deducted $186,000 in traveling expenses and $120,000 in accounting fees. At the Seneca-Cayuga hall, Wayne Newton Enterprises was clearing $20,000 to $30,000 a month, according to Don Deal, who used to work for the company and saw the accounting sheets, while the tribe earned next to nothing. The Winnebagos of Wisconsin got a Halloween party and a back-taxes bill from the IRS for $800,000 but have yet to get any profits from their management company, the Genna Corporation.

Even worse, gambling has cut off the little federal support the Winnebagos had before gaming, says tribal chairwoman Jo Ann Jones. Allegations that the Genna Corporation has bought off half of the Winnebagos' tribal council in lieu of sharing the profits has so riven the tribe that members have been unable to meet and approve applications for government programs. Since June 1, 1990, all their federal grants for housing, education, and other social services have ceased.

So are the Genna Corporation and those other management companies corrupt? No one—neither the tribes nor the government—has taken the trouble to find out. While in Nevada and New Jersey the mere scent of ill repute will get one barred from even the lower echelons of casino management, aspiring Indian casino managers are currently disqualified only if the FBI—which runs fingerprint checks on request—discovers a felony conviction. The NIGC is supposed to be doing more sophisticated background checks, sniffing out the mafia and making sure tribes are getting a fair count from their management companies. But the commission is clearly not doing enough homework. Wayne Newton Enterprises' only other experience in Indian gaming, with the Santa Ynez of California, ended in bankruptcy. Emmet Munley was unable to get a gambling license through the Nevada Gaming Control Board on two occasions because he associated "with persons of questionable and unsavory character." (The NIGC's colleague, the Bureau of Indian Affairs [BIA], which must approve any contract between a management company and a tribe, has also been less than vigilant in sifting out undesirables. Indeed, it was a BIA agent, Thomas Burden, who originally recommended Emmet Munley when the Mohawks were searching for investors.)

What has the NIGC been doing since it was written into existence in 1988? Mostly finding office space; it wasn't until February 1991 that it settled on permanent quarters, and even then it needed an additional eight months to publish its first set of regulations. It has yet to hire field operatives and has no legal ap-

paratus to make and enforce its decisions. The man Bush appointed to run the commission, Tony Hope (adopted son of enter-
tainer Bob Hope), plans to have the commission up and running
by this spring. In the meantime, most Indian casinos proliferate
and run in a regulatory vacuum. "When we started having problems with our management company," says the Winnebagos' Jo
Ann Jones, "we didn't even think of calling [the NIGC]."

Slow motion is a standard feature of federal bureaucracies,
but the commission has also been hindered by the combined resistance of Indian leaders—many of whom see the commission as
patronizing and unnecessary—and the states, which have their
own interest in making sure the halls are functioning responsibly.
Adjudicating between two sovereign entities makes painstaking
debate on the commission's every move inevitable. A set of revised
regulations on what types of electronic machines will be allowed
in bingo halls was heatedly debated for months in hearings in five
cities across the country.

Even after it publishes all its regulations, the commission will
probably remain ineffective. For one, it is woefully underfunded.
Today the New Jersey Casino Control Commission employs 400
people and spends $23 million per year to keep an eye on Atlantic
City's 12 casinos. The Indian Gaming Commission will hire 25
people and spend $3 million per year to oversee more than 150
halls. And what the NIGC lacks in financial way, it won't be making up with regulatory will. Hope intends to preside over a relatively hands-off commission. "There will be no micromanage-
ment from D.C.," he insists.

The style is the legacy of a Republican policy, initiated by
Nixon in 1970 and expanded upon by Reagan and Bush, to encourage Indian self-determination by allowing tribes to make their
own decisions wherever possible. When James Watt headed the
Department of the Interior, he instructed BIA to review contracts
between Indians and bingo hall managers only when tribes re-
quested it, even though long-standing law requires that all such
contracts get BIA approval. The NIGC is headed for a similarly
minimalist approach in its role as watchdog.

That the growth of Indian gaming coincides with this new
governmental disinterest is a historical accident and not a very
fortunate one. Washington's libertarian impulses may arguably be
long overdue in other realms of Indian life, but they are mis-
placed in gambling, an industry that constantly tempts those involved with large sums of immediately available cash and easily

fudged ledgers. What is true for the owners and managers of casinos in Atlantic City and Las Vegas is true for the Indians: Without strong, vigilant, and impartial oversight, they are easy marks for the mob and all types of hustlers.

Santee clause

The most recent opportunists have been Nevada entrepreneurs. The legitimate gambling industry, after years of casting an alarmed and disapproving eye on its down-market competitors and pressing Congress to legislate the Indians out of its domain, appears ready to adopt an if-you-can't-beat-'em-join-'em strategy. The first proposal was perhaps the most audacious. It came from Harvey's Wagon Wheel Inc., a Lake Tahoe resort hotel and casino that caters to 2.5 million visitors annually.

Harvey's and the Santee Sioux, a small and impoverished tribe in northeast Nebraska, hatched a plan to petition the federal government to take into trust three acres of land in Council Bluffs, Iowa, a small town just across the river from the 600,000 residents of Omaha. When the petition is approved by the BIA, the land will become sovereign territory, allowing the Indians to permit Harvey's to build a casino on it. Then Harvey's will buy 47 surrounding acres to build a $67 million hotel and convention center, cutting the Indians in on the action once the dollars roll in.

Sound dubious? Not to the tiny Kickapoo nation of Horton, Kansas, which is currently negotiating a similar deal with the massive Mirage Hotel and Casino. Since the Las Vegas-based company approached tribal leaders back in August 1991, the project has gotten a lot of popular support (the governor included) and made the tribe of barely 1,500 members some new friends. "We used to be 'those Indians,'" says Verna Finch, the tribal vice-chair. "People would not even use our name. Now we have a lot of folks acting like they've always been our buddies."

The Mirage deal is clearly good for the Kickapoo leaders' egos. Less clear is whether it is good for the Kickapoo rank and file, who suffer from a 60 percent unemployment rate. Although the nearby town of Hiawatha has offered to donate 70 acres of land within the tribe's ancestral boundaries to build the casino locally, the Mirage has made it clear that it's no dice unless the land is near Kansas City, an hour and a half away.

Because many Indians currently rely on far-flung, low-paying migrant work to survive, the promise of jobs is often a major incentive to tribes considering gaming. But these Vegas-scale operations will not ease unemployment. They need to be located near or within easy access of major population centers; most reservations, however, are in the hinterlands.

Regulation roulette

The jobs issue is even more important than it first appears because it is most often those halls and casinos employing and involving tribe members that succeed. While the Winnebagos went broke and the Mohawks turned to gunplay in squabbles over outside control, several tribes have been quietly fulfilling the gaming act's promise of more jobs and social services by operating their own shops.

Before the Mille Lacs Chippewas of Minnesota opened their Grand Casino in April 1990, 60 percent of their families lived below the poverty line; 45 percent were unemployed. By December, only a handful lived in poverty, virtually none were unemployed (most had gotten jobs in the casino), and the tribe had become the county's biggest employer. A modern sewer system, school improvements, and a health clinic are on the way.

The Oneidas, also from Minnesota, watched their unemployment rate fall from 40 percent in 1976 to 17 percent in 1991, thanks to their gaming facility—which is run with no outside management help. "I can't imagine why so many tribes are willing to give away 40 percent," says Bobby Webster, part of the tribal management team. With proceeds from their bingo hall, they have built a $10.5 million hotel and convention center and an environmental testing lab that has won state and federal contracts. They've subsidized their own Head Start program and built their own K-8 grade school. A high school is now in the works. While most reservations have been losing members, the Oneidas have seen their numbers swell by a third in the past 15 years.

Still, even when it works this well, gambling is no panacea for deep social ills that could be billions of dollars and decades away from a cure. Even among the Oneidas unemployment is still high, and drug and alcohol problems persist. But if a few tribes can make a little progress through gaming, perhaps more can. And in the absence of other sources of funding, it means a few more Indian kids educated and employed and fewer houses with trash-bag roofs.

Yet in their current hands-off mode, the NIGC and the legislators who created it are repeating the mistakes of previous would-be benefactors who threw plots of land, and then money, at tribes. By their passivity, they're effectively ensuring that good programs are flukes, not formulas—and that beggared but eager tribes like Eagle Bend's Kickapoos will be playing against the odds.

Keeping decent information about what works and what doesn't, and then providing technical assistance for start-ups, should be the minimal role of the slumbering NIGC. But it's not enough. While some Indians might paint any oversight effort as an infringement on their rights of sovereignty, this is the wrong moment for the government to be daunted by that charge. After a green light from the federal courts, program-slashing by successive administrations, and a reluctant thumbs-up from Congress, the government now has an obligation to tribes to make sure that gaming is run legally and in the interests of the people it was intended to help—in short, that gambling is the "means of promoting tribal economic development, self-sufficiency, and strong tribal governments" Congress declared it would be in the eighties. The last thing the Kickapoos need, after all, is another broken promise.

INCIDENT AT AKWESASNE[2]

Akwesasne is a place of rivers: the Raquette, the Grass, the Saint Regis and the Saint Lawrence. Water was lavished on this ground, which is why for centuries Akwesasne, the 28,000-acre reservation straddling the U.S.-Canada border near Massena, New York, has been a home of the Mohawk nation. The rivers are still there, of course, sweeping past the long grasses that grow to their banks; they are wide, gentle, rippling, like the land around them, but they run scared and forgotten now, except as receptacles.

In days past, the rivers of Akwesasne gave rather than re-

[2]Article by Daniel D'Ambrosio. From *Gentlemen's Quarterly*, Nov '93. Copyright © 1993 by Daniel D'Ambrosio. Reprinted with permission of the author.

ceived. Bullheads were pulled from the Saint Lawrence with a hayfork, so full was the big river with life. The rivers made the land surrounding them fertile: Crops grew, and cattle grazed the fields. But Akwesasne has no fishermen now, few farmers. On the doorstep of the reservation, three industrial plants—Reynolds, Alcoa and General Motors—have created one of the largest PCB-contaminated sites (other than military bases) in the United States. Agriculture, which made the Mohawks self-sufficient, was slowly destroyed. Fluoride caused cows to lose their teeth. The PCBs seeping into the groundwater and soil made anything grown at Akwesasne suspect. The fish that survive in the Saint Lawrence are no longer edible, so laden is the river with heavy metals. The marshes, once productive hunting and trapping grounds, were flooded by the completion, in 1959, of the Saint Lawrence Seaway.

Route 37, a two-lane blacktop highway with narrow, sloping shoulders, rolls impatiently through Akwesasne, irritated by the necessity of bothering at all with the place. The businesses along the road range from the pitiful to the passable. Here, in a peeling white plywood shack with hand-lettered signs out front ("SAVE ON CARTONS!"), is a smoke shop, the legal tip of the illegal cigarette-smuggling iceberg that thrives on the reservation. There, in a grease-stained building painted an ugly shade of green, is a gasoline station. These are the twin pillars of Akwesasne's retail-business community: cheap cigarettes and cheap gas.

Just before an intersection known as the Four Corners, or Hogansburg, where vacant storefronts stare glassy-eyed at you, there is an enormous steel structure. This is a bingo palace. Large hand-painted signs, reminiscent of the former Eastern bloc, hang high on the sides of the building. One reminds you "THIS LAND IS INDIAN LAND." You may not even notice the warnings, however, because this is a place where you will slow down only because you have to, wonder what the hell went wrong here, then hurry on your way to some other town in the Adirondacks or beyond. Before you leave, you may catch a glimpse of one of the rivers, flowing gently toward the Saint Lawrence Seaway.

About halfway through the reservation stands Tony's Vegas International (TVI). The casino is closed now, overgrown, huge, dull and sinking fast. For 300 years, despite wars, environmental degradation, unemployment and pervasive drunkenness, the Mohawk nation had remained essentially cohesive, tribal. But it could not survive TVI and the other gaming houses that sprang up along Route 37. The reservation divided irreparably into two camps over the casinos.

The Warriors saw gambling as economic salvation for the Mohawks and the way to true sovereignty. The Seminoles of Florida were, after all, earning millions of dollars, and other tribes in other states—Wisconsin, Oklahoma, California, Arizona, Connecticut—were following suit. The Warriors were led by a generation of men and women in their forties who had challenged the whites in the late Sixties and early Seventies, inspired by the civil-rights struggle of black America. They had occupied land in the Adirondacks and won the rights to it. They had refused to accept the governments foisted on them by the Americans and the Canadians and gained a greater degree of independence.

The Antis, guided by the tribal elders, were adamant in their opposition. To them it was simple: Gambling went against the Mohawk way. It was immoral.

This split began as a kind of family dispute, a spat that led to hard feelings but little more. But it soon spun out of control in a way that can happen only in a place where there has been an overpowering need left unmet for a long, long time. Money would fill the empty heart of the Mohawk people.

In the early Eighties, as gambling came to Akwesasne, violence broke out between the two camps. There were brutal beatings, drive-by shootings that left slugs within inches of sleeping children, houses burned to the ground. And then, in the spring of 1990, roadblocks, put up by the Antis to prevent gamblers from reaching the casinos; barricades, thrown up out of whatever was at hand—logs, toolsheds, shacks, sawhorses, big barrels used to burn firewood. Cutting off Route 37 both east and west of town, the barriers were an expression of the complete frustration of the Antis, who had pleaded for months with federal and state authorities to do something about the casinos, which were operating illegally.

The roadblocks were a major irritant to the Warriors, many of whom had an economic stake in the casinos. On the night of April 24, 1990, they overran the western roadblock and crossed the Raquette River Bridge on Route 37, approaching the eastern roadblock, leaving many vehicles flaming in the cold spring night. As they marched across the bridge, the Warriors banged their baseball bats and lead pipes against the railing, letting those manning the remaining roadblock know what they were in for. If that unspoken message wasn't clear enough, they called ahead on a captured Anti radio: "We're coming to get you, you fucking Antis! You're gonna die!" And then, according to law-enforcement sources, the rounds started coming in, including armor-piercing slugs, which penetrated the lowered snowplow on a three-quarter-ton truck. Vietnam vets working at the U.S. customs checkpoint on the international bridge across the Saint Lawrence listened and thought they were back in the DMZ.

The violence that marked the fall of the roadblocks changed everything on the rez. Doug George, editor of a reservation newspaper and one of the leaders of the Antis, remembers a palpable sense of dread settling on Akwesasne. The line had been crossed. Anything was possible.

After the roadblocks fell, an estimated 2,000 Antis fled Akwesasne for Canada's Cornwall Island, leaving everything they owned behind, believing that the authorities—the Royal Canadian Mounted Police, the New York State police, the FBI, somebody—would restore order and prevent property damage.

The next morning, George began throwing books, papers and clothes into the trunk of his brother Dennis's car. He was leaving Akwesasne. The Warriors were in control now, and no one was intervening. But before he could get out, a message reached him: His brother Davey had shot someone.

Davey George was a special obsession of the Warriors'. Whereas Doug George had infuriated them with his newspaper stories, Davey, a mason who stood five-nine and weighed 220 pounds, had been a physical threat. Now Doug knew he could not leave the reservation. He and Dennis headed to Davey's house.

They found Davey there, along with their brother Dean, their brother-in-law Cartoon and a cousin, Perry Thompson. Davey had decided to take a stand. Refusing to leave his home, he had blown out the tires of a Warrior car that was cruising in front of his house (hence the report of a shooting). Warriors had been gathering in the woods surrounding Davey's house ever since.

That first night, according to Doug George, the gunfire was sporadic. The Warriors never stormed the house directly but shot at it from the road. Mostly they partied. The six men in Davey's house couldn't see them, but they could hear them. As the two sides settled for this symbolic, open-ended confrontation, the Georges were monitoring Warrior radio transmissions, and the Warriors knew it. And so, interspersed with the normal chatter that goes with running a loosely knit military organization, came special messages to Davey, low, coarse whispers.

Davey, you fuck with the people, you fuck with the Warriors.

For three days, this went on. The Warriors dug in and kept their sights on this last vestige of opposition. There was scattered gunfire, especially at night, and outbursts of violence, as when Davey set a Warrior car on fire. During the day, the Antis would ferry in food and occasionally weapons to the Georges. Some of them would stay. By the fourth day, there were eleven men in the house. And, constantly, the radio messages.

Lover boy, you're a pussy. Warrior women cut your nuts off. Hey, lover boy, c'mon over so we can stick that AK right up your asshole.

On the final night of the standoff, the gunfire began around nine-thirty and went on almost continuously until eight the next morning.

"You could hear [the gunfire] all over the rez," remembers Darren Bonaparte of the Mohawk Council of Akwesasne. "I was up all night. I called Québec police, and they said they wouldn't go [to Davey George's house] because they had to go through the United States, and the New York State police wouldn't come on the reservation to escort them."

In the last hours of the gun battle, under clear skies and a sun that was already hot by 6 A.M., a young Mohawk named Matthew Pyke, 22, was shot in the back with a .223-caliber bullet, suffering massive internal injuries. He died after four hours in a hospital in Malone, New York. Pyke had brought food to the men in Davey's house two days earlier and, according to the Georges, had come to help evacuate a woman and child thought to be trapped in the cross fire of the battle, in which, by some estimates, 5,000 rounds were fired. J.R. Edwards, 32, a noted Mohawk dancer who was neutral in the dispute, as he was in life—everybody's friend, a drinker—died sometime, somewhere, for some reason, probably the previous night or in the predawn hours. The actual time and place of his death are unknown—his body had been moved to the spot where it was found, lying on the ground behind a house, two hand-sized smears of blood on the wall above it.

Shortly after the deaths, hundreds of New York State troopers swarmed onto the reservation, shut down the casinos and restored order. Doug George was arrested for the murder of Edwards. Almost immediately, all charges were dropped and Doug was released. The murders remain unsolved, and barely investigated, to this day.

Doug George had feared all along that it would come to this —that gambling, this bone tossed by the society that had surrounded, overwhelmed and suffocated the Mohawks, would stick in the throats of his people and choke them to death. He knew that all that was good about his culture was too fragile after 300 years of oppression to withstand the onslaught of gambling.

As editor of *Akwesasne Notes*, the respected reservation newspaper, George consistently revealed the essentially corrupt nature of casino gambling. It was not, he pointed out in article after article, a benign enterprise. The quick cash came at a price: Drugs, prostitution and organized crime went with it.

Within months of taking over *Akwesasne Notes*, he learned that most of the money behind the proposed Mohawk Bingo Palace came from a man named Emmett Munley, not the two Mohawks, Guilford White and Buddy Cook, who were the front men for the operation. Traveling to Carson City, Nevada, George discovered that Munley had been denied a gaming license in Nevada two times because one of his former partners was linked to organized crime. Munley has denied having any such links.

Eventually, Munley was driven out of the Bingo Palace operation by the continuous articles in *Notes* and protests staged on Route 37 outside the building. It was George's next revelation, however, that made him the focus of Warrior hatred and divided the longhouse—the traditional Mohawk government, cultural and religious center—foreshadowing the events of April 1990.

Loran Thompson, a handsome, charismatic former subchief who became a mentor to the Warriors, had grown up in the customary way. His father had been a chief for more than forty years and his mother had been a clan mother. He was well-known at Akwesasne for his involvement in the confrontations that the longhouse had had with outside law-enforcement agencies over jurisdiction on the reservation, beginning in the late 1970s.

In April 1986, Thompson brought a contract to the longhouse for a bingo parlor, called the Bingo Jack, to be financed by an outside investor. Profits would be split 51-49, with the larger share going to the tribe. Thompson had negotiated a 10 percent cut for himself, which would come out of the investor's share.

Doug George, investigating the Bingo Jack contract as he had investigated all the other gaming contracts, discovered that the investor represented to the chiefs was a front. The real backer was a man in Tell City, Indiana, who, much to George's surprise, said he was of the opinion that Thompson represented the Nation

Council chiefs, the longhouse. He also said he had the signatures of three clan mothers, endorsing the Bingo Jack, on his contract. Thompson, in fact, did not represent the Nation Council chiefs, and the clan mothers, by secretly signing the contract, had betrayed the longhouse. George ran the story.

"After that, there were two distinct sides in the longhouse," says George. "Those who were part of Loran Thompson and his element, and the chiefs and people who didn't want anything to do with this gambling stuff. We began to fall apart real quickly after that. Gamblers began to crystallize around Loran and his gang. They began to buy the guns and defend themselves against any attempt by us or anybody else to control what they were doing. Violence began to escalate."

The war came because the Mohawks couldn't agree among themselves. Should they take easy money from the hated and foolish whites or not? What were the alternatives, besides going on the dole, either in Canada or in the U.S., depending on which side of the Saint Lawrence you happened to live? Farming was gone. Fishing was gone. A furniture-building business had sputtered, then died. There was a lumberyard and a computer store of sorts and, of course, gas stations and smoke shops. Whites would come for cheap cigarettes and gas. But they wouldn't come for much else. Except gambling. For gambling, they would come by the busload. Five daily from nearby Montréal—21,000 whites every week for TVI alone. Hit the mall just outside Massena for bargains, go gambling on the rez. Another fun day in the U.S.A.

Suddenly, there were jobs—a thousand jobs for Mohawks by the time nine casinos had opened along Route 37. There was money, lots of it—money for those who owned the casinos and even for those who worked there, who might make $1,400 in a week.

The economic argument was irrefutable. And it could easily be transmuted into an argument for the revitalization of Mohawk life.

Darren Bonaparte is a slight man outfitted in Levi's Dockers, with delicate, slender white fingers and a stylish haircut. He understands the lure of gambling.

"It was like, all of a sudden, Las Vegas in your hometown. This place went from being a boring old damn rez to suddenly having white people coming in, sometimes some hot chicks, white people flashing the bucks. It was just a big, lovely, wonderful thing," he says. "But there's those angry people in the streets with signs, pissed-off.

"Outside governments have screwed us left and right, every chance they got," Bonaparte continues. "Stole our land, whittled it down to nothing. We're living on a pillowcase, basically, and finally, because of the white man's greed for gambling, his addictions, cigarettes, cocaine, drugs, guns, whatever, suddenly, we're able to make a profit off their misery. That's a potent argument. We're shoving it back down their throats.

"They take your land, your culture, your language, everything. Even your history, your collective knowledge of who you are. Then they leave you with nothing, so it's wide open for something else to come in and fill that void. That's what the Warrior movement did. Average people didn't know that. They didn't know they had those gaps in their lives. Suddenly, somebody filled it, and they felt great."

Doug George lives in a double-wide mobile home beside Highway 46, just north of Oneida, New York, in rolling, grass-covered hills dotted with ponds and attractive country homes. Within fifty yards of his house, which he shares with his wife, Joanne Shenandoah—a gifted singer and performer and the daughter of an Onondaga chief—sits the Oneida Indian Nation Bingo Hall.

A single dirt road leads west from the hall for perhaps half a mile into the surrounding meadows. Mobile homes, dug in to stay, line both sides of the lane. This is the Oneida Indian reservation —about 800 acres. Doug George's home is the first one on the right, just past the speed bump that separates the residential and business districts of the reservation. It is a supreme irony that George, driven away from his home, his family and his life at Akwesasne, lives here, in the shadow of a bingo hall.

Doug George had been forced to leave Akwesasne many times before. The first time was at the hands of a Canadian-government official. George's mother had died of cancer and his father worked in Rochester as a stonemason. A housekeeper stayed with Doug and his eleven brothers and sisters during the week. At the time, the Canadian government had dictatorial power over the Mohawk people. The official decided that the family should be split up and that Doug should be placed in a residential school. He was 12 years old.

He spent two years at the school, waiting for a white home to go to. Indian children were never placed in Indian homes, no matter what the merits of those households. During the next four years, George lived with fifteen white foster families. Whenever possible, he would run away, back to Akwesasne.

"I created tremendous amounts of trouble for the foster parents," remembers George. "Sometimes I was placed in these homes where weeks and literally months would go by and I'd never talk to these people. I wouldn't say anything to them. You have your dinner and you just grunt something, and then you go back to your room, and you never talk to them. Never.

"You can't imagine how physically ill it makes you when you know you are there not as someone to be welcomed into a family. You're there because there is a financial incentive for taking you. You realize quickly what the scam is."

In one home, Silent Doug lasted only two days. The last time he was placed, at the age of 17, was with a woman who was a preacher at a fundamentalist church at Akwesasne. After four years of running back at every chance, George had finally returned to Akwesasne officially.

He immersed himself in the longhouse. The Akwesasne longhouse itself is a white rectangular building just off Route 37, with a black roof and tall, skinny cinder-block chimneys centered at each end. Its wooden steps and faded plywood door face due east, toward the rising sun. Inside, it is Spartan: wood stoves at either end of the single room, simple wooden benches running the length of each wall. Clean white panels cover the ceiling, and four shuttered windows let in light. There is nothing else.

The lure for George was irresistible: "I was part of a society that was basically good. It was very secure at its heart. It was very tolerant. It was a good life that these people had lived. It was based upon respect for each other. It was based upon respect for the land in which they found themselves."

By the age of 19, George was one of the longhouse people. He went to Syracuse University and later completed two and a half years of law school before dropping out rather than swear allegiance to the U.S. Constitution, as he would have been required to do to join the bar. Like many Mohawks, Doug George does not consider himself an American citizen. He is a citizen of the Iroquois Confederacy.

In the mid-Eighties, George was named the fourth editor of *Akwesasne Notes*. And in that role, he became the point man for the antigambling forces.

In the small breakfast nook of his mobile home, 120 miles

from Akwesasne, George sifts through the pieces of the struggle: snapshots of vehicles rammed in confrontations between Warriors and Antis, of bullet holes in windshields and windows, of his brother-in-law Cartoon raising a weapon over his head in celebration after surviving the four-day standoff with the Warriors. For three hours, George roams the length and breadth of his nation's history, recalling treaties and battles with the United States of America, dates and places of significant events in the surrounding countryside, just over that ridge or just beyond that river, and the Iroquois Confederacy, a dominant force on the Eastern seaboard from Montréal to Albany, with the Mohawks entrusted with guarding the Eastern Door and the Senecas entrusted with guarding the Western Door. (Among the Antis, the roadblocks at Akwesasne came to be known by the same names.)

George, now 37, quiet, unassuming, his black shoulder-length hair pulled straight back from his high forehead, speaks matter-of-factly about the demise of his people.

"It's a division in philosophies and how people see themselves and their communities," he says. "Our community, Akwesasne, was the worst. Things happened there, people were actually killed. Because we had gamblers and smugglers come in and try to run the community."

George draws a crude map of Akwesasne, indicating the curves of the rivers that cradle the reservation, the single highway, the local roads and, with an X, the location of his brother Davey's house.

"I never go back there now," he says when the map is finished. He's afraid that if he does, he'll be beaten, or killed.

Tony Laughing was also exiled from Akwesasne. Of all the Mohawk casino owners, Laughing was the most adamant in his conviction that gambling was the future of his people. He was also the most successful, Laughing says, with Tony's Vegas International generating more revenue than all the other Akwesasne casinos combined.

When I meet Tony Laughing at the Federal Correctional Institution in Ray Brook, New York, about eighty miles from Akwesasne, he is weeks away from finishing a twenty-seven-month sentence for various gambling-related offenses.

He is a small man, perhaps five feet six, with a blank, coarse face, showing little emotion. Like Doug George, Laughing spent many years away from Akwesasne. Unlike George, Laughing does not wax philosophical about Mohawk tradition and culture.

"The government, there's three things they don't like," he says intently, leaning slightly forward in an orange plastic chair in the small, overheated receiving room. "One, they don't like an Indian that has any brains. Number two, they don't like the Indian that has any money. Number three, they sure as hell don't like one that has balls. And I had all three. That is a major problem."

After being away from Akwesasne for twenty-six years and starting his own steel-erecting business in Cleveland, Laughing returned to the reservation in 1986 to visit his sick mother. He had become an ironworker at the age of 13, hitchhiking to Detroit to join his brother and a friend. He took to ironworking naturally, he says, even though he knew nothing about it.

"We all ate at this JoJo's restaurant on Third Street, a bunch of us, forty or fifty Indians, we sat and bullshitted for hours," says Laughing. "On paper, they were showing me my hand signals, what I had to do, how I'd have to climb a column and everything else. I learned in the restaurant what I'd have to do the next day."

Balls. Big ones. And they served him well when he realized Akwesasne had suddenly become the land of opportunity. "I'm not ashamed to say I made $2 million in 1986 in the cigarette business, which I put into my casino," says Laughing, a smile creeping across the flat cardboard that is his face. "I made $2 million, and I built my casino."

The "cigarette business," as Laughing euphemistically puts it, is cigarette smuggling. Canada imposes a tax on cigarettes that drives the price of Canadian cartons up to nearly $40. Cigarettes exported to the U.S. are exempt from the tax. Mohawk smugglers buy the tax-exempt cigarettes and store them on the American side of Akwesasne, then haul them back across the river, usually at night, to supply the black market in Toronto, Montréal, Québec and other Canadian cities.

Laughing quickly got back the money he put into TVI during its first year of operation, 1988. In 1989, he netted $4 million, and in the four months he was open in 1990, before his arrest and the closing of TVI, he netted more than $12 million. Or so he claims. Laughing's figures cannot be substantiated.

Laughing also claims that in 1988 he donated more than $1 million back to the community at Akwesasne. In 1989, he says, he gave back more than $2 million. He gave money to the volunteer fire department. He sponsored all eight Little League teams. Behind his casino, he built a day-care center (which never opened).

Everything was done informally, the way Laughing wanted it. You asked, and Tony gave.

And he says he wanted to give more. He wanted to build a go-cart track and a big gymnasium with a pool and a lit ball field—all of the things he'd never had while growing up. None of these things happened.

"[The casino owners] had millions, millions, of dollars," says a longtime Mohawk activist. "They could have put up their arena, redug all the ditches. I mean, things that need to be done to bring the land back to some sort of richness. They could have done it."

In June 1993, John Loran and David Jacobs, two of the three elected chiefs on the American Mohawk Tribal Council, signed the compact negotiated with the state of New York that will bring casino gambling back to Akwesasne. And this time, it will be legal and it will be big-time, beyond even Tony Laughing's wildest dreams.

Chief Loran, a young, aggressive businessman who took the lead in the negotiations, talks of cutting a deal with a "big-name, well-reputed gambling contractor," once the compact is signed by Governor Mario Cuomo and Secretary of the Interior Bruce Babbitt. Loran talks of a gaming "complex" at Akwesasne that will cost between $20 million and $80 million. He talks expansively about the programs that the gambling profits will fund—education, health services, a municipal water project, a municipal sewer project and even, he claims, a lobbying effort to repeal the federal law, passed in 1948, that gives New York State law-enforcement jurisdiction over Akwesasne.

But what happens at Akwesasne if Chief Loran's gambling complex actually opens? No one *wants* to believe there will be a return to the insanity of 1990, that the Warriors and the Antis will take up arms again. That was too heavy a price to pay, everyone says, and no one is willing to revisit that nightmare.

But one night, eight months earlier, near the end of 1992, in a darkened office, the shades drawn against Warrior spying, a Mohawk law-enforcement official offered a different opinion.

"We've been getting ready for the last two or three years," he said. "It's going to be a lot quicker and a lot bloodier. Decisions are going to be made a lot quicker this time, because with the firepower on both sides now, nobody's going to back down. People are going to get wiped out."

Doug George and others have a different vision of the future of the Mohawks. Buy land in New York's Mohawk Valley, the aboriginal homeland of his people, and start over. Rebuild the nation. Farm. Bring food from the earth for the Mohawk people and share—share everything. That's how it used to be. Everyone ate or no one ate. Everyone was housed or no one was housed.

Recently, George saw that dream come closer to becoming a reality, when a small group of Mohawks led by Tommy Porter, a close friend of his, bought Montgomery Manor, a Montgomery County-owned complex in the Valley. The property includes 300 acres along the Mohawk River, land that belonged to the tribe more than 200 years ago. The Mohawk families that are moving to the property will try to live off the land, as do about forty Amish families in nearby Palatine. Gambling, even bingo, will be forbidden. Doug George and Joanne Shenandoah are searching for a piece of property nearby.

I crossed the Saint Lawrence at night, on the eve of Thanksgiving, my last day at Akwesasne. The weather was terrible, spitting snow and rain, and I felt suspended in midair on the big arc of the bridge. Below me, cloaked in the black expanse of the Saint Lawrence Seaway, were Mohawks—maybe coked-up, maybe drunk, definitely armed to the teeth—speeding across the water in 300-horsepower boats loaded with cases of bootleg cigarettes. When the casinos closed down, after the death of Pyke and Edwards and the arrest of the casino owners, smuggling picked up as the Mohawks were forced to scramble for other ways to make a living.

Sometimes the smugglers crash into one another in the flat blackness of the river. No one runs with lights. And they regularly rob one another, usually while still on the water, like pirates. That's 100 percent profit. Gunfire rings out most nights, sometimes as a signal to comrades on the opposite bank of the river, sometimes to intimidate other smugglers. Occasionally, an Indian mother with a missing son calls, and Canadian customs officers find an empty, bloodstained boat on the Saint Lawrence. Inside, there's an AK-47 assault rifle, but no cigarettes and no body. They drag the river, without success.

In the bitterly cold winter, when the Saint Lawrence ices over, the smugglers run it in snowmobiles, and a few have vanished before they reached the other side, disappearing, sledful of cigarettes and all, through a hole in the ice, taking with them the hopes of a nation.

REVENGE OF THE INDIANS[3]

Along narrow, winding Route 2A in southeastern Connecticut, not far from the old whaling port of Mystic, clouds of red dust billow above the birch trees.

These woods once concealed the comings and goings of Mohicans, Narragansetts, and Pequots, who took part in the bustling trade among early English and Dutch settlers.

Indians are still in these woods, but most of those who live on the Mashantucket Pequot reservation are hardly recognizable as such. None is native to the reservation, and what they trade is mostly illusory. They are here, some 250 strong, because of a sprawling sandstone casino that promises to make them all millionaires and forever change the popular perception of Indians as "downtrodden."

There is no basket-weaving, no pottery or firewood for sale here. Near the casino, a luxury hotel is being completed. At the edge of the reservation, giant cranes loom above the tree line. Dump trucks queue in long formations, kicking up clouds of clay-lined soil as work progresses on yet another hotel, a wastewater-treatment plant, a golf course, a monorail system, a shopping mall, and a multiplex movie theater. Serving all of this is a parking lot so large that shuttle buses ferry people back and forth between its outer edges and the casino. On an ordinary Monday afternoon, almost every parking space is taken.

Inside the crowded casino—quiet by Las Vegas standards, but too loud for many New Englanders—are acres of newly installed slot machines and dozens of blackjack and craps tables. Amidst a lavender-and-aqua color scheme, tellers take bets for nearly every horseracing track in the land; above a bar, television monitors display the latest results from Chicago, New Jersey, Florida, and Maryland. Downstairs, poker players eat seafood served by waitresses dressed in short, beaded tunics.

At one end of the building is the place where it all began, the bingo hall. But this is not ordinary bingo. Some of these games cost $350 to enter; most cost $25 or so. Like the rest of the casino,

[3]Article by Kim I. Eisler. From the *Washingtonian,* August '93. Reprinted with permission.

the bingo parlor is filled with Yankee gamblers. The stream of money they pour into the casino has not let up in 18 months.

On the side of the casino is a booth marked "Gaming Commission."

"Are you from the state or the federal government?" I ask.

"We are a sovereign nation," comes the reply. The casino operates under no state rules or regulations. Best of all for the Indians, they are not required to pay one dime in federal taxes.

In this area of New England, the Pequot reservation has defied 200 years of failed Washington policies on Indian affairs to emerge as a powerful economic force. Now one of the largest employers in the state, the Pequot tribe is growing so wealthy that its biggest problem is figuring out how to spend its money. It has begun by providing cradle-to-grave social services for its 250 members; building apartments, houses, and health clinics; and providing free ambulance service. It has also begun planning a $300-million theme park. After all these expenses, the tribal council still had enough cash on hand last year to award every member on the reservation a check ranging from $5,000 to $50,000.

All this on a reservation that just fifteen years ago was down to its last elderly resident. Now, instead of watching forlornly as their children leave the reservation, Pequots have hired a genealogist to study the stacks of applications that have poured in from people claiming membership in the tribe. Instead of selling off their land to survive, the Pequots are buying out their neighbors. In place of pickup trucks and subsistence housing, Jaguars and boats dot the front lawns of split-level homes.

If Indians historically were cheated out of their land in part because of alcohol, they have now recognized their old adversary's vulnerability. As the stream of customers continues, it is gambling that may secure the Indians' belated triumph over the white man.

It has been 350 years since the Pequots last wielded influence in these forests. Mighty warriors and shrewd traders, they commanded thousands of acres and played an important role in the fur-and-wampum trade. But in 1637, in a massacre that lasted an hour, the tribe was nearly extinguished by British musket fire. Most of the Pequots who survived were assimilated into the Narragansett or Mohican tribes; others were sold into slavery by the British and shipped to the West Indies. For the few who remained, a 2,000-acre reservation was created by the colonial government of Connecticut in 1667.

By the 1970s, the reservation had been whittled to 178 acres. Only one elderly Pequot remained alive, and the state of Connecticut planned, when 78-year-old Elizabeth George died, to declare the reservation abandoned and convert the land to a state park.

Elizabeth George had lived a long and full life. But she knew that her death would mean more than her own passing: It would mean the end of the Pequot nation.

Her daughter, like all her children and those of her five sisters, had left the reservation and married outside the tribe. But from the time he was a toddler, her grandson, Richard "Skip" Hayward, had come to visit. He seemed mesmerized by her tales of Pequot history. His father was a Navy corpsman who traced his lineage back to the Mayflower. Hayward also had been in the Navy, and then had worked in nearby Groton as an executive at a plant that made nuclear submarines.

In August 1975, Elizabeth George called her grandson and told him, as she had before, what would happen to their land when she was gone. Hayward promised her that he would move onto the reservation and keep the state parks department at bay.

Hayward, a man experienced in working with government grants and contracts, declared himself chairman of the Pequot Tribal Council and began pursuing federal funds. With HUD grants he hired crews to build fifteen houses and an apartment building for relatives to live in.

Hayward also began work on a greenhouse for growing vegetables. He put out a call to the children and grandchildren of Elizabeth George and her sisters to join him.

Lured by the promise of free housing, several returned. Among them was Joey Carter, a black man from Rhode Island who was going through a divorce and whose father was dying of cancer; he figured he didn't have much to lose. By 1981, Hayward had convinced 29 Pequot descendants to come to the reservation. They grew and sold lettuce, tapped maple syrup, and sold firewood. It was progress, but Hayward figured there had to be a better way. He went to the Seminole Indian reservation in Hollywood, Florida, to find it.

Seminole Chief James Billie was a visionary. For years the Seminoles had run small-time bingo operations. Charity bingo was tightly regulated by the state. Jackpots couldn't exceed $100.

A student of Indian law, Billie had taken notice of a 1976 Supreme Court ruling that an Indian reservation constituted a sovereign nation. A state's interest in the reservation's legal affairs could extend to criminal felonies, Justice William J. Brennan Jr. had declared, but a state trooper had no power to, say, go onto the reservation and enforce civil regulations.

Shortly after his election as chief, Billie reasoned that if the state could not even enforce non-criminal traffic laws on the reservation, the Seminoles could not be compelled to live under Florida's restrictions on bingo. If the state already permitted charity bingo, he argued, then the Seminoles could set their own hours and the size of their own jackpots. In 1979, after three years of feuding with state officials, he won his case in federal court.

High-stakes Indian bingo, with six-figure jackpots, opened to packed houses on the Seminole reservation in July 1979. Suddenly, Indian bingo was big business.

Hayward saw this when he visited the Seminole operation. Connecticut, he knew, also allowed charity bingo games. Chief Billie assured him that under the federal court ruling, the Pequots could not be prevented from operating their own high-stakes bingo parlor.

Hayward returned to the Pequot reservation. "He came back with flaming arrows trying to convince us that bingo was the way to go," Joey Carter recalls.

It was not an easy sell. Many of the reservation's inhabitants, who by then numbered around 50, were Jehovah's Witnesses; others were non-gambling Baptists. Bingo wasn't what their return to the reservation had been about.

While Hayward argued with his cousins, he scurried around Connecticut trying to line up $2.5 million in bank financing to build a bingo hall. In a region where even the building of a new convenience store draws protests, no local banker dared to back a bingo parlor. So Hayward went to New York City and made his pitch to the Arab-American Bank.

The novelty of bingo appealed to the Arab bankers, and they didn't share the fear that conservative New Englanders would not play bingo. Their only concern was that $2.5 million wouldn't be enough; they wanted Hayward to build a $5-million, 46,000-square-foot bingo hall. There was little risk; law prohibited the Indians from putting up their land as collateral, so Hayward already had secured a promise from the Bureau of Indian Affairs that the federal government would guarantee the loan.

"We weren't betting the reservation," says one tribe member. "We were playing with the federal government's money."

While he pursued financing and continued to entice Pequots to come home, Hayward also worked to restore the reservation's historic 2,000 acres. With the help of Connecticut Congressman Sam Gejdenson, who served on the House Interior Committee, the Pequots won a $900,000 appropriation under the Native American Claims Act to help restore the reservation nearly to its original size.

With land, financing, and a growing number of hands to pull weeds and help build a building, the Pequots in 1985 began work on their bingo parlor. The state of Connecticut blocked the opening for more than a year with legal maneuvers. In January 1986 the Pequots won permission in federal court to open their high-stakes bingo parlor. Drawing on the meaning of the name Pequot —"fox people"—and Mashantucket—"muck-wooded land"— they called it Foxwoods.

With the lure of such prizes as a $22,000 Cadillac Coupe deVille, the people came. Charging a $25-per-person admission fee, the tribe figured to gross $6 million a year.

As bingo boomed, Hayward discovered that Connecticut law also allowed charity casino nights. If the reservation could operate a bingo parlor, why not blackjack, craps, and roulette tables?

The Arabs weren't interested; blackjack and craps are not familiar to their culture. So Hayward tried Lim Goh Tong, a casino magnate in Malaysia.

An ethnic Chinese, Lim owned the only casino-hotel complex in predominantly Muslim Malaysia. His operation, Genting Highlands, was an adult fantasy world in the rain forest, 6,000 feet above sea level and 35 miles from the capital, Kuala Lumpur.

Lim was eager to enter the US market. The closest he had come was with a $100-million casino-hotel complex near the Subic Bay naval base in the Philippines. Listening to the pitch presented by Hayward and his attorneys, Lim felt confident. His Malaysian casino had surmounted many of the same obstacles: Foxwoods, like Genting Highlands, was in a remote location, and it would be met, as the Malaysian operation was, with local and state opposition. Lim brought in gamblers by cable car and tour bus; once they arrived, Genting Highlands offered lakes, golf courses, and swimming pools.

He agreed to lend the Pequots $65 million to expand the bingo parlor into a casino. Hayward hired an Atlantic City lawyer to operate it. By 1990 the casino was ready to go. Again the state went to court to block the Pequots, but again they were defeated, this time on the basis of both a 1987 ruling by Justice Byron White, affirming the earlier Brennan ruling, and the 1988 Indian Gaming Regulatory Act, which required that state governments negotiate gambling agreements in good faith with federally recognized tribes.

The federal court rules in early 1991 that Connecticut, in its drawn-out efforts to block the Pequot casino, had acted in "bad faith," and basically gave the tribe license to open the casino and run it as it pleased. The only thing the tribe couldn't do was operate slot machines, which had never been allowed in charity nights.

When the Foxwoods casino opened in February 1992, plans were to operate it eighteen hours a day. It never closed. This year the tribe negotiated a deal with Connecticut allowing slot machines—in exchange for payment to the state of about $100 million a year or at least 25 percent of the slot-machine revenue.

Even before the slots were added, customers shoved $1 billion through Foxwoods' windows, and the casino netted more than $100 million in its first year of operation. Slot-machine revenue is expected to push the take to more than $500 million a year—all to be shared by residents of the reservation.

After a year of casino operations, the Malaysians were financing two new hotels at the Indian reservation. The name of one is Two Trees Inn, which Hayward has explained describes the strong relationship that has been built between Lim and the Pequots. Tribal sources say that the tribe's original debt of $60 million to Lim is now $240 million and climbing.

Because of their "sovereign nation" status, none of the Pequots' deals have required disclosure about their partners to the Securities and Exchange Commission. Nor are their private financial arrangements a matter of public record. The Lim family is said to like it that way. Although little is known in this country about the family and its international connections, it attracted attention in 1992 by buying into Lonrho PLC, a British hotel company with ties to Libya. Lim also is said to have had extensive business contacts with the governments of China and Vietnam. Connecticut officials had no comment on Lim, saying they were in the middle of a background check.

A spokesman at the Interior Department scoffed at questions about the Malaysians. "They came to the rescue when nobody in Connecticut would give them a dime," says Bureau of Indian Affairs spokesman Carl Shaw. "They deserve credit for that."

As news of the tribe's wealth has reached even the Bahamas, many of the new applications for membership have come from Bahamians claiming that their ancestors were the Pequots sold into slavery 300 years ago. The Pequot Tribal Council has assigned tribal clerk Debbie Frankovich to rule on who qualifies for membership in the tribe.

Most of the 250 Indians are one-eighth Pequot at most, the minimum required by the tribe for acceptance as a member. The Interior Department says it's none of the US government's business who is and isn't an Indian. "Each tribe is allowed to be arbiter of its membership qualifications," says department spokesman Robert Walker. "The federal government does not dictate the standards for membership."

Nor does Washington have much to say about the Indians' financial partners.

"I don't think the Indians are being used," says Walker. "I think both sides are using each other. They obviously needed capital to get the gaming operation going."

The Federal Government has no objection to the construction of Indian-owned casinos and bingo parlors, which now number nearly 175. But some people do, including people already in the business. According to testimony at a recent congressional hearing, Indians now control 3 percent of the $600-billion gambling industry. By 1998, experts say, that share will triple.

Some opponents of Indian casinos voice concern about the seemingly unchecked spread of gambling, with state governments powerless to regulate casinos. When its expansion is complete, Foxwoods will be the largest casino in the United States.

And more are on the way. At the Oneida reservation, near Syracuse, a $10-million casino is scheduled to open Labor Day weekend. Out west, casinos are becoming as common as smoke-shops on reservations, with twelve in Minnesota and others in Washington, the Dakotas, and Iowa.

Opponents have brought their case to Congress, but it has been damaged by the perception that their arguments were based not on concern about the evils of gambling but on fear of competition. The original anti-Indian-casino coalition—which had hired Washington public-relations firm Burson-Marsteller—lost credibility when it was revealed that the campaign was funded by existing casinos and the racing industry. As one spokesman for Indian gaming said, "It was kind of hard to make the argument that gambling was evil when your clients were racetracks and casinos."

Anti-casino efforts by the Nevada Resort Association, a lobby of corporations with gambling interests, also have fallen flat. This spring, several big Las Vegas operators decided to break ranks and work with Indian reservations to develop and manage their properties. Now the major casino operator challenging the Indians is Donald Trump, owner of Atlantic City's Taj Mahal, who has filed suit asking that the federal court overturn its precedents.

The Nevada Resort Association is said to have halted its lobbying campaign and no longer has a position on Indian gaming. A sign of the way things are going is that Washington lawyer-lobbyist John Rafaelli, who has represented the casino industry on tax matters, is now working for a Connecticut tribe, the Paugusetts, who are trying to win federal tribal status so they, too, can open a casino.

Nevada Senator Harry Reid wants to rewrite the law to regulate Indian casinos and to make it harder to open new ones, provisions likely to be included in a bill drafted by Senator Daniel Inouye, chairman of the Senate's Select Committee on Indian Affairs.

But proposals to make life difficult for the Indians are not likely to win Interior Department support. "Our position," says spokesman Walker, "is that at last the Indians are getting into something that is self-supporting. If the Indian has an advantage finally, it's about time."

Individual states could take action, but not easily. When the Connecticut legislature had a chance to halt the Pequot casino by repealing the state's charity "Las Vegas Night" regulations, church groups were among the strongest opponents of repeal. The bill failed by two votes in the legislature.

Although the forces arrayed against them are formidable, the Indians have proven adept at politics. They recently hired Reid Walker, of Kaufman Public Relations in Washington, to coordinate their public-relations offensive. Walker himself is Indian; his father, Washington lawyer Hans Walker, was born at the Three Affiliated Tribes reservation in North Dakota.

The tribes also have set up a Washington lobbying office on Pennsylvania Avenue. During the presidential campaign, the Pequots made a $100,000 soft-money contribution to the Democratic National Committee. They have even patched things up with Connecticut state officials, who were so hostile to the tribe at first that they had refused to post road signs to the reservation. Relations were improved by the deal allowing slot machines at the casino in exchange for the payments to the state—and Governor Lowell P. Weicker Jr.'s promise not to allow casinos in Hartford and Bridgeport.

While their gambling enterprises flourish, the Pequots are looking to the future—and laying groundwork for a time when gambling revenue dwindles. Richard Hayward and his cousin Joey Carter are headed to China to negotiate a deal that might bring a 325-acre, $350-million Chinese garden and theme park to reservation land, a project similar to the one under construction at Genting Highlands. They are using their cash reserves to buy property around the reservation. Other plans include a cable-television network, and there has even been talk of buying a major-league sports team. Some Indians joke about buying back Manhattan.

Meanwhile, the casino has boosted the fortunes of the surrounding region. Neighbors may avail themselves of the reservation's free health clinic and ambulance service. Local banks that first spurned the tribe's business are now asking for deposits. The tourist town of Mystic, which was experiencing a slump, is bustling again; Washingtonians planning to stop on the way to Cape Cod are advised to make hotel reservations in advance.

The explosion of wealth has been hard for some residents of the reservation to handle. Although everyone receives the year-end bonuses, tribe members receive salaries only if they work on the reservation. Not that the Pequots are parsimonious. Bonus money for children is placed in interest-bearing trust accounts to be used for college educations. Senior members of the tribe get luxury cruises to Jamaica, among other destinations.

Most year-end bonuses are pegged to the amount of work performed during the year. But many jobs at the casino are beyond the reach of tribe members. Of the 250 or so certified Pequots, only a handful have an education beyond high school, says Carter. Operating a blackjack or craps table requires skill; dealers handle thousands of dollars in chips.

Although no members will voice it publicly, the situation has caused resentment on the reservation. High-paying, skilled jobs go to outsiders while descendants of the original Pequots are relegated to janitorial or gardening positions, one tribe member complained to me.

The success of Foxwoods is certain to make many Indian tribes take a second look at the potential of gambling. But don't expect to see Indian casinos sprouting up in the Washington area.

There are no federally recognized Indian reservations in Maryland, Delaware, or West Virginia. Virginia—home of the state-recognized Mattaponi and Pamunkey tribes—has no charity gaming laws. Even if it did, leaders of those conservative tribes say that opening a casino is the furthest thing from their minds.

"We're church people here, and we disapprove of gambling," says Curtis Warhorse Custalow, a member of the Mattaponi tribal council.

But tribes like the Mattaponi and Pamunkey are in the minority. Many more believe they have seen the promised land. Just as Richard Hayward once traveled to Florida, other Indian leaders now journey to Connecticut to see what their own future might be. "Once again," says an Interior Department official, "they have hope."

CASINO WARS: ETHICS AND ECONOMICS IN INDIAN COUNTRY[4]

The "Ghost Trail" weaves through 7,000 acres across one of Washington state's largest Indian reservations. My informant tells me it carries no visible markings. For outsiders the path remains a hidden part of that indigenous community's spiritual geography. I'm told that some Salish avoid crossing the trail casually. They regard it as one that their forest spirits travel. Only initiates into the *Seyouwin,* or winter dance society, continue to perceive the trail; those who practice the thousand-year-old secret rituals are pledged to protect and honor it.

I stand in a parking lot with a longtime employee of the tribe's Treaty Protection Task Force, who musingly points out that the ghost trail ends a few yards in back of me at the doorway to the tribal casino, which operates 24 hours a day. This is my second visit to the tribe's gaming enterprise. We casually wander over to the renovated warehouse that now houses bingo games, roulette wheels and blackjack tables. The central image on a cedar totem pole near the entrance is a bear holding a deck of cards. Next to the door a world map invites visitors and customers to mark their

[4]Article by Jon Magnuson. From *Christian Century,* February 16, '94. Copyright © 1994 Christian Century Foundation. Reprinted with permission.

points of origin. Hundreds of red and green tacks fill the display, representing dozens of countries in Europe and Asia, as well as North America. Approaching the casino's entrance, I lift my hand to trigger a motion activator hidden inside a Halloween skeleton. The "Addams Family" theme song echoes from a speaker mounted just out of sight.

It's busy this afternoon. As in big-time casinos, there are no windows, no clocks and no places to sit down apart from gaming and bingo tables. Employees are cordial, floors spotless. State regulations prohibit liquor from being served here, and although food is available, it's apparent that no one has come to linger, eat or socialize. The atmosphere reminds me of Las Vegas and Reno. There is a feeling of peculiar seriousness in such establishments, perhaps because the rules seem so straightforward. This is about winning. And money.

As is true on most Indian reservations, this casino is leased to a national gaming organization, with a contract stipulating that it turn over full operation to tribal leaders in three or four years. Meanwhile, plenty of sophisticated marketing techniques have been put into place. Not long ago this nondescript warehouse was an empty building on the edge of a bay next to a lonely ferry dock. What was once an abandoned storage area is now an expansive, neatly ordered parking lot filled bumper to bumper with cars and vans. Each day hundreds of bingo and blackjack fans enter what was once a sleepy tourist and fishing town, oblivious to ghost trails, Indian treaty rights, or the ancient masked dances that still go on near here on rainy winter nights. I get myself some coffee, and my friend introduces me to a young tribal woman dressed in medieval jester's garb, working as one of the hostesses. She is friendly, and mentions with pride that 60 percent of the employees are tribal members. She's a single mother with three children. The pay is good, she says. My colleague, one of the tribe's cultural specialists, points, smiling, to a blackjack table. He says the dealer, a man with long dark hair, is one of the leaders of the *Seyouwin*.

This small but obviously lucrative casino is only one example of the sudden growth of legalized gambling on Indian reservations. It is also a sign of the sweeping shift in public morality that is under way in virtually every municipality, Indian and non-Indian, across the country. Gambling has become an acceptable form of mass-market entertainment. In 1992 Americans spent more on legal games of chance than on films, books, amusement attractions and recorded music combined. That same year Americans spent three times as much money at Indian gambling casinos as on movie tickets. According to Wall Street forecasts, spending on gambling will double within a decade. "If there weren't more demand than supply, we'd all be doing something else," says Bruce Turner, a casino analyst for Raymond, James, and Associates.

Twenty states now have Indian gambling, ranging from bingo parlors to casinos as big and glamorous as those in Nevada. Fifty-eight tribes are currently involved in gaming ventures. The Foxwoods casino in Connecticut is the single largest contributor to that state's tax coffers; it alone will provide the state with $113 million this year. Minnesota, with its Native American gambling halls, currently has more casinos than Atlantic City. Eager to jump aboard the economic boom, a promoter in northwest New Jersey has recently offered to donate land to the Delaware Indians if a few members of that tribe will come back from Oklahoma to sponsor a casino.

The use of reservation lands for large-scale commercial gaming designed to attract non-Indian players is a relatively new trend. Two court cases in the early 1980s set the standard for states: In both *Seminole Tribe v. Butterworth* (in Florida) and *State of California v. Cabazon* the courts used the "criminal-prohibitory and civil regulatory" test. This test holds that if state law criminally prohibits a form of gambling, then the tribes within that state may not engage in that form of gaming free of state control. To further regulate tribal gaming, Congress passed the federal Indian Gaming Regulatory Act in 1988. This act affirms Indian sovereignty over gaming based on provisions established by the country's first interactions with tribal entities. Supreme Court Justice John Marshall, who shaped the earliest federal policy toward Native Americans at the beginning of the 19th century, wrote that Indian tribes are "domestic dependent nations, recognized as sovereign within their territories, with power of self-government over activities on their reservations." The legal ramifications of this position have proved to be complex, and subject to modifications by the reservations' federally appointed trustee, the Bureau of Indian Affairs. The 1988 act, for example, places restrictions on tribes that are not imposed on state gaming operations. It ensures that tribal governments are the sole owners and primary beneficiaries of gaming. It further states that tribes may not conduct casino-type gambling without a valid tribal-state compact regulating such issues as what games are played and the percentage of payoffs.

For many Native peoples, gaming has become the method for building the strong economic base that they claim they need for their independence. For others, the proliferation of gaming is a spiritual cancer eating away at what is left of the soul of Native American communities.

Driving south from Minneapolis, we take Highway 42 west off Interstate I-35. My companion, a former church worker for Indian ministry in northern California, says, "You gotta see this." He's right. Mystic Lake is Minnesota's most spectacular new gaming facility. Owned by the Shakaopee Mdewakanton Dakota tribe, Mystic Lake is a $15 million gaming entertainment center, the largest gambling casino between Las Vegas and Atlantic City. Crowning the facility is a tepee formed by searchlights extending hundreds of feet into the sky. The 135,000-square-foot casino boasts more than 75 blackjack tables and 1,000 video slot machines. One of its promotion brochures proclaims, "The excitement of Vegas . . . Without the desert." The Twin Cities' *Southwest Metro Entertainment Guide* reads, "If it's big money you're looking for, Mystic Lake Bingo offers games with mega jackpots. Megabingo starts at $500,000 and grows each night until someone cashes in." This is the pinnacle of Indian bingo, a dazzling feast of lights and sound where a new car is given away every night, where the food and beverage service is elegant and sophisticated, and where free shuttles from Minneapolis and St. Paul hotels arrive around the clock.

Walking through the doors, I'm taken aback by the glitter and noise of hundreds of slot machines and video games. The structure's circular design, our host says, symbolizes "the great circle of life, the four seasons, and the three cycles of life. Within the concentric circles of the main casino, all seven tribes of the Sioux nation are represented." I wander into the 1,100-seat Bingo Palace located at the west end of the structure and pause, disoriented by the mixture of spiritual and cultural images that frame this setting. A clergy friend from northern Minnesota had told me that the radio advertisements for Mystic Lake use a drum and the voice of an "authentic" shaman to lure customers to its gaming tables. Mysticism of a kind abounds here, but I'm not sure it is exactly what Black Elk had in mind.

On one level, the Native American boom in commercial gaming looks like a sure bet. In Minnesota, gambling is well on its way to becoming one of the state's largest employers, having created over 10,000 jobs. Members of some Indian nations receive checks as a share of casino profits. Three Dakota communities in southern Minnesota give out payments that vary from $2,000 to $4,000 per month, depending on profits, to each enrolled member of the tribe. The figures are staggering. After a lengthy legal struggle to regain the tribe's original 2,000-acre reservation, the Pequot nation finally got a financial guarantee from the Bureau of Indian Affairs and a loan from the Arab-American Bank in New York. Its casino opened in 1992 and is expected this year to earn over $500 million for tribal members. The tribe has had to open a genealogy office to judge the claims of long-lost relatives to membership in the group, which is now up to 256 members, all of whom are at least one-eighth Pequot by blood.

Some of the tribes, like the Oneidas of Wisconsin, have gained respect and admiration from both Indian and non-Indian groups as they collectively have made decisions about how to use their windfalls of revenue. Thanks to their new gaming facility, the Oneidas' unemployment rate fell from 40 percent in 1976 to 17 percent in 1991. With proceeds from their bingo hall, they have built a $10.5 million hotel and convention center, as well as an environmental testing lab that has won state and federal contracts. They have also subsidized their own Head Start program and built an elementary school. Other tribal councils, like Washington State's Suquamish, are using proceeds to purchase back reservation lands that were long ago taken away by state and federal policies. An attractive, state-of-the-art pamphlet for Mystic Lake concludes with some direct advocacy: "Tribal governments realize that casino gaming is not an end in itself. It is a means to achieve what no other federal economic development program has been able to in more than 200 years—the return of self-respect and economic self-sufficiency to Indian people."

The varied responses to Indian gaming emerging from Christian churches warrant special attention. As a non-Indian and a member of the clergy, I believe these responses reflect important deeper issues about ethics, spirituality and the complex face of racism and cultural identity. An immediate and common response was related to me in the form of a question by a denominational executive not long ago. "What are we going to do about Indian gambling?" he asked. In light of his strong, sensitive record of supporting treaty rights for Northwest tribes, he was finding himself in a moral quandary. He was pondering the dilemma of how the Christian community could affirm the proliferation of what has long been considered a vice by most Protestants. To best answer this question it is important to acknowledge that the issue poses several ethical and moral dilemmas. The first, and perhaps the most elemental, is the right of Native peoples to decide their own destinies, a right protected by treaty provisions. Only in states that already allow gambling are commercial Indian games of chance legal.

In the larger social context, it is unsettling that there has been so little opposition by church leaders to the proliferation of state lotteries. The exploitation of low-wage workers and the abdication of any corporate public commitment to building a solid, equitable tax system is dismally evident to economists, whatever their political loyalties. It might be good to clean one's own house before suggesting that Native Americans should clean theirs. For historical reasons, America's 200 Indian reservations face overwhelming internal and external conflicts in developing strategies for survival. As Rick Hill, Oneida tribal chairman, stated in his welcoming speech to the Native American Journalists Association in 1992, "We have been reduced to gaming, but I feel at this time it offers the only chance we have for economic self-sufficiency."

Some perceive the results of Indian gaming as a humorous kind of revenge. Thomas Donlan, writing recently for the financial weekly *Barron's,* reminds us that one of the fundamental principles of economics is that a fool and his money are soon parted. What can be said in favor of a gambling casino, he says, is that it concentrates fools, money and those who would part the two, thus contributing to economic efficiency through moral decay. Donlan enjoys the irony. The people who were "defeated by imported alcohol and disease," then corrupted by paternalistic management, he writes, "now find themselves, through a legal loophole, able to erect institutions to corrupt their oppressors."

A second popular response to the rise of gaming in Indian country is often moral indignation and masked anger. This is voiced quietly by many political liberals and whispered privately by progressive church leaders. Such an emotional response is probably rooted in what anthropologists call "nostalgic imperialism," an unconscious sentimentalizing and romanticizing of that which a dominant culture has destroyed. It is a fascination with indigenous people and culture, *exclusively* from an historical and artistic point of view. Such an "emblematic" relationship with Native cultures, anthropologists suggest, is a form of racism that

many of us, including many Native Americans, share. In other
words, others in the culture can gamble, but not the "noble American Indian."

While creative, powerful traditional values are still embodied
in the remnants of Native spiritual religions and customs, it is
important to remember there is no more "pure," unblemished
spiritual teaching in indigenous cultures than there is in the vari-
eties of Christian expression. The question "How could Indians
be involved in commercialized gambling?" betrays our own long-
ings for an innocent culture in touch with the best of earth and
heaven. A good corrective might be to recognize that among
Native Americans there is no consensus on the commercial gaming boom. The Mohawks of New York State have broken out in
armed conflict over casino operations. The struggle to protect
big-time tribal operations from organized crime continues. Tra-
ditionalists around the country grapple with tribal governments
over the direction in which their communities are moving.

A third response to the increase in commercial Indian gaming
is the plea by some for an "even playing field." The accusation
that Native Americans have been given special privileges reflects
a superficial reading of American history, as well as an ignorance
of treaty rights and the historical relationship of tribes to the U.S.
government. One of the more entertaining legal struggles against
the explosion of Indian gaming has been waged by Donald Trump,
seeking better odds for his own gambling ventures. Trump has
sued the federal government for supposedly giving tribes regulatory breaks. His testimony before the federal courts was embar-
rassing and amusing to many Native American journalists, as he
showed little if any understanding of the peculiar but critical
history of the tribes' right of sovereignty, which has been affirmed
since the earliest days of the Constitution. The defense of aboriginal rights in courts has been won over and over again in the last half
of the 20th century. That legacy will undoubtedly remain part of
our country's ongoing jurisprudence.

I'm on my way to British Columbia for a two-day stay at a
Benedictine monastery. I turn on my car radio and hear an ad-
vertisement for the Lummi Indian casino 50 miles to the west.
Switching stations, I find a public radio broadcast of a speech in
Vancouver by a recent recipient of the Visiting Scholar Award
sponsored by Simon Fraser University's Institute for the Human-
ities. The announcer introduces the speaker as Ovide Mercredi,
grand chief of Canada's 600,000 aboriginal people. Although

schooled as an attorney, his thoughts are expressed in typical Native style, in a personal, informal and somewhat circuitous way. Mercredi's closing remarks are about the future of his people, the recovery by his children and grandchildren of their culture, traditions and religion. "We're growing stronger," he says. "When we reclaim what once was ours, you will see us differently. We will win it back, buy it back, the land that was taken from us. You will hear our voices. Our Indian culture is renewing itself. In the years ahead," he concludes almost matter-of-factly, "you're not going to like us very much."

IV. WHEN GAMBLING BECOMES A PROBLEM

EDITOR'S INTRODUCTION

The articles in this section deal with the problem of aberrant gambling behavior and how to define it. Is so-called problem gambling a mental disorder or an uncontrollable addiction? Or is it simply a bad habit that can be broken by sheer will power? Questions of treatment, funding, and personal and governmental responsibility and liability all surface in the ongoing debate.

The chief proponents for either side are represented in this section. Dr. Henry Lesieur, in "Compulsive Gambling," reprinted from *Society*, defines the parameters of pathological gambling and discusses the costs to individuals, families, insurance providers, and society at large. Besides the financial costs, he also considers the consequences of compulsive gambling on mental and physical health, at the workplace, on spousal and parental relationships, and upon criminal behavior. Lesieur concludes with an outline for state and federal responsibility and a call for national awareness of what he deems an escalating problem.

Dr. Richard Vatz and Dr. Lee S. Weinberg, in "Refuting the Myths of Compulsive Gambling," reprinted from *U.S.A. Today Magazine*, argue against the "gambling-as-disease" model presented by Lesieur. It is their position that this model has won too easy acceptance from the public because the mass media have failed to present scientific data to the contrary. They further claim that the image of the addicted, compulsive gambler may ultimately be no more than a way to avoid personal responsibility.

The next article is a chapter from the book *Pathological Gambling* by Dr. Martin C. McGurrin, in which the author discusses not only the "disease model" for pathological gambling but also issues dealing with its treatment. McGurrin explores alternatives in a discussion of abstinence versus controlled gambling (in the U.S., the treatment mode is usually centered on a program similar to Alcoholics Anonymous, which calls for total abstinence). He also considers hospital and out-patient treatment and the effects on loved ones and family.

Finally, *20 Questions*, reprinted by permission of Gamblers Anonymous, presents what is considered a standard litmus test to assess whether one has a gambling problem and should consider getting further help.

COMPULSIVE GAMBLING[1]

In 1974, the number of Americans who gambled was 61 percent of the total population. They wagered 17.4 billion dollars legally. In 1989, the Gallup organization reported that 71 percent of the public gambled, while the gross legal gaming handle was 246.9 billion dollars for the year. This represents a 1,400 percent increase in dollar volume in just fifteen years. Currently, forty-eight states (all but Utah and Hawaii) have some form of legalized gambling. The California lottery alone is a 2.5 billion dollar-a-year operation.

Not only did the number of states involved increase, but the variety of gaming offered has moved up as well. In addition to the state of Nevada and Atlantic City, New Jersey, local casinos have opened in Deadwood, South Dakota, and were approved for three mining towns in Colorado, and on the Mashantucket Pequot Reservation in Connecticut. Iowa, Illinois, and Mississippi authorized riverboat or dockside casinos; Video Lottery Terminals (VLTs), similar to slot machines, have been approved for Iowa, South Dakota, and West Virginia; charitable gambling has increased at a similar rate. For example, Minnesota with bingo run by charities and recently legalized pull tabs (called "paper slot machines") had gross sales of 1.2 billion dollars a year in charitable gaming in 1989.

Evidence suggests that in areas where more forms of gambling are legal, the incidence of problem and pathological (compulsive) gambling is also higher. In 1974, fewer than 1 percent of the adult population in the United States were recognized as compulsive gamblers while the comparable rate for Nevada was 2.5 percent. Recent surveys done in New York, New Jersey, Maryland, and Iowa and in Quebec, Canada, revealed that problem

[1]Article by Henry Lesieur. From *Society*, May/June '92. Copyright © 1992 Transaction pub. Reprinted with permission of Transaction pub.

and pathological gambling in Iowa, where there is less legalized gambling, was about half that in other states and Quebec, where the studies were made.

Given the recent increase in legalized gambling, it is important to determine the potential impact such legalization on the segment of the population prone to developing problems. So far, no systematic analysis of the costs of pathological gambling has been made.

What is pathological gambling? The American Psychiatric Association defines it as chronic and progressive failure to resist impulses to gamble, and gambling behavior that compromises, disrupts, or damages personal, family, or vocational pursuits. While the terms pathological and compulsive are technically not synonymous—for psychiatrists a compulsion is a behavior that is involuntary and in gambling this does not occur until quite late in the problem gambler's career—professionals and lay persons use them interchangeably.

While pathological gambling does not involve the use of a substance, research conducted by numerous scholars has noted similarity with other addictive behaviors. For example, pathological gamblers state that they seek "action" as well as money or a means of escaping from problems—an aroused, euphoric state comparable to the "high" derived from cocaine or other drugs. Action means excitement, thrills and tension—"when the adrenalin is flowing." The desire to remain in action is so intense that many gamblers will go for days without sleep, without eating, and even without going to the bathroom. Being in action pushes out all other concerns. During the period of anticipation, there is also a "rush," usually characterized by sweaty palms, rapid heart beat, and nausea.

Pathological gamblers, like alcoholics and drug addicts, are preoccupied with seeking out gambling; they gamble longer than intended and with more money than intended. There is also the equivalent of "tolerance" when gamblers have to increase the size of their bets or the odds against them in order to create the desired amount of excitement.

Researchers in Australia, Germany and the United States have noted "withdrawal-like symptoms" in pathological gamblers who stop gambling. Hence, while not physiologically addicting, gambling has addictive qualities. Because of this, excessive dependence on gambling is often called an "addiction." Like substance abusers, pathological gamblers make frequent unsuccessful attempts at cutting down and quitting. While gambling does not produce intoxication or physical impairment and consequently does not have an impact on social, educational or occupational obligations in that way, the obsession with gambling has been noted to impair performance in these spheres.

The American Psychiatric Association is proposing new diagnostic criteria for pathological gambling for inclusion in its *Diagnostic and Statistical Manual.* Maladaptive behavior is indicated by at least four of the following: 1) preoccupied with gambling— preoccupied with reliving past gambling experiences, handicapping or planning the next venture, or thinking of ways to get money with which to gamble; 2) needs to gamble with increasing amounts of money in order to achieve the desired excitement; 3) is restless or irritable when attempting to cut down or stop gambling; 4) gambles as a way of escaping from problems or relieving dysphoric mood—feelings of helplessness, guilt, anxiety, depression; 5) often returns another day in order to get even ("chasing" one's money) after losing; 6) lies to family or others to conceal the extent of involvement with gambling;) engages in illegal acts such as forgery, fraud, theft, or embezzlement, committed in order to finance gambling; 8) has jeopardized or lost a significant relationship, job, educational or career opportunity because of gambling; 9) relies on others to provide money to relieve a desperate financial situation caused by gambling (a "bailout"); 10) repeats unsuccessful efforts to control, cut back, or stop gambling. "Dimensions" for each of the criteria are: preoccupation, tolerance, withdrawal, escape, chasing, lies/deception, illegal acts, relationship/job disruption, financial bailout, and loss of control.

Most gambling is merely a reshuffling of resources from one player to another with no net loss to the system as a whole. However, there is a redistribution of resources from losers to winners and from losers to the operators of the gambling activities. In some instances the operators are illegal bookmakers, people who run card rooms illegally, and so on. More recently, with the increasing legalization of gambling, the operator has been the state. State (as well as charity or corporate) profits therefore represent player losses.

Cost of Pathological Gambling

Some people gamble more than others. These people, including pathological gamblers, account for a greater share of the state profits than the typical player. Most of this money comes out of paychecks and savings and is difficult to measure, particularly since the average gambler does not always lose but experiences a roller-coaster relationship with wins, losses and breaking even. Because losses outweigh wins in the long run for pathological gamblers, they typically borrow in order to finance continued play or to recover past losses. This debt can be examined.

Researchers have reported on different rates of indebtedness of pathological gamblers in treatment. The mean gambling-related debt (excluding auto loans, mortgages, and other "legitimate" debts) of individuals in treatment ranges from 53 thousand dollars to 92 thousand dollars. Female Gamblers Anonymous (GA) members have a lower level of gambling related debt, averaging almost 15 thousand dollars. This is only the debt they accumulate and does not include the debt they pay off. For an estimated 18 percent of males and 8 percent of females in studies of treatment samples and members of Gamblers Anonymous, this eventually led to bankruptcy. Other defaults on indebtedness and civil suits also need to be added to the costs.

Since the data are limited, it is not possible to estimate the total debt, bankruptcy, and other civil problems produced by pathological gambling in the United States per year. Using a twenty-year gambling history and estimates of the number of probable pathological gamblers in New Jersey, I estimate that over 514 million dollars are accumulated in debt by compulsive gamblers in that state alone per year. This, however, is based on the assumption that pathological gamblers not in treatment are similar to those in treatment. Yet, it does not include the costs of bankruptcy proceedings, attempts to garnish paychecks, and other civil actions related to indebtedness.

Gambling-related debts appear to be a reflection of easy credit and check cashing policies of the casino and the racing industry in New Jersey. Based on a review of the literature as well as discussions with members of Gamblers Anonymous, the following policies by gambling establishments appear to exacerbate the debt of pathological gamblers: 1) check cashing services at gambling facilities; 2) holding a check for months or allowing gamblers to "buy back" their checks at a later date rather than cashing them right away; 3) cash machines at the gambling location or within easy walking distance from the casinos; 4) credit in any form associated with gambling; 5) one-time credit checks on the gamblers rather than a periodic review of credit required; 6) no total review of credit when a payment for a marker has "bounced" or is overdue; 7) loan sharks operating in or near the gambling facility; 8) drinking in association with gambling which produces irrational play and increases debt. This is based on overall assessments of debt-related problems of GA members and those in treatment. A review of the interaction of these policies in other states and the gambling patterns of the broader gambling public would prove useful in guiding public policy.

Medical and Insurance Costs

Pathological gamblers also borrow from life insurance policies, surrender their policies, and allow them to lapse or be revoked. This is costly for the insurance companies and the insurance buying public as well as the gamblers' families. Gamblers operate uninsured automobiles, get into accidents, and become disabled or die without insurance. While these costs have not yet been calculated, one study of (primarily male) GA members found that 47 percent had engaged in insurance related fraud or thefts where insurance companies had to pay the victims. The average amount of fraud was 65 thousand dollars. Pathological gamblers engage in an estimated 1.3 billion dollars in insurance-related fraud per year.

Pathological gambling has adverse health and emotional consequences. In the later stages of their gambling, pathological gamblers experience depression, insomnia, intestinal disorders, migraines, and other stress-related diseases. In a study done at Taylor Manor Hospital in Maryland, researchers compared chemically dependent patients with chemically dependent patients who were also pathological gamblers. They found that the chemically dependent gamblers reported more chronic medical problems, conflicts with family members, and more psychiatric symptoms than the non-gambling chemically dependent patients. In addition, studies have reported rates of suicide attempts by GA and hospitalized pathological gamblers that range from 15 to 24 percent—five to ten times higher than for the general population.

Psychiatric Disorders

Recent evidence reveals that pathological gambling overlaps with other psychiatric disorders. Richard McCormick and colleagues examined the rates of major affective disorders and schizophrenia among fifty inpatients at the Brecksville Veterans Administration medical center in Ohio. Seventy-six percent of the subjects were diagnosed as having major depressive disorder and 38 percent as having hypomanic disorder—thirteen patients (26 percent) met the criteria for both major depression and hypomanic disorder. Eight percent had manic disorder—three patients (6 percent) also met the criteria for major depressive disorder, and one patient (2 percent) had schizo-affective disorder, depressed type. Only four patients (8 percent) did not meet the criteria for another disorder.

In a study of twenty-five male members of Gamblers Anonymous, researchers used different methods but arrived at similar results. Eighteen of the subjects (72 percent) had experienced at least one major depressive episode. Thirteen (52 percent) had recurrent major affective episodes. There was a high rate (20 percent) of panic disorders also. In addition, twelve (48 percent) met the criteria for alcohol abuse or dependency. One recent report of hospitalized psychiatric patients found that seven out of 105 patients surveyed (6.5 percent) were pathological gamblers. This is a rate four times higher than for the general population.

The high rates of other psychiatric disorders in both hospitalized and non-hospitalized male pathological gamblers indicate that some of these individuals may have been treated for these disorders prior to the recognition that they had a problem with gambling. Some evidence for this comes from studies of Gamblers Anonymous members which show that 24 to 40 percent of males and 58 percent of females surveyed had been treated by mental health professionals prior to attending GA. Most were not referred by these professionals to GA or gambling-specific treatment.

General psychiatric populations, particularly those with major affective disorders, need to be screened for pathological gambling. Mental health professionals need to be educated about pathological gambling and Gamblers Anonymous. With the exception of small scale efforts by the National Council on Problem Gambling, its state affiliates, and a few other organizations, this need is not being met at present.

Multiple Dependencies

Systematic studies of pathological gamblers reveal rates of alcohol and other substance abuse problems ranging from 47 to

52 percent. Some research has been done on substance abusing populations to find out the extent of their problems with pathological gambling. These studies have uncovered rates of 9 to 14 percent of the patients diagnosed as pathological gamblers and 19 to 28 percent as problem or pathological gamblers. These rates are six to ten times higher than for the general population. Further research is needed on the overlapping social worlds of the drug-using gambler and the gambling drug user.

Pathological gambling appears to compound the already high costs of psychoactive substance use dependence. Current evidence suggests that chemical dependency combined with a gambling problem may place pathological gamblers at greater risk of incarceration. In addition, substance dependent patients who are also pathological gamblers have higher rates of stress-related diseases and serious psychiatric problems including suicide attempts.

Family Issues

The pathological gambler's financial burden is partially borne by the family. Added debt means fewer family expenditures are possible. Payment of mortgage, rent, gas, electricity, telephone and other bills may be late or overdue. In extreme cases, utilities may be shut off, automobiles or furniture may be repossessed, and household items may have to be sold. The family may be evicted from their apartment or the mortgage may be foreclosed. Compulsive gambling creates other problems for family members as well. Researchers and clinicians have described patterns of exploitation of family finances, lies, distrust as a consequence of the lies, periodic arguments, separations and divorce threats, all related to excessive gambling. Valerie Lorenz of the National Center for Pathological Gambling in Baltimore has conducted most of the systematic research in this area.

The bulk of Lorenz' subjects were wives of compulsive gamblers attending Gamblers Anonymous/Gam-Anon Conclaves (regional conferences). Her data show serious problems within the family including harassment by bill collectors (experienced by 62 percent of the spouses in Lorenz' 1981 study), insomnia related to gambling-produced difficulties (78 percent), physical violence by the spouse against the gambler (62 percent), and suicide attempts by the spouse. The suicide attempt rates of 11 to 14 percent she has reported are three times higher than the reported rate of suicide attempts in the general population.

In more recent research, Lorenz and her colleague Robert Yaffee examined the psychosomatic, emotional and marital difficulties of pathological gamblers and their spouses. Five hundred questionnaires were filled out at Gamblers Anonymous/Gam-Anon Conclaves. Of these, 215 were completed by spouses. They found very high incidence of the following illnesses when compared with studies of female hospital patients: chronic or severe headache, bowel disorders (excessive constipation or diarrhea), asthma, depression, and suicide attempts. Aside from Gam-Anon, present resources to help families cope with gambling-related problems are nearly nonexistent in most states. While there is a growing body of literature on pathological gambling itself, relatively little is known about the children of compulsive gamblers. What is known tends to point to serious problems in the children as well as their parents.

The children of compulsive gamblers are caught in a situation of extreme behavior by their parents. At times the gambler dotes on them, then ignores them. This seesaw relationship has been portrayed in the few accounts of the dynamics of the family of pathological gamblers. The children feel angry, hurt, lonely, guilty, abandoned, and rejected. According to Robert Custer and Harry Milt (in *When Luck Runs Out*) their teen years are troubled, they run away from home, use drugs, become depressed and experience psychosomatic illnesses. However, when they asked in their study of spouses of pathological gamblers about psychosomatic illnesses of the children, Lorenz and Yaffee did not find a statistically significant difference between the rates of these children and the general juvenile population. More systematic research of this issue is needed.

Some studies have found serious psychosocial maladjustment in the children of pathological gamblers. Durand Jacobs, in a study of California high school students, found compulsive gambling in the parents of students were abusing stimulant drugs and tended to overeat. These students were also more likely to report having an unhappy childhood, having a legal action pending, being depressed and suicidal, and showing other signs of psychosocial maladjustment than children without troubled parents. Studies done in New Jersey and Quebec found that high school students whose parents had a gambling problem were more likely to have a gambling problem themselves than those whose parents were not reported to have a gambling problem. These studies reinforce the need for state-mandated education about pathological gambling in the schools.

In her study of spouses of compulsive gamblers, Lorenz asked about the parents' relationship with their children. Eight percent of the gamblers and 37 percent of spouses of gamblers physically abused their children. A more recent study has shown that children of Gamblers Anonymous members in the United States are more likely to be abused than children in studies of the national population.

The Workplace

Little systematic study has been done on the pathological gambler in the workplace. Previously, I have described differences between supervised, less supervised, and self-employed male compulsive gamblers. The lower the level of supervision on the job, the more likely the compulsive gambler is to exploit the time and finances the position grants. This has been found to be the case with female compulsive gamblers as well.

Extended card games and casino venture cause lateness and absences from work; lunch hours are lengthened for off-track betting (OTB); the gambler's mind may not be at work because of heavy losses, indebtedness, and intense preoccupation with getting even; irritability, moodiness, and poor concentration on work are added consequences. Many gamble on company time including card playing, betting on numbers, and acting as runners, writers, or bookmakers for a gambling operation at work. Money is borrowed from fellow employees; advances are taken on paychecks; paychecks are garnished. As a last resort, the employee may steal from the company or engage in illegal activities on company time. Those who own a business exploit it and drain its assets as well as those of suppliers and other creditors. The exact cost of these activities to employers, employees and fellow employees is not known, but it appears to be rather extensive. This aspect too needs further research.

In spite of these problems, very few employee assistance programs are actively screening troubled employees for a gambling problem. Systematic education is sorely needed.

Gambling and Crime

Ultimately, pathological gambling results in crime. Studies conducted to date, uncovered a wide variety of illegal behaviors among compulsive gamblers we interviewed. Jay Livingston found compulsive gamblers involved in check forgery, embezzlement, theft, larceny, armed robbery, bookmaking, hustling, running con games, and fencing stolen goods. My research uncovered similar patterns. In addition, I found gamblers engaged in systematic loan fraud, tax evasion, burglary, pimping, prostitution, selling drugs, and hustling at pool, golf, bowling, cards, and dice. Compulsive gamblers are engaged in a spiral of options and involvements wherein legal avenues for funding are utilized until they are closed off. Dependent on personal value systems, legitimate and illegitimate opportunity, perceptions of risk, the existence of threats (for example, loan sharks) and chance, gamblers become involved in more and more serious illegal activity. For some, the amount of money involved runs into the millions of dollars.

Studies of prisoners, alcohol and drug abusing inpatients, female members of Gamblers Anonymous, and a study of Veteran's Administration inpatients and Gamblers Anonymous members provide useful comparative information. In all four studies, the subjects were asked if they had engaged in a range of financially motivated crimes in order to gamble or to pay gambling debts.

Approximately two-thirds of non-incarcerated and 97 percent of incarcerated pathological gamblers admit engaging in illegal behavior to finance gambling or pay gambling related debts. White collar crimes predominate among treatment samples while street crimes and drug sales are more frequent among imprisoned compulsive gamblers. The total cost of this crime is unknown at present. An estimated 10 to 30 percent of prisoners are probable pathological gamblers. Most are also addicted to alcohol and/or other drugs. We need to find out what percent of their drug-related crimes are actually produced by gambling in combination with drug use. Treatment programs that address multiple dependencies are vitally needed in prisons and diversion programs, and halfway houses are needed for individuals on probation and parole.

Given the high level of property crime among pathological gamblers, to what extent do they engage in violent behavior? In a study examining nonviolence among pathological gamblers, Iain Brown surveyed 107 Gamblers Anonymous members in England and Scotland and found that thirty-five of them (33 percent) had criminal convictions. He examined these convictions to find out whether pathological gamblers had patterns of crime which were more similar to alcoholics (with a mix of violence and property offenses) or drug addicts (primarily property offenders). Theft and fraud offenses accounted for 94 percent of all criminal convictions. An additional 4 percent of convictions were for armed robbery. Fewer than 1 percent of convictions were for non-property violence offenses. Brown concluded that pathological gamblers are primarily nonviolent and their crime patterns are closer to those of heroin addicts who exhibit primarily property oriented crimes than to alcoholics who have high rates of violent crime.

Cost Assessment

Estimates of the percentage of probationers and inmates who are pathological gamblers range from 14 to 30 percent. There is no accurate estimate of how many got there as a result of gambling-related offenses. In one study, 13 percent of both male and female prisoners stated they were in prison as a result of gambling-related debt. The cost of arrest, prosecution, probation, parole, and imprisonment must also be figured into the total cost of pathological gambling to the general society.

The relatively high rate of illegal activity among pathological gamblers and its obvious social cost makes it imperative that probationers, parolees, and inmates be screened. Treatment for gambling should be provided along with treatment for alcoholism and for drug addiction.

How does one measure the cost of pathological gambling? The financial costs seem fairly straightforward. If the 514 million-dollars-a-year figure for New Jersey can be believed, even one-third of this figure extrapolated to the United States would mean billions of dollars in loans every year. If the 1.3 billion dollars in insurance fraud is accurate, this must also be added to other theft and fraud engaged in by pathological gamblers. The costs to employers is also immense and has not yet been measured. Similarly, the expense of prosecution, probation, prison, and parole for pathological gamblers driven to crime to support their obsession has not been studied. However, if the 13 percent figure arrived at in New Jersey (or even half of it) is accurate, these costs are enormous as well.

While financial costs can be assessed, how does one measure the cost of a suicide attempt, an ulcer, a child filled with anger and hatred for a parent or using drugs to obliterate painful memories? We could conceivably measure these in terms of cost of medical care, psychiatric care, marriage counseling, suicide prevention, drug prevention and other counseling. The greatest difficulty lies in measuring the intangible. Loss of trust in a marriage, divorce and separation, heart wrenching tears, burning anger, shame, resentment and guilt, all leave emotional scars wrought by gambling-related problems.

No statistical evidence exists that confirms that the legalization of gambling increases the rate of pathological gambling. However, as noted above, there is an association between legalization and the extent of gambling problems. Calls to hotlines in Maryland, New Jersey, and New York reveal that the majority of callers are dependent on legalized forms of gambling. In New Jersey, for example, 62 percent of the callers mention problems with casino gambling, 33 percent with horse racing, 38 percent with state run lotteries, 10 percent with bingo, and 8 percent with stocks and commodities. (These figures add up to more than 100 percent because many pathological gamblers have problems with more than one type of gambling.)

State Responsibility

Gambling problems are not evenly distributed across the general population. Epidemiological surveys indicate that the problem is greater among the poor and minorities than other segments of the population. There is also evidence that the poor, minorities, and women are grossly underserved by available treatment resources. There are long waiting lists (up to six months) in states with some treatment services to pathological gamblers and their families. In spite of enormous gaming revenues the states receive and the enormous expenditures for advertising to attract new customers or repeat business, these same states devote nothing or only meager resources to education and training of professionals and the general public about problem gambling.

At present, only Massachusetts, Connecticut, New York, New Jersey, Maryland, Iowa, Minnesota and Delaware parcel out money to deal with problem gambling. Connecticut, Maryland, and Delaware spend less than 100 thousand dollars per year each. Massachusetts and Iowa recently cut the budget devoted to the issue and the governor of New York proposed wiping it out altogether while floating plans to legalize sports gambling to ease the fiscal crisis. In the 1990/91 fiscal year, the New Jersey state treasury took in a net sum of 783 million dollars from various sources (after winners were paid out and other expenses), yet the state spent only 260 thousand dollars for all compulsive gambling-related programs combined—in other words, only 3/100 of a percent of its gambling revenues—this in a state where compulsive gamblers accumulate an estimated 514 million dollars in gambling-related debts per year. The irony is that New Jersey is one of the most generous states. Nevada, for example, contributes nothing to education, training, research, or treatment of problem gambling.

Surveys indicate that approximately 1 to 2 percent of the adult population are probably pathological gamblers and 2 to 3 percent are problem gamblers. We have *no* estimates of what percentage of total gaming revenues are produced by problem gamblers. Given that they expend much more money than the typical player, it would not be unreasonable to estimate that at least 10 percent (and possibly as much as 50 percent) of gaming revenues are produced by problem gamblers.

Given this simple reality, I propose the following steps to be taken: 1) No new forms of gambling should be legalized without first providing treatment on demand for gambling-related problems in all localities of a state. A no-waiting-list policy should be adopted whereby all costs of treatment should be derived from gambling revenues. This does not mean that the state should be responsible for the gamblers' debts, but it should be responsible for providing adequate treatment programs for the gamblers and their families.

2) No promotion of gambling should be allowed without a warning label and an 800 helpline number to call for those with gambling problems. The full cost of the helpline would be derived from gaming revenues or specific gambling fees (possible sources include but are not limited to unclaimed prizes, taxes on gaming machines, entree fees, and so on).

3) Careful epidemiological studies of all gamblers should be conducted to gain an estimate of what percentage of the money wagered is being wagered by problem gamblers.

5) A percentage of the revenues lost by problem gamblers (and hence, are added to state coffers through state gambling taxes) should be devoted to education, treatment, and research.

National Attention

Gambling has national implications and consequences. Gamblers from Minnesota, Illinois, and Florida travel to Las Vegas, Atlantic City, Deadwood, and other gambling heavens. People from the Dakotas, Iowa and Wisconsin venture to race tracks in neighboring states and vice versa. In some instances the local lottery ticket agent in an adjoining state is closer than the one from your own state. Players win money in one state only to lose it in another. They also lose money and make cash transfers from their home state to the host. In some cases they lose money in one state and steal in another in order to repay their debts. The common feature of interstate gambling is that most benefits, such as increased jobs and the "voluntary tax" revenues, appear to be local while some (though by no means all) of the problems are exported. Pathological gambling is clearly a problem with costs that cross state boundaries.

Gambling is not just an interstate problem. It also has implications for one of America's most poverty stricken and oppressed minorities—Native Americans. On the federal level, the Indian Gaming Regulatory Act of 1988 has allowed Indian tribes to operate any form of gambling currently legalized in the state in which the tribe resides. Ironically, this opportunity for entrepreneurship and self-reliance has improved the lot of some tribes—which now have their own unemployment insurance and poverty relief programs funded by gambling proceeds—and has the potential of reducing federal aid to the tribes involved. On the other hand, Indian gambling has its victims as well. Like the states with neighbors who gamble, most of the benefits appear to be localized while the problems are exported. The major question then becomes, how can we allow people who want to gamble, and groups that need the economic benefits that can accrue from operating gambling operations, pursue their goals with a minimum amount of disruption to potential pathological gamblers and their families?

A national commission on compulsive gambling is needed to investigate the issues discussed. Short of this, federal legislation is needed to provide education, treatment and research into pathological gambling. Ideally, the National Institute on Drug Abuse and the National Institute on Alcoholism and Alcohol Abuse would have another counterpart, a National Institute on Problem Gambling. If governments benefit from gambling revenues, they have an obligation to help those who are hurt by their actions.

REFUTING THE MYTHS OF COMPULSIVE
GAMBLING[2]

Robert Terry, the *Philadelphia Inquirer's* chief police reporter, borrowed money from that city's police commissioner and other department officials. Despite the fact that such borrowing creates a blatant conflict of interest, Terry was suspended *with pay,* with no decision made on a final disciplinary action. His managing editor, James Naughton, accepted Terry's explanation that it was a "disease" of gambling that put him in sure dire straits. Naughton stated that he would await the outcome of a therapy program intended to cure Terry's "disease" before rendering final judgment.

In 1992, former "ABC Monday Night Football" producer Chet Forte was given a suspended sentence for bank fraud and income tax irregularities after Gamblers Anonymous testified at his sentencing hearing.

Former Baltimore Colt quarterback Art Schlichter went from object of scorn to one of pity in 1983 when it was claimed that his wagering, which had cost him hundreds of thousands of dollars, was the result of the "disease of compulsive gambling" (sometimes called "pathological gambling"). The late psychiatrist Robert Custer, often referred to as the father of compulsive gambling, stated, "Art has suffered the full effects of his disease."

In mid 1989, it was revealed that baseball hero Pete Rose dropped more than $500,000 through heavy gambling. It also was reported that he had to sell treasured memorabilia because of his debts. After weeks of bad press following a denial that he had a problem with gambling, Rose made a public statement that he had what his recently acquired psychiatrist called "a clinically significant gambling disorder" that rendered him powerless over his gambling. He then went on a media tour, during which he was greeted by a lengthy standing ovation from Phil Donahue's television audience and congratulations for his "admission" from Barbara Walters. Rose had gone from miscreant to courageous victim.

[2]Article by Richard E. Vatz & Lee S. Weinberg. From *USA Today Magazine,* Nov '93. Copyright © 1993 by the Society for the Advancement of Education. Reprinted with permission.

Since then, press attention to compulsive gambling—with uncritical acceptance of its being an illness and uncontrollable—has abounded. It has been heralded as the "Addiction of the 1990s." In the *Journal of Gambling Studies (JGS)*, the major academic journal on gambling and social issues, editor Henry Lesieur wrote quite accurately in 1992 that "Not a day goes by . . . without something appearing in the professional literature or mass media about compulsive gambling."

The groundwork for the successful promotion of the disease model for heavy gambling was laid firmly more than a decade ago. After years of what *JGS* called his "unflagging advocacy," Custer persuaded The American Psychiatric Association in its 1980 update of the *Diagnostic and Statistical Manual (DSM-III)* to elevate gambling to one of its categories of impulse disorders or, more specifically, a "Disorder of Impulse Control not Elsewhere Classified." This act was heralded in articles and media appearances by prominent gambling researchers as establishing that heavy, self-destructive gambling was a disease, the medical identity that was seen as necessary for sympathy for heavy bettors, and status and financial support (third-party payments, grants, etc.) for the researchers themselves, of whom few were—or are—medical doctors. If such gambling were a disease (the manual uses the term disorder, but its "nomenclature" specialist, Robert Spitzer, claims that it may be considered the same as disease), it was axiomatic that it was beyond the individual's control.

The problem is that there is no evidence that compulsive gambling is a disease (a point psychiatrist Thomas Szasz has made for decades) or uncontrollable. Revealingly, there are indications that, at least as far as the disease claim is concerned, many gambling researchers don't believe it either. Moreover, the consequences of accepting compulsive gambling as addictive or uncontrollable may be to hinder efforts of heavy gamblers to resist their urges.

Psychiatry's diagnostic manual lists no medical criteria in its "diagnostic criteria" for pathological gambling, only those referring to frequency of wagering and its social, financial, and legal consequences. Put simply, heavy gambling is not an illness in the sense that most people think of one. There is no credible evidence whatsoever of any neurochemical or neurophysiological status causally linked to heavy gambling, only changes such as increased adrenaline or palpitations caused by the excitement of the action. No study has found any neurobiological status specific to compulsive gamblers as contrasted with other excitable people. Yet, the finding of neurobiological correlates—especially if they were specific to heavy gambling—would constitute a Holy Grail for researchers, providing a basis for maintaining that it is a disease and uncontrollable.

Thus, it was discouraging to gambling researchers in the late 1980s (and confirmed in recent follow-ups) when a year-long study at the National Institute of Alcohol Abuse and Alcoholism showed no differences in serotonin levels between compulsive gamblers and normal men. A positive finding could have been used to argue that such gamblers lacked impulse control.

In 1989, however, gambling researchers argued that they finally had their "proof." A study published in *The Archives of General Psychiatry* found that 17 heavy gamblers had neurochemical elevations correlated with their "extroversion." The article was —and continues to be—heralded by gambling researchers and the popular press as evidence that gamblers' biology is destiny. *The New York Times* headline read: "Gambling: Biology May Hold Key," and a piece in the February, 1992, *Harvard Mental Health Letter* argued that the 1989 study demonstrates that "The gambling addiction may even have a physiological basis."

Even this study, the gambling researchers' best evidence that chronic gambling is compulsive and a disease, proved little beyond what one would expect—namely, that gamblers are excitable personalities who evidence heightened neurological measures of excitement. It demonstrates neither that such biological differences are causal nor that they are specific to compulsive gamblers or even gamblers at all. As the study's senior researcher, psychiatrist Alec Roy concedes, the gamblers "were not compared to other groups, so we cannot answer the question with regard to specificity." He adds that no follow-up studies have been done or currently are being done to his knowledge.

Responsible gambling researchers do not maintain that there is any proof of biological causation in compulsive gambling. Sirgay Sanger, [former] president of the National Council on Problem Gambling, admits in *The Journal of the American Medical Association* what one rarely, if ever, reads in gambling researchers' quotes in the popular press: Pathological gambling "has the smell of a biochemical addiction in it," but, he admits, "there is no research proof."

The most prominent medical doctor promoting the gambling-as-disease concept is psychiatrist Sheila Blume, the medical director for the alcoholism, chemical-dependency, and compulsive gambling programs at South Oaks Hospital, Amityville, N.Y. She often talks about heavy gambling as an illness, but there is reason to believe she doubts the claim herself and uses medical language only for strategic purposes.

In an article in *JGS*, Blume makes a remarkably frank recommendation that, regardless of objections to the medical model, heavy gambling should be considered an illness for practical benefits for gamblers and their doctors: "It is concluded that the many individual and social advantages of the medical model make it the preferred conceptualization of our present state of knowledge." Lesieur also has cited the strategic importance of public acceptance of pathological gambling as an illness, arguing that, without it, the gamblers themselves are less likely to accept the disease model, an acceptance he views as crucial to successful treatment.

Valerie Lorenz is executive director of the National Center for Pathological Gambling and one of the most vocal promoters of the illness model for gambling in her constant beseechings for governmental and other source funding. She sees the acceptance of gambling-as-illness as critical to legal exculpation and counsels that "the expert witness for the compulsive gambler facing legal charges" must "educate" judges and others as to the "illness" of the "compulsive gambler" in legal trouble, in order to avoid the unfair punishing of those who are "seriously disturbed" and "out of control."

Significantly, Norman Rose, a professor of law and vice-president of the California Council on Compulsive Gambling, who, according to *JGS*, is the "nation's leading authority on gambling and the law," disputes the medical model for compulsive gambling. In an interview, he expressed skepticism regarding the notion that heavy gambling can be a disease: "I have a lot of trouble with that idea, especially within the law, where it is used as an excuse." In terms of insanity-like defenses, wherein people are found not guilty of crimes by virtue of suffering from pathological gambling, Rose says, "It just doesn't work anymore," even though the plea still is attempted. What does work to some degree—and probably is increasing in usage—is its employment in criminal cases to provide alternative sentencing programs comparable to alcohol treatment programs, as well as in divorces, tax problems, and bankruptcy.

Regardless of questions of validity, the public appears conditioned to call any deviant behavior disease if the situation entails sufficient poignancy. In an article in *Good Housekeeping* titled "When Gambling Becomes a Disease," the magazine asserts that "It is only when gambling overtakes a person's life that it moves from recreation to an illness." However, does gambling *really* overtake people's lives?

Is compulsive gambling treatable?

In the wake of the claim of the astronomical prevalence (almost six percent of all adults in Maryland—more than one in every 20) of problem or pathological gambling, legislation was passed in Maryland to require all state lottery tickets to carry the following warning: "Compulsive gambling is a treatable illness." Those six words concede all three of the major disputable claims of the gambling researchers: that heavy, self-destructive gambling is an illness, is uncontrollable, and is treatable, which implies that treatment programs have been shown to be significantly helpful to those who seek aid to resist the urges. (The study was fueled by a National Institute of Mental Health study using a broad definition of pathological gambling, nearly guaranteeing a large claim.)

Researchers who argue that compulsive gambling is beyond control believe the proof to be self-evident by virtue of the devastating consequences of such activity and confirmed by the participants' claims that they can not stop. How, they wonder, could people willfully gamble themselves into such financial, legal, and family problems, consequences that define for the most part gamblers' "chronic and progressive failure to resist impulses to gamble" as required for psychiatry's current diagnostic manual (*DSM-III-R*)? This is, of course, a circular definition, as no one can verify a person's ability to control his or her behavior. Let us look at that assertion with reason as a guide.

When we wrote an article several years ago that "control" is not accessible or measurable except through the potentially self-serving claims of gamblers, Blume responded by accusing us of saying that gamblers could not be believed. Leaving aside that researchers invariably insist that lying is one of the cardinal signs of the compulsive gambler, the point is that a claim of inability to control one's gambling—even if made sincerely—can not logically confirm such inability. At most, the statement might reveal his or her honest belief.

Chet Forte, who gambled himself into millions of dollars of

losses, has asked rhetorically how anyone could think he willfully would have "gone through the money" or "destroyed my family"? The answer is twofold. First, his stated concern for his family notwithstanding, many heavy gamblers—including, perhaps, Forte, according to a letter written to us by his first cousin, Anne Perrin, and her husband—simply don't care so much about their families.

Gambling researchers themselves are aware that the image of the heavy gambler whose actions destroy what otherwise would be a great family man (most heavy gamblers are men) is simply a myth. Most compulsive gamblers are not committed family men, with or without their gambling. Perrin stated that Forte defrauded her family, despite his being "someone my mother helped put through college and whose parents were constantly helped financially by my parents!" She adds that Forte has no real remorse and quotes him as saying that he learned that, "when you are stealing, steal big." Along a similar line, gambling researchers who attribute great social costs to gambling, such as those to businesses due to lost productivity, do not consider the possibility that a compulsive gambler who wasn't gambling would not be very productive or might have high absenteeism regardless.

Second, gambling is exciting for many reasons, including the risks and opportunities it provides for "big wins," as well as extensive losses. Heavy gamblers often engage in "chasing," which involves a type of exponentially increasing betting that can win back losses quickly, even substantial ones. Gamblers don't expect to lose.

The assumption that they can not control their urges figures largely in gambling treatment programs, as it does with those for other behavioral "addictions." In fact, the first in the well-known Twelve Steps of Recovery common to such programs is that the addict must admit that he or she has a problem (or illness) and is powerless to resist it. Despite the exaggerated claims of the promoters of groups like Gamblers Anonymous (GA) and Alcoholics Anonymous, there is little or no evidence of their widespread success. With respect to compulsive gamblers, anecdotes exist in abundance, but there are few studies available on the outcomes of such group-oriented treatment.

What studies there are reveal very limited success in achieving gambling abstinence. The astronomical dropout rate of 70% and more in GA and other groups makes it appear that whatever success there is—and sometimes high rates are claimed—is due largely to the high level of commitment of those who stay in the program, rather than the program itself. Neither is abstinence verifiable.

It is time for at least some skepticism regarding the unquestioned need for addicts to admit powerlessness over their own behavior. It is worth considering whether such admissions constitute a self-fulfilling prophesy—that is to say, the belief that a habit is uncontrollable actually may discourage people from trying to stop behaving in a self-destructive manner since it is beyond their control.

Assertions that heavy, destructive gambling is a disease, uncontrollable, and treatable simply do not withstand close scrutiny. Questionable research, reasoning, and evidence are used to criticize the existence of state lotteries, exculpate irresponsible behavior of heavy gamblers, and, in the case of treatment, perhaps undermine efforts to help people resist the urge to gamble. That the unique excitement and risk-taking motivates some people to neglect many important aspects of their lives is intriguing, but not overly surprising. It is the medicalizing of heavy gambling that makes it seem so utterly mysterious.

The debate about compulsive gambling, like that about other self-destructive or socially unacceptable behaviors ranging from compulsive drinking to compulsive shopping (a supposed new disorder whose advocates urge its inclusion in the next review of psychiatry's diagnostic manual), ultimately comes down to a single question: Should individuals who engage in these behaviors be excused on the grounds that they suffer from a disorder that produces urges they are unable to resist? Without further evidence, we believe the answer to be no.

Whether talking about newspaper employees who have a conflict of interest due to borrowing to pay off gambling debts, people who defraud banks and associates, or athletes who bet on games in violation of league rules, there should be no general moral or legal recognition of compulsive gambling disorder as a valid reason for such behavior. The practical effect of recognizing disorders is to make these excuses significant because they are alleged disorders while rejecting other exculpatory claims.

The implication of this position, however, is not that no differences exist among individual cases of misconduct or self-destructive conduct. Quite the contrary. For instance, the employee who embezzles money to pay for a child's medical care may be entitled to more consideration than the one who pleads compulsive gambling. While both should be made to repay the stolen money, perhaps the former, not the latter, is entitled to a second chance. This much is clear: it is time to stop all special consideration for those whose excuses are sympathy-provoking only because they bear the unscientific "disorder" imprimatur of psychiatry.

TREATMENT OF PATHOLOGICAL GAMBLING[3]

Abstinence Versus Controlled Gambling

The prevailing goal of most treatment programs for pathological gambling is total abstinence from gambling. This goal is a further indication of the conceptual and organizational resemblance between Alcoholic's Anonymous and Gambler's Anonymous. It is common in each group respectively to speak of the "recovering alcoholic" or the "recovering pathological gambler," but never "recovered." Both groups invoke a particular version of the disease model which dictates that once stricken, never cured. Even the National Council on Problem Gambling's motto, "Compulsive gambling is a treatable disorder," does not include the additional notion of *cure*.

Inpatient and residential rehabilitation treatment programs generally reflect this underlying assumption of the chronic and incurable nature of pathological gambling. In these programs, counseling and group therapy are used to develop what they maintain is necessary insight in the pathological gambler about the ongoing risk of remission and to support the recovering gambler's resolve to live the rest of his or her life without gambling. Generally, participation in group therapy means a mixture of attendance at GA meetings and participation in other group sessions led by a trained counselor. Regular participation at GA meetings is usually considered to be the most significant step a pathological gambler can take in the process of recovery because

[3]Article by Martin C. McGurrin, reprinted from *Pathological Gambling: Conceptual, Diagnostic and Treatment Issues*, 36–58, by Martin C. McGurrin, Sarasota, Fla.: Professional Resource Press, 1994.

GA members are considered, by GA at least, to be the "true experts" in helping pathological gamblers in the recovery process.

Advocates of the treatment goal of total abstinence have had almost exclusive control over the formulation of policy and treatment goals for all public-sponsored treatment programs for pathological gamblers in the United States. This dominance has been granted to these advocates because of the general acceptance of GA's other major foundational argument that pathological gambling is a disease. The uncritical conceptualization of pathological gambling as a disease with primarily biological causation rather than as a behavioral disorder resulting from a complex process of behavioral conditioning and/or psychological conflict has thus far resulted in most inpatient and residential treatment being managed under a medical model of care and decision-making authority. The bias of the disease model has been criticized for limiting the range of treatment and research on pathological gambling. Debate over both the validity and utility of the disease model of gambling and the related medical model of treatment has been waged with the same level of intensity and lack of rational resolution as has been true in the field of alcohol and drug abuse. A critical review of the literature on the comparative analysis of gambling as a disease versus a behavioral disorder is beyond the scope of this guide, but it is important . . . to realize that this debate remains a volatile issue and has very strong implications for treatment programs and techniques.

The overall effectiveness of treatment focused exclusively, or even primarily, on total abstinence has definite limitations and may even be counterproductive to the effective treatment of problem gamblers. Although GA's use of the term disease implies a rather uniform causal dynamic underlying pathological gambling, there is already a sufficient body of clinical and research data to suggest that any single cause and single treatment is naïve and excessively simplistic.

The emphasis on uninterrupted abstinence as the primary indication of treatment success can actually backfire when pathological gamblers experience episodic relapse into gambling activity. Although attendance at GA meetings often provides sufficient peer support to achieve temporary remission, the recurrence of gambling activity is fairly common and may lead recovering gamblers into self-defeating gambling binges because they feel they will never succeed in sustained abstinence. Rather than attempting to control their gambling during these relapses, they seem to prefer instead "the voluptuousness of giving oneself up for lost." Several investigators have reported on the high dropout rate from GA. Additionally the fact is that some categories of persons such as women, racial minorities, and adolescents usually do not even join GA because they feel uncomfortable about their under-representation.

Controlled Gambling. The alternative to total abstinence and life-long involvement in GA is generally referred to as *controlled gambling*. Like its counterpart in the treatment of alcohol abuse, *controlled drinking*, it represents a minority position and is generally criticized more as ideological heresy than an alternative treatment approach that should be evaluated scientifically. One of the primary supporters of treatment designed to develop a capacity for controlled gambling has been John Rosecrance. He has based his own approach on work done outside the United States where both controlled drinking and controlled gambling have enjoyed more widespread and objective reception among treatment and research professionals. Specifically, he cites the British and Australian successes in controlled gambling programs. The Australian reports are especially noteworthy because controlled gambling has been part of comprehensive treatment programs for over 5 years.

Rosecrance's central argument for treatment goal alternatives to abstinence is that

current treatment programs by demanding abstinence often cause delays in seeking treatment since troubled gamblers are reluctant to permanently give up an activity that serves as an important source of excitement and camaraderie in their lives. At present, gamblers assume that if they want treatment they must first agree to give up gambling. Therefore, only desperate losers are willing to seek help. It seems wasteful to discourage all but the most severely troubled from seeking assistance. Controlled programs, by offering an alternative approach, are capable of reaching gamblers who have not yet hit "rock bottom" but who nevertheless are experiencing serious problems related to gambling.

Following Oldman's model of problem gambling ["Compulsive Gamblers." *Sociological Review* 26, 1978 349–370], Rosecrance virtually rejects the concept of *pathological* gambling and any underlying uncontrollable impulse to gamble and argues that problem gambling results from inappropriate gambling strategies rather than psychological disorders. The proper response to correct this problem is to educate so-called pathological gamblers to utilize more appropriate strategies in their gambling activity.

This never happens in the current conventional gambling treatment programs in the United States because treatment staff not only reject the basic concept of controlled gambling, but also because of:

1. Lack of knowledge concerning appropriate gaming strategies and/or money management.

2. An inability to develop empathy for gamblers who want to maintain participation in an ongoing treatment program while continuing to gamble.

3. The fact that inappropriate strategies are manifested outside of a counseling setting.

4. Failure to be aware of sources that could aid gamblers in developing appropriate strategies.

Rosecrance has provided a general description of the basic components of a controlled gambling rehabilitation program but has not yet reported or made available a fully detailed program manual that can be used for establishing such a program. Basically, the staff includes some mental health professionals such as psychologists, psychiatrists, or psychiatric social workers. The core counselors, however, are active gamblers who are able to provide empathic understanding of the problem gambler's plight and also can provide objective and technically informed evaluation and correction of the problem gambler's inappropriate gambling strategies. The mutual understanding of the gambling experience that exists between this peer counselor and client supposedly allows them to relate on both a cognitive and affective level. Problem gamblers are highly motivated to learn new strategies and modify their gambling behavior because the peer counselor is not focused on extinguishing gambling activity, but instead is perceived by clients as a knowledgeable compatriot who is providing useful and relevant counsel that will allow clients to resolve a *gambling problem* without having to give up gambling. Rosecrance ["Controlled Gambling: A Promising Future." *in* H.J.S. Laffer et al. *Compulsive Gambling* pp. 147–160] reports substantial success with at least one controlled gambling program that rehabilitated 50 clients who met the [the American Psychiatric Association's] criteria for pathological gambling. Certainly additional application and evaluation of this rehabilitation model is required before it can be reasonably appraised as an effective alternative to abstinence, but initial results suggest that it may be useful for at least some pathological gamblers.

Synoptic Model. Other less radical rehabilitation models have been proposed as alternatives to the orthodox disease model of pathological gambling with its requirements of total abstinence. These models are conceptually related to social learning theory and basic cybernetic or cognitive feedback principles.

One example of these alternative models is Abt, McGurrin, and Smith's synoptic model [*Journal of Gambling Behavior, 1,* 1985, 79–80]. This model regards pathological gambling as the outcome of the gamblers' failure to integrate the norms of the gambling situation with their own motivations and to use feedback provided in the actual gambling situation to correct their increasingly problematic behavior. Gambling is conceptualized as social behavior that achieves meaning by reference to the contexts in which it occurs. For example, the apparently objective monetary costs and benefits of gambling are often regarded within the reference frame of gambling as symbols of the gambler's willingness to sacrifice in order to achieve the ecstasy and release of "the action." Judgments about the irrationality of betting in the face of unfavorable odds may be very incomplete without also calculating the other rewards which the gambler achieves simply by participating in the process of gambling. Gamblers play under many different conditions and for many different reasons. The synoptic model focuses, therefore, on a gambler's evaluation of the meaning of gaming activities within a social context. It regards the gambler's information processing activity as the principal mechanism that integrates societal (macro level) and individual (micro level) causes of gambling behavior.

The synoptic model represents the gambler's reality with eight interrelated sets of variables.

The macro level of the gambler's social reality consists of

1. status variables such as socioeconomic status, marital status, and disposable time and income;

2. situational variables such as opportunity to gamble and number of gambling colleagues;

3. contextual variables such as local gambling regulations and statutes;

4. social transformation rules which are the social norms that define the general values and conduct of the gambling environment; and

5. gambling event variables such as type of equipment and odds.

The micro level consists of

6. psychological variables such as self-esteem, personality disorder, and locus of control;

7. the gambling action such as actual gambling styles and strategies; and

8. social feedback signal variables such as peer approval and perceived cost/benefit outcomes after a series of wagers.

The application of the macro and micro level transformation rules by gamblers in a particular situation is the means by which gamblers produce a framework of meaning to evaluate the degree to which their conduct and its consequences are validating their self-image as a successful gambler. For example, if a gambler receives feedback that he or she is being a *poor loser,* this will also signal that he or she is a poor gambler, because manifest discontent about losing is a deviation from the universal gambling norm that calls for stoic acceptance of loss as an integral part of the action. Accepting random losses gracefully shows character and style which is itself a basis for winning respect from fellow gamblers. As with many other forms of social behavior, unfavorable peer evaluation based on the gambler's failure to *play by the rules* may be experienced as a far greater loss than a financial loss on a series of gaming outcomes. In the long run, a gambler's sense of success or failure at gambling usually depends on an interrelated set of variables and not just on calculated financial gains or losses as may be the case for nongamblers.

McGurrin (1989) has developed some treatment applications of the synoptic model. One of these applications can be demonstrated by continuing with the example of the *poor loser, poor gambler* situation. Because many pathological gamblers are found to have low self-esteem and are very reactive to the judgment of fellow gamblers, the therapist should first assess the particular client's level of self-esteem and sensitivity to issues of self-worth. If the client has low self-esteem, the therapist hypothesizes that the client's practice of escalating bets after losses is not only a method of attempting to recover financial loss, but also and especially a means of accentuating the gambler's style of remaining cool and unthreatened in the face of recurring lost bets. The therapist then employs a simulated gambling situation with the client in which the client is allowed to increase amounts bet in response to losses but is given feedback by the therapist that a strategy that increases risk of further losses suggests a loss of control and indicates panic in the client. The therapist then substitutes the feedback of reduced approval of gambling style with each loss. After a series of five or six such bets and feedback messages, the therapist involves the client in discussion about motives for increasing the amount of money bet in each play of the game. The therapist points out that the client would have just as likely gained respect from other gamblers if the client had accepted his or her losses and not tried to recover large amounts on a single bet. The therapist also suggests that the client could have quit at any time and resumed betting at some other time. This decision to stop gambling temporarily could be viewed by others as a sign of good gambling judgment worthy of respect. This exercise is repeated at least several times depending on how responsive the client is and how much insight seems to develop each time it is carried out.

In a second example of synoptic applications, the therapist informs the client that he or she will be required to guess the numeric identity of a card drawn from the top of a set of five ordinary numbered playing cards. After the therapist shuffles the cards, the client is asked to identify the top card and the therapist then reveals the card's numeric identity. Let us assume that the client correctly guesses the card's numeric identity on the first shuffle. Whenever the card is correctly identified, the client is asked to read aloud the following printed message provided by the therapist:

I have just correctly identified the top card before you turned it over. That is not easy to do and you and I know it. I like the feeling I get from winning at games of chance. Let us try it again to see whether I guess it right or wrong.

After the client reads the message, the therapist reshuffles the cards and asks the client to guess the top card. This continues until the client incorrectly guesses the card's identity.

Whenever the client guesses the card's identity incorrectly twice in a row, the client is asked to read aloud the following printed message provided by the therapist:

I have just incorrectly identified the card twice in a row. I do not know why I should continue guessing if I am losing. If I were betting money, I would be losing money also. Usually when I lose, I lose money and I lose the feeling of excitement from winning.

After the client reads the message, the therapist asks the client to explain what is wrong with the message. The dialogue typically takes the following form:

Therapist: Tell me what is wrong with that message you just read.
Client: Nothing, I guess. You know it makes sense.
Therapist: No, tell me what is wrong with it.
Client: What? I don't know.
Therapist: Yes you know, you said the message makes sense, but you don't act that way. Don't you make sense?
Client: Oh, you mean my compulsive gambling?
Therapist: Yes, what makes it different from the message?

The therapist keeps directing discussions about discrepancies between the message and the client's acknowledged gambling behavior by requesting that the client explain his or her motivation for continuing the discrepancies when the client gambles. The therapist concludes each such discussion by emphasizing that normal gamblers set an early limit on continuing losses and win other people's respect for doing so. The card selecting, message reading, and related feedback discussion are repeated several times in a session.

Applications such as the two examples just presented are included in as many sessions as the therapist judges to be useful in assisting the client to recognize and utilize corrective feedback regarding problematic gambling behavior. The therapist should anticipate that many clients will experience these applications as simplistic and artificial compared to actual gambling situations. The client should be told at the outset that the primary purpose of the application is to enhance the client's use of feedback rather than providing a gambling opportunity.

The synoptic feedback approach provides a means by which the therapist becomes a relevant source of information and influence in changing the client's gambling behavior without totally separating the client from gambling through required abstinence. The synoptic technique is not used as a total replacement for other aspects of therapeutic intervention with the pathological gambler, but is intended as a supplemental approach in cases where controlled gambling is a tentatively accepted treatment goal. More conventional techniques that focus on affective issues and family dynamics should also be included in the treatment plan.

The synoptic technique has not been used with any pathological gamblers during inpatient rehabilitation. It has been found to be partially successful with some pathological gamblers who entered outpatient therapy without any previous inpatient care, and with some pathological gamblers who had inpatient care but did not sustain abstinence during aftercare outpatient therapy. There is currently insufficient data to reliably evaluate the long-range (i.e., 10 years) effectiveness of the controlled gambling and synoptic model techniques in treating pathological gamblers. These techniques may be limited in effectiveness to pathological gamblers who have not yet lost complete control over the impulse to gamble. They are available, however, to all persons who need to modify their gambling activity and would participate in treatment so long as it does not require abstinence. There are a substantial number of problem and pathological gamblers to whom this condition applies.

Inpatient Treatment

The majority of pathological gamblers begin treatment in specialized inpatient programs because they have denied the need for treatment until major life disruptions have seriously affected their personal, marital, and vocational functioning and financial status. Typically, there will be a crisis that involves several of these areas simultaneously. By this point, gamblers may already have experienced several months of increasingly intense and frequent anxiety attacks, periods of insomnia, and recurrent alternation between manic and depressed affect. They recognize the developing crises in their life and understand their inability to continue avoiding or escaping the consequences of their gambling activity. Gamblers may also report dissociative-like experiences or feelings of derealization that create great difficulty in concentrating and completing routine tasks. Thoughts of suicide, or even threats of suicide to family members and friends, are fairly common at this point.

The most widely accepted model of the natural course of pathological gambling has been developed by Custer. This model represents the development of pathological gambling disorder as a passage through sequential phases of loss of control over gambling and increasing personal and social problems related to gambling. A final "hitting bottom" phase occurs when the gambler's life is in general crisis and often warrants inpatient treatment.

Inpatient admission based on a primary diagnosis of pathological gambling is rare because of the difficulty in acquiring private health insurers' preapproval of payment for inpatient care of an individual with this diagnosis. Because the gambler at this point of crisis is usually suffering from acute anxiety, depression, and suicidal ideation, and may have been abusing alcohol or drugs sufficiently to require detoxification, the more typical admitting diagnosis is appropriately one of the several Mood Disorders or Psychoactive Substance Use Disorders. At private hospitals with specific programs for treatment of pathological gamblers, the gambler and a family member are often interviewed separately by telephone in advance of actual admission to determine if the gambler can be admitted under an appropriate diagnosis. If accepted, the gambler is then evaluated and assigned an official diagnosis by a staff psychiatrist as a part of the official admission process.

Most formal inpatient and rehabilitation programs are 20 to 30 days in length and have a treatment cost ranging from $20,000 to $28,000. Patients typically receive basic medical, psychiatric, and psychological assessments preliminary to the assignment to a treatment team and development of a treatment plan. Treatment teams usually consist of a staff psychiatrist, a primary therapist or counselor, and a social worker who coordinates and acts as a liaison to family, employers, and other significant persons who are outside of the hospital. Primary therapists or counselors are often master's level psychologists, MSWs, psychiatric nurses, or addiction counselors.

Treatment objectives during the first week generally involve stabilizing the patient emotionally, selecting and monitoring medications if indicated, and orienting the patient to hospital and treatment program regulations. Patients are required to follow highly structured schedules of daily activity which can include prohibiting all contact with family members or others outside of the hospital until the treatment team allows such contact. Telephone use is a scheduled and closely monitored privilege during most of the treatment program. This enforced, detention-like atmosphere is maintained to prohibit access to alcohol, drugs, or the opportunity to place bets or gamble. The total abstinence from addictive substances and behavior is a control goal of most treatment programs, and is usually a requirement for being allowed to remain in the program.

By the middle of the first week, the patient is involved in group therapy sessions. These focus on reducing the patients' denial of their inability to gamble in a normal, controlled manner. It is important for them to recognize that what they had believed were their own private techniques for beating the odds in gambling are essentially the same unsuccessful techniques employed by the other pathological gamblers in the group. Groups often include a volunteer who is a recovering gambler as a means of introducing the patient to the concept of peer counseling or sponsorship on the part of GA.

There is usually a strong educational component introduced into treatment by the second week. Patients are required to attend sessions in which they are counseled on personal finances and money management. Often they must develop a time schedule for paying back the debts incurred through gambling. It is thought to be very important that the patient accept responsibility for paying back debts without financial assistance from family or friends. This requirement not only confronts patients with issues they will encounter after they have left the hospital, but also discourages resumption of co-dependent relationships with family members, which have been interrupted by inpatient treatment.

During the first 2 weeks of treatment, family members are seen collaterally by a member of the treatment team. The goals of these sessions are to (a) educate them on the disorder of pathological gambling, (b) inform them about the goals of the patient's treatment plan, (c) allow the treatment team member to develop impressions of the family's dynamics, and (d) provide initial supportive therapy to family members (especially the spouse) who may be dealing with mixed feelings of resentment, guilt, and neglect in the face of all the attention and support that is being directed toward the patient.

By the third week, many programs include spouses and, sometimes, other key family members, in group sessions. This allows both patients and family members to recognize the common features of pathological gambling that have affected other patients and their families. Pathological gambling, as with other pathological behavior, is typically the "great family secret" that family members do not discuss and that they collectively deny. Sessions involving patients and family members are very useful in teaching families to acknowledge the problem gambling and discuss it in a healthy and constructive manner. These sessions also encourage the emotional expression that has often been avoided by the family. The therapist can offer assurance that such expression may benefit them, that they will not be allowed to exceed the limits of the therapeutic situation, and that, over time, they can integrate the material in a meaningful way.

Many inpatient programs schedule GA meetings in the hospital several evenings a week. This allows patients to begin attending meetings as well as to have further contact with peer counselors. It also helps develop the practice of attending meetings which will be important to patients after their release.

Outpatient Treatment

Outpatient therapy may begin under either of two different conditions. First, and most common, the client has recently completed an inpatient rehabilitation program and has been referred to an independent outpatient therapist as a part of the aftercare plan. Usually the client also will have been enrolled in a GA group. The client is typically motivated to attend at least several outpatient sessions because therapy is accepted as a continuation of the inpatient program. The client's spouse and family usually have been counseled by the inpatient treatment team leader to expect and support follow-up psychotherapy after the pathological gambler has been discharged from inpatient treatment.

The client's GA sponsor also may encourage the client to participate in outpatient therapy depending on the attitude of the sponsor and the particular GA group. GA's ideology on pathological gambling often has no practical significance for the independent psychotherapist and treatment techniques. There are times, however, when GA's somewhat evangelical themes (public confession before peers, recovery of self-worth through self-criticism and abstinence, dealing with life only one day at a time, and achieving a vaguely defined form of spiritual redemption through surrender to a greater power) may create conflict with the goals of a particular outpatient treatment plan.

The second condition for beginning outpatient psychotherapy occurs without the client having "hit bottom" and gone through hospital care. This client is often threatened with divorce, loss of employment, or other conditions if he or she does not become involved in therapy. Usually such an individual is not strongly self-motivated to seek help. Strong denials that gambling is out of control usually exist. Typically, the client is extremely cordial and cooperative, expressing a somewhat patronizing and indulgent attitude toward family members who have communicated concern, as well as toward the psychotherapist. The opportunity to demonstrate a basic control over the therapy situation by skillfully conducting a hustle of all parties involved becomes a welcomed challenge to the client. During the early sessions, a self-imposed but limited period of abstinence from gambling is often volunteered by the client to demonstrate capacity for control. The client entering outpatient therapy under this second condition is usually far more difficult to work with, at least initially.

Miller's Four-Phase Approach ["Individual Outpatient Treatment of Pathological Gambling." *Journal of Gambling Behavior*, 2, 1986, 95–107] utilizes a four-phase individual outpatient treatment technique that views recovery from pathological gambling as a process whereby the pathological gambler chooses to lose an addiction to gambling, while mourning the loss of the gambling as one would any severe loss. Miller's model is a very useful generic approach to outpatient psychotherapy for the pathological gambler even if the therapist chooses not to include the additional assumptions of a parallel between discontinuing gambling and the experience of grief and mourning a severe loss.

Phase one of this approach focuses on inducing gamblers to commit themselves to abstinence. It is crucial at this phase for the therapist to confront the gambler's denial and minimization of his or her inability to control gambling behavior. At the same time, it is important that the therapist not become manipulative or too adversarial because of the risk of the client's premature withdrawal from therapy. The therapist must be authentic, involved, and supportive, but also firm on the issue of abstinence. Anxiety must be managed carefully so that clients remain motivated to change, but not so overwhelmed by anxiety related to discontinuing gambling that treatment is terminated or gambling behaviors return.

In the second phase, the client must be enabled to identify and confront the problems that have been caused by gambling. Continued abstinence is important and the therapist should support the client's ability to cope with the increasing distress resulting from abstinence. The focus of sessions will often be on managing urges and thoughts about gambling. Engagement is a difficult but crucial issue at this phase. Most pathological gamblers have been so dishonest and manipulative with other people that an honest and open emotional relationship with the therapist may be difficult to develop initially.

The third phase focuses on longer term problems. Developing greater internal control over behavior and accepting greater intimacy in relationships, with more direct and expressive recognition of feelings of anger, sadness, and guilt related to gambling, become important issues in this phase. Sufficient structure and direction by the therapist must be maintained to prevent regression.

In the fourth phase, therapy is less structured and similar in process to open-ended, client-centered therapies. The client should be able to tolerate increasing amounts of anxiety and acknowledge his or her personal limitations in controlling gambling.

Other Approaches. A variety of different models of outpatient psychotherapy have been utilized over the past 20 years in treating pathological gambling. [One] describes successful results with couple's group therapy with treatment lasting about 1 year. They claim that there was typically a reduction of chronic anxiety, depression, and destructive criticism within couples. The couples also developed more effective defense techniques, became more spontaneous and authentic in interpersonal relations, and assumed more responsible and appropriate marital roles.

[There have been reports of] limited success with aversion therapy. Tepperman (1985) reports substantive success using short-term (12 weeks) conjoint group therapy using the Gamblers Anonymous 12-Step program materials as topics of group discussion. Each session began with one or more members reading aloud one of the steps and then group members each discussing the meaning the step had for their respective lives.

Role of Family in Cause and Treatment of Pathological Gambling

The significance of family dynamics in treating and explaining pathological gambling has received increasing attention since about 1970. The initial recognition of the importance of providing some support to the gambler's family was prompted by GA's further imitation of the basic AA model, which includes Al-Anon, a support group for alcoholics' families. In 1960, the first Gam-Anon groups were formed, although there were no support techniques specific to the issue of pathological gambling that distinguished Gam-Anon from Al-Anon. Even today, the basic focus of Gam-Anon is to separate the family members from feelings of guilt, responsibility, and other inappropriate emotional reactions toward the pathological gambler's gambling activity. The problem of codependency and enabling the addict seem apparent in many relationships between pathological gamblers and their family members regarding the different ways in which they may be influencing the gambler's behavior without either party consciously realizing the nature of the involvement.

The intentional inclusion of the pathological gambler's family in professional mental health treatment lagged behind the peer support group approach substantially. Custer's innovative treatment program for pathological gambling at the Brecksville, Ohio, Veterans Administration Hospital did recognize the significance of the family in the recovery process, but the inpatient structure of the program greatly limited opportunity for family member involvement. Furthermore, because the first several programs were provided through the Veterans Administration Hospitals, access to these programs for both the gambler and family was limited to veterans.

The first treatment program for pathological gamblers that was open to the general public was offered by Taylor Manor Hospital in Elliot City, Maryland, in 1979. Both the inpatient and aftercare portions of their program placed increasing attention on the gambler's family. By 1982, New York State funded outpatient programs at St. Vincent's North Richmond Community Mental Health Center on Staten Island and the Rochester Health Association in Rochester, New York. Subsequent increased state funding for outpatient programs for pathological gamblers has expanded services to Queens, Manhattan, and Buffalo, New York. Other states which have provided some funding for outpatient programs are Nevada, Massachusetts, New Jersey, Iowa, and Connecticut. Currently there are approximately 45 formal treatment programs for pathological gamblers and their families nationally.

Family of Origin. Although most interest in the significance of family dynamics for explaining and treating pathological gambling has focused on the conjugal family in which the gambler participates as an adult spouse and parent, there has been limited interest in the gambler's family of origin where the formative experiences of infancy, childhood, and adolescence occurred. This relative lack of interest in the etiological significance of pathological gamblers' experiences within their families of origin may be a reflection of two assumptions about pathological gambling that have recently been challenged conceptually and empirically. First, until Jacobs' recent research documenting the extent of late childhood and early adolescent gambling activity ["Teenage Gambling." *In* H.J. Sheffen, et al. *Compulsive Gambling* 249–292], it was generally assumed that pathological gambling was an adult phenomenon. Clearly, this assumption is no longer valid because of the increasing research findings that document childhood and adolescent gambling for money on sports and other types of games of chance previously thought to be restricted to adults.

Second, the primary sources of influence to gamble were related to persons and events that existed outside of the family of origin and did not become effective until the gambler became a young adult and separated from the family of origin. Recent data have shown, however, that approximately 40% of adult pathological gamblers first gambled in the company of an adult family member or older sibling, and approximately 45% came from families in which one or both parents were active gamblers. These data suggest that positive values and attitudes toward gambling as well as opportunity to learn gambling behavior may begin within the gambler's family of origin. Furthermore, [it has been] report[ed] that women pathological gamblers tend to have had very dysfunctional families of origin. Forty-two percent had an alcoholic parent or were from an alcoholic family. Forty-two percent had parents who gambled excessively. Thirty-three percent reported being physically abused by their parents, and 29% claimed that they had been sexually abused as children.

The importance of knowing more about the experience of pathological gamblers within their family of origin becomes increasingly apparent as knowledge of gambling phenomena in general increases. Certainly the literature on the etiology and treatment of personality disorders could provide a fruitful basis for designing further research on the significance of early childhood experiences in the development of pathological gambling, because, at least conceptually, personality disorders and pathological gambling have been linked. The limited amount of formal research and even published clinical case analyses on the issue of the causal role of family of origin and pathological gambling is a serious shortcoming in the analysis of pathological gambling. Clinicians and research scientists should both be encouraged to investigate and report on this aspect of pathological gambling.

Conjugal Family. As an adult, the pathological gambler's family roles are often those of spouse and parent. Since demographic studies have reported such a disproportionate number of male pathological gamblers, the majority of family studies have viewed the effects of pathological gambling on wife, mother, and children. More recent research has revealed, however, that as many as a third of pathological gamblers are female and many are married. Research on the female pathological gambler as wife and mother is very much needed to expand our knowledge of the effects of pathological gambling on family life.

Effects on Spouse. The tensions between the gambler and spouse develop over time and have been classified into stages of worsening symptoms and progressive decline in the marriage. The first phase is characterized by one spouse's early realization of the other spouse's gambling problem combined with an attempt to deny its significance. The wife usually keeps her concern to herself, considers her husband's gambling activity as a passing interest, and is easily reassured by the gambler that he is in control of his gambling. In fact, at this stage the gambler is often successful in concealing the extent of his gambling and the wife tacitly agrees not to create tension by confronting the gambler with her concerns about the possible problems related to continued gambling.

The transition into the second phase begins when unpaid bills and financial crises can no longer be denied by the wife. She experiences increasing rejection by the gambler and accusations of harassment and spousal disloyalty. The wife also attempts to control the consequences of the gambling by arranging partial loans from friends and relatives. This strategy simply enables the pathological gambler to continue gambling and results in isolating the wife from her own support system of friends and relatives because she ignores their advice to leave the gambler to face the legal consequences of debt on his own. The combination of rejection and isolation often leads to early stages of depression for the wife.

In the second phase, the continued gambling and worsening financial condition increase the wife's efforts to arrange bailouts and to make excuses to creditors, family, friends, and others affected by the gambler's debt and continued gambling. If the gambler and spouse are parents, the mother must now provide explanations to the children about their father's increasing absence and uncaring behavior. The children begin to experience both emotional and material deprivation because of the gambling problems. The spouse begins to be emotionally and physically exhausted by her unsuccessful efforts to control the gambler's activity and to forestall financial foreclosure. She experiences episodes of acute anxiety, confusion, and resentment followed by extended periods of depression.

In the third phase, the spouse experiences the undeniable realization that she cannot control her husband's gambling, nor can she protect herself and her children from its manifold adverse consequences. She may alternate between panic and rage.

Shortly thereafter, she enters a fourth phase which is the spouse's version of "hitting bottom." In her own feelings of extreme hopelessness, she may begin abusing alcohol or prescription medications. She often begins preparation for divorce and may even consider suicide. There is a strong sense of hopelessness and loss of control over life.

Effects on Children. The effects of pathological gambling on the gambler's children are quite similar to those observed in many dysfunctional families, especially the alcoholic's family. The children respond to pressures from both parents, and many children experience severe role conflicts. As family tensions increase from the progressively worsening gambling, children may become scapegoats, peacemakers, or strive to replace the failing parents by becoming the overresponsible children who try desperately to restore order to the deteriorating family environment. Often with their own feelings of anxiety, anger, and depression, these children assume responsibility for the emotional tensions of the family. Unable to reduce the family's conflicting emotions, these children inevitably begin acting out. Several common ways are through inconsistent academic performance with under- or overachieving, substance abuse, and even gambling activity. Jacobs' (1989) research on children of pathological gamblers has revealed consistently a higher propensity for use of tobacco, alcohol, and a range of narcotics than their classroom peers with average parents. These children also had an earlier age of onset for behaviors such as gorging food and gambling activity. In fact, [according to Jacobs] "children of problem gamblers showed what may be inferred to be a greater drive state to escape reality and a greater propensity for seeking mood-elevating substances and stimulating experiences than did their peers with average parents".

The family environment may have a variety of related interpersonal tensions, all of which create a progressively stressful environment for the children's psychosocial development. Frequent disappointments result from unkept promises by the gambling parent who finds it easier to make promises for shared activity than to keep them. The children's repeated experience of abused trust in the parent inculcates psychosocial defenses which protect the child from psychic pain while also tending to excuse the parent's behavior. In fact, the child's fear of being abandoned by the gambling parent may actually motivate him or her to excessive efforts to please this parent in return for any possible approval or love from the parent. Herein lies the basis of the dynamics of the "enabling" child who protects and excuses the parent's problematic behavior. Children may also experience severe conflict when solicited by the mother into alliances of mutual protection from the bad father. Children and mother begin to look to each other for emotional security and satisfaction which should be provided to them respectively by a mature adult male filling the roles of husband and father. The substitute alliance often generates feelings of guilt and shame among the children and mother. They feel an uneasy sense of disloyalty to the pathological gambler who may occasionally rebuke the family for locking him out of their lives.

These children are also unusually sensitive about relationships with persons outside of the family. The family usually attempts to conceal the "shameful" problem of the gambler and consequently remains very guarded about how close to allow friends and neighbors to approach them in relationships in which the family's secret might be at risk of disclosure. . . .

TWENTY QUESTIONS[4]

---

1. Did you ever lose time from work due to gambling?
2. Has gambling ever made your home life unhappy?
3. Did gambling affect your reputation?
4. Have you ever felt remorse after gambling?
5. Did you ever gamble to get money with which to pay debts or otherwise solve financial difficulties?
6. Did gambling cause a decrease in your ambition or efficiency?
7. After losing did you feel you must return as soon as possible and win back your losses?
8. After a win did you have a strong urge to return and win more?
9. Did you often gamble until your last dollar was gone?
10. Did you ever borrow to finance your gambling?
11. Have you ever sold anything to finance gambling?
12. Were you reluctant to use "gambling money" for normal expenditures?
13. Did gambling make you careless of the welfare of yourself and your family?
14. Did you ever gamble longer than you had planned?
15. Have you ever gambled to escape worry or trouble?

[4]From *Twenty Questions* by Gamblers Anonymous, 1980, Los Angeles, CA: Gamblers Anonymous. Copyright © 1980 by Gamblers Anonymous.

16. Have you ever committed, or considered committing an illegal act to finance gambling?

17. Did gambling cause you to have difficulty in sleeping?

18. Do arguments, disappointments or frustrations create within you an urge to gamble?

19. Did you ever have an urge to celebrate any good fortune by a few hours of gambling?

20. Have you ever considered self destruction as a result of your gambling?

BIBLIOGRAPHY

An asterisk (*) before a reference indicates that the material or part of it has been reprinted in this compilation.

BOOKS AND PAMPHLETS

Allison, Loraine. When the stakes are too high: a spouse's struggle to live with a compulsive gambler. Abbey. '91.

Clotfelter, Charles and Cook, Philip J. Selling hope: state lotteries in America. Harvard Univ. '89.

Colbert, James. God bless the child. Atheneum. '93.

DeMaris, Ovid. How greed, corruption, and the mafia turned Atlantic City into the boardwalk jungle. Bantam. '86.

Eadington, William and Cornelius, Judy A. (eds.) Gambling & public policy: international perspectives. University of Nevada. '91.

Eadington, William and Cornelius, Judy A. (eds.) Gambling behavior & problem gambling. University of Nevada. '91.

Esquinas, Richard and Distel, Dave. Michael & me: our gambling addiction —my cry for help! Athletic Guidance Center. '93.

Estes, Ken. Deadly odds: the compulsion to gamble. Edgehill publications. '91.

Galski, Thomas (ed.). The handbook of pathological gambling. Charles C. Thomas. '87.

Noland, Jane T. Gamblers Anonymous: a day at a time. CompCare. '94.

Orford, Jim. Excessive appetites: a psychological view of addiction. Wiley. '85.

Rosecrance, John. Gambling without guilt: the legitimation of an American pastime. Wadsworth. '88.

Sasuly, Richard. Bookies and bettors: two hundred years of gambling. Holt, Rinehart & Winston. '82.

Shaffer, Howard J., Stein, Sharon, Gambino, Blase & Cummings, Thomas N. (eds.) Compulsive gambling: theory, research & practice. Free press. '89.

Sifakis, Carl. The encyclopedia of gambling. Facts on file, Inc. '89.

Spanier, David. Inside the gambler's mind. University of Nevada. '94.

Thompson, William N. Legalized gambling. A B C-Clio, Inc. '94.

Walker, Michael G. The psychology of gambling. Pergamon Press. '92.

ADDITIONAL PERIODICAL ARTICLES WITH ABSTRACTS

For those who wish to read more widely on the subject of gambling, this section contains abstracts of additional articles that bear on the topic. Readers who require a comprehensive list of materials are advised to consult *Reader's Guide to Periodical Literature* and other Wilson indexes.

Lotteries and sin taxes: painless revenue or painful mirage? Richard A. McGowan, *America* 170: 4–5 Ap 30 '94

Many local and state governments are trying to pay for increasingly expensive public services through lotteries and "sin taxes," but these new revenue sources may not be the quick and easy fixes that they seem. Thirty-seven states and the District of Columbia now run lotteries, and a growing number of cities allow casino gambling. Meanwhile, several state governments, encouraged by the pronouncements of the Clinton administration, have raised excise taxes on tobacco or alcohol. However, lotteries usually fill only a small percentage of a state's budget needs, decline in popularity over time, and encourage the legalization of other forms of gambling. Sin taxes, for their part, can either reduce the demand for the product or increase tax revenue, but not both. Even if sales do not fall, such tax increases are unlikely to bring in enough additional revenue to subsidize important new programs.

Gambling's advocates are right—but for the wrong reasons. Gary Stanley Becker, *Business Week* 14 S 6 '93

Financially strapped state and local governments should forget about legalized gambling as a fail-safe way to fill their coffers. Whereas legalizing gambling would enable those who wish to place bets to do so without patronizing illegal establishments or facilities controlled by criminals, it would nevertheless cause a big increase in the number of communities competing for limited tax revenues from gambling. As a consequence, new establishments would not be able to duplicate the financial successes of Las Vegas, Atlantic City, and the Indian reservations that have legalized gambling. An argument in favor of state-run gaming that has merit is that arguments against it, such as the contention that gambling is sinful, are specious.

Will too many players spoil the game? Ronald Grover, *Business Week* 80+ O 18 '93

As more operators get involved in the gambling business, existing casinos and gaming resorts are suffering. The gaming and casino business is one of the hottest industries, taking in $10.2 billion in 1992, and gambling experts think that figure will double by the end of the decade. State and local governments, hungry for the tax revenues they can draw from gambling, are allowing new casinos at various locations around the country. The increased competition, however, ensures that someone will be hurt. New casinos in Las Vegas, for example, usually thrive at the expense of existing ones. Atlantic City, meanwhile, is feeling a pinch, in part because of Foxwoods, a new Native American-run casino in Ledyard, Conn. Overbuilding in newly opened territories is prompting a shakeout, which could accelerate as gaming giants with well-heeled marketing operations move in. Nevertheless, size alone does not guarantee success.

Under the Boardwalk. Joseph Nocera, *Esquire* 114: 69–70+ O '90

The social problems facing Atlantic City have been blamed on the gambling industry, but in truth, the city's problems are like those of many other American cities. Gambling has done what it was intended to do—produce jobs and prosperity. Casinos have created close to 48,000 jobs and have led to an economic boom in southern New Jersey. The state has benefited, as 8 percent of the gross profits from the casinos goes back to the state and another 1.25 percent goes to urban renewal projects in Atlantic City. Although the state has been eager to take the money from the casinos, it has passed regulations that have promoted the enforced separation of the city and the casinos. Atlantic City's population has dropped by 20 percent in the past 15 years; residents moved to the suburbs once they had enough money.

A bit of a flutter. Mark Clapson, *History Today* 41: 38–44 O '91

Though prohibited for over a century, off-track betting remained a popular pastime among the working class in Britain. Lower class gambling was considered an incitement to crime, impoverishment, and an 1853 act of Parliament forbade assembly in places other than the race track for purposes of betting. This law merely shifted much of the betting from shops to the streets. Despite further legislation against it in 1874, off-track betting increased, becoming part of the general commercialization of leisure that resulted from rising wages and a shortened workweek. The class bias of antigambling laws was exemplified by the 1906 Street Betting Act, which cracked down on street transactions while permitting rich clients to bet by mail and over the phone with impunity. Recognizing that most gambling was moderate and that legislation against it was a source of resentment among bettors, the government allowed licensed betting shops to open in 1961.

The dark side of charity gambling. David Johnston, *Money* 22: 130–1+ O '93

Americans spend $10 billion a year at charity-sponsored bingo and casino games, but only a fraction of that money actually goes to the needy. Americans are spending record amounts on games sponsored by local charities and affiliates of groups like the American Cancer Society, the

American Red Cross, and the National Kidney Foundation. Although the gambling helps a wide array of worthy causes, only about 10 percent of total charity-gambling revenues go to the people they are designed to aid. The increasingly high costs of running gambling operations, lax enforcement of charity-gaming laws, cheating by professional players, and an influx of scam artists and mob associates who skim money from charities are all contributing to the problem. A sidebar presents tips on participating in charity gambling.

Casino clout for Native Americans. Carroll Bogert, *Newsweek* 123: 24 Mr 28 '94

In just 2 years, the Mashantucket Pequot Indians of southern Connecticut have used their growing gambling empire to gain immense political and economic influence in the state. The tribe's Foxwoods casino in Ledyard is hugely successful, bringing in more than $1 million a day, and the Pequots have big plans for expanding. A new bingo hall and concert arena are under construction, and the tribe may also undertake an amusement park, golf courses, another casino, and a third hotel. The Pequots' success has allowed them to voluntarily contribute a minimum of $100 million a year to the state budget, making the tribe Connecticut's largest contributor outside of the federal government. The tribe also employs more than 8,000 people, aids nonprofit groups, and helps local governments. Some non-Indian local residents, however, have complained that the Pequots are encroaching on their way of life.

Fools gold in Black Hawk? Carroll Bogert, *Newsweek* 123: 22–4 Mr 28 '94

Politicians and citizens all over the country are turning to gambling to solve financial and social problems, but recent developments in the town of Black Hawk, Colorado, illustrate the unanticipated pitfalls of this strategy. In 1990, voters approved a state referendum allowing casino gambling in the town and 2 other sites in Colorado. Black Hawk residents hoped that the increased revenues and tourism would bring jobs, lower taxes, and money for local improvements. The vast revenues now generated each year by Bullwhackers Casino and other gaming establishments have indisputably accomplished these aims, but casino development has also led to crime, congestion, pollution, and unsightly construction. Property values have become so inflated that local businesses are being driven away, and many residents are unhappy with the general environment promoted by the gambling business.

The gambling man. Mark Starr, *Newsweek* 121: 72–4 Je 14 '93

Michael Jordan's search for challenges may cause him an image problem. Jordan, who reportedly earned $35.9 million in 1992, is a frequent and ardent gambler. At practice with the Chicago Bulls, he wagers on trick shots, and on the Bulls' plane or on the road, he runs card games that sometimes last all night. The National Basketball Association gave him a reprimand at the beginning of the season for gambling on golf games with unsavory characters, including a convicted felon. Now, the New York Times has reported that he gambled late into the night in Atlantic City, New Jersey, before a New York game, and San Diego businessman Richard Esquinas has alleged that Jordan lost $1.2 million to him during a 10-day golf binge in 1991. In his book, Michael and Me: Our Gambling Addiction. . . My Cry for Help!, Esquinas says that Jordan still owes him $100,000. Jordan admitted to betting with Esquinas but said he had no records of the amount.

Recovery fever. Melinda Blau, *New York* 24: 30–7 S 9 '91

The popularity of Alcoholics Anonymous (AA) and the development of the large number of spinoff groups have prompted questions about the programs' effectiveness. AA's primary purpose has always been to "stay sober and help other alcoholics to achieve sobriety." Today, however, the baby boomers and social club kids who are flooding AA and its spinoffs seem self involved and less willing to help out at meetings or to even reach out to newcomers. Moreover, some people question whether the AA prescription, which was originally designed around complete abstinence, can work for such behavioral problems as compulsive gambling (Gamblers Anonymous), sex addiction (Sexaholics Anonymous), or food disorders (Overeaters Anonymous). A sidebar provides a partial listing, taken from the 1990 edition of The Self-Help Sourcebook, of the more popular groups that have spun off from AA.

Doing the BOPTROT. Bobbie Ann Mason, *The New Yorker* 70: 46–8+ My 9 '94

An F.B.I. sting operation code-named BOPTROT has made Kentuckians wary of the prospect of instituting gambling casinos to boost the horse-racing industry. Operation BOPTROT, which began in 1990, initially targeted lawmakers who were willing to be bribed for their influence in helping a troubled harness track compete against a rival Thoroughbred track for more gambling opportunities. Several of the state's politicians have been convicted of taking bribes to influence racing legislation. The investigation spread to other areas of public business and has forced Kentuckians to confront their history of tolerating public corruption. Amidst this atmosphere of self-consciousness, horse-racing tracks were unable to get casino gambling legalized this year. Still, given the fact that casinos are thriving in nearby states, Kentuckians will likely have to grapple with the issue again.

After the New Age: the recovery trend. Lys Ann Shore, *Skeptical Inquirer* 15: 227–8 Spr '91

The recovery trend, which emphasizes Alcoholics Anonymous-style 12-step treatment programs for gambling, drug addiction, sexual addiction, and any number of other problems, has been called the new spiritual movement of the 1990s. The trend is also a major growth industry, particularly for publishers and booksellers of recovery literature. The trend's link with the New Age movement and its focus on parent-child relationships, a key concern of the baby boom generation, may partially account for its popularity. A backlash to the idea that virtually everyone is in permanent recovery from something has already started to take hold.

Deeper and deeper. Jill Lieber, *Sports Illustrated* 72: 50+ F 12 '90

Tommy Gioiosa, a former friend of banned-for-life ballplayer and manager Pete Rose, has stated that Rose bet on baseball as far back as 1984 and that Rose had bookies in such cities as New York, Chicago, and Los Angeles. A U.S. district court in Cincinnati recently sentenced Gioiosa to five years in prison for conspiracy to distribute cocaine and conspiracy to hide part of Rose's $47,646 in winnings from a 1987 Pik Six ticket at Turfway Park in Florence, Kentucky, from the Internal Revenue Service. Gioiosa said that Rose, whom he has known since 1977, bet on games involving the Cincinnati Reds, the team Rose managed. Rose, who claims that he is being treated unfairly for a gambling addiction, says that Gioiosa is lying and that he is trying to make a name for himself at Rose's expense.

A losing bet. William F. Reed, *Sports Illustrated* 75: 124 Ag 26 '91

Legalized sports gambling should not be expanded. Some people argue that because illegal sports gambling is already at least a $38 billion a year industry, it should be taken away from criminals and used by cash-starved state governments as a lucrative source of revenue. The United States already has too much legal gambling, however. Aside from the moral contradictions and the concerns that the passion to get rich quick through gambling will replace devotion to hard work and saving, expanding legal gambling would promote an increase in gambling addiction, boost fan hostility toward athletes, damage the horse racing and dog racing industries, fail to drive illegal bookmakers out of business, and not make sense from a practical standpoint.

High stakes. *Sports Illustrated* 78: 13 Je 14 '93

In the wake of new gambling allegations against Michael Jordan, the NBA should issue a statement condemning both gambling and Jordan's involvement in it. A book by San Diego businessman Richard Esquinas titled Michael & Me: Our Gambling Addiction My Cry for Help! states that Jordan and Esquinas bet on golf matches and that the Chicago Bulls star owed Esquinas $1.25 million at one point. This sum is not pocket money even to Jordan, who allegedly welshed on paying up, and it is certainly big enough to attract the sort of heavy-duty gamblers who might try to use IOUs to gain inside information in wagering on NBA games. Also troubling is Esquinas's suggestion that Jordan is a compulsive gambler. Although Esquinas comes off as an opportunist at best, Jordan's response to these and previous gambling allegations has damaged his credibility.

Gaming guru. Anna Esaki-Smith, *Success* 34–6 Ja/F '93

Part of a cover story on renegade entrepreneurs. Lyle Berman's casinos have foiled critics who said that gaming wasn't appropriate on Indian land. Grand Casino Mille Lacs opened on the Mille Lacs Indian Reservation, about 70 miles north of Minneapolis, in 1991. After only 10 months of operation, the casino had generated $56.3 million in revenues and $11.2 million in profits. The original casino and a newer facility in Hinckley, Minnesota, employ about 600 Indians.

Chasing the super red sevens. Sue Raffety, *Time* 137: 15 My 6 '91

Slot machines, a booming market in the gambling industry, account for 58.4 percent of gross revenues at Atlantic City casinos. By law, the machines are required to pay out a minimum of 83 percent of what they take in. A slot machine tournament held at Trump's Castle Hotel and Casino in Atlantic City is described.

Las Vegas, U.S.A. Kurt Andersen, *Time* 143: 42–51 Ja 10 '94

A cover story profiles Las Vegas, Nevada. Las Vegas is currently caught up in its biggest boom since the 1950s and 1960s. Tourist inflow has nearly doubled over the past decade and the area is among America's fastest-growing. With its high-tech amusement park spectacles, its convenience, its classlessness, its aura of fantasy and wealth, and its universally understood cultural references, Las Vegas drew some 20 million Americans and 2 million foreigners in 1992. Las Vegas is also drawing more families than ever before: The city has become virtually a mirror image of the nation itself, where gambling, 24-hour commercial culture, and Vegas-influenced entertainment forms have become widespread in recent years. The history, attractions, and huge new casinos and resorts of Las Vegas are discussed, and the contributions of Steve Wynn and other Las Vegas developers are detailed.

It's a sin to buy a lottery ticket. Mitch Finley, *U.S. Catholic* 55: 12–17 S '90

Buying a lottery ticket is wrong because state lotteries constitute a sophisticated social and economic evil. According to Charles T. Clotfelter and Philip J. Cook in Selling Hope: State Lotteries in America, playing state-run lotteries helps perpetuate an implicit tax that hits the poor the hardest. Lotteries encourage superstition, lead many people to a gambling addiction, and undermine the ethic of honest work for an honest dollar. Moreover, state lotteries contradict the New Testament's teaching about the danger of riches and contribute to an unsavory image of government.

In sum, playing state-run lotteries renders people incapable of fulfilling duties incumbent upon them by reason of justice and charity. The results of a poll of U.S. Catholic subscribers on the appropriateness of playing state lotteries are presented.

Indian casinos hit the jackpot. Ruth Denny, *Utne Reader* 35–7 N/D '92

Articles in the March 1992 Washington Monthly, the April 1992 issue of the Minneapolis-based Native American newspaper the Circle, and the March/April 1992 issue of Colors, a Minneapolis journal for writers of color, discuss gambling operations run by Native American tribes. The Indian gambling industry is big business; for example, the 14 casinos operated by Minnesota's 11 sovereign Native American nations together generated an estimated $900 million in 1991. The industry can benefit Native Americans, but there are social costs: In some cases, such problems as suicide, high dropout rates, alcohol and drug abuse, and tribal government corruption have risen along with profits. Discussed are how the Seminole tribe in Florida pioneered big-stakes reservation gambling by testing the limits of tribal sovereignty, the controversy over the Indian Gaming Regulatory Act, how Native communities deal with their casino profits, and the potential political cost of Indian gambling.

The lure of gambling's "easy" money. Robert McClory, *Utne Reader* 60–1 S/O '92

Part of a cover story on people's financial anxieties. Gambling has become the addiction of the 1990s. Gaming and Wagering Business reports that in 1990, Americans bet $286 billion—more than was spent on health insurance, dentists, shores, foreign travel, and household appliances combined. Charles T. Clotfelter and Philip J. Cook, authors of Selling Hope: State Lotteries in American, blame state lotteries for much of the rise in gambling. They note that lotteries use misleading advertising, offer terrible odds, generate revenues far less important to the states than people realize, and turn millions of people into gamblers. Studies show that suicide rates are higher among compulsive gamblers than for any known addicted group and that gambling is popular among the poor, who are most damaged by losing.